TRANSFORMATIVE LEADERSHIP

SELF-MASTERY FOR THE
NEW VOICE OF BUSINESS SUCCESS

JILL "GIGI" AUSTIN

FEATURING: MITSY ANDREWS, JAMES M. BLAZAR, MARK J. BOHEN, DASHA ALLRED BOND, DAN COBB, AMY MOUDY COMEAU, KATHY L. DIVIS, JEAN DOUGHERTY, JOEL ENGLISH, DAVID A. FEINBERG, DANIEL FELL, CARRIE FRESHOUR, JENNY GLADDING, SUSAN S. HOLT, ELY JONES, LAURA LEE JONES, MARY KIPP, KIRAN LAKSHMAN, MIKE MILLIGAN, KARRI MORGAN, GARY MUELLER, CHRISIE SCOTT, DON STANZIANO, CAMILLE STRICKLAND

TRANSFORMATIVE LEADERSHIP

SELF-MASTERY FOR THE NEW VOICE OF BUSINESS SUCCESS

JILL "GIGI" AUSTIN

FEATURING: MITSY ANDREWS, JAMES M. BLAZAR, MARK J. BOHEN, DASHA ALLRED BOND, DAN COBB, AMY MOUDY COMEAU, KATHY L. DIVIS, JEAN DOUGHERTY, JOEL ENGLISH, DAVID A. FEINBERG, DANIEL FELL, CARRIE FRESHOUR, JENNY GLADDING, SUSAN S. HOLT, ELY JONES, LAURA LEE JONES, MARY KIPP, KIRAN LAKSHMAN, MIKE MILLIGAN, KARRI MORGAN, GARY MUELLER, CHRISIE SCOTT, DON STANZIANO, CAMILLE STRICKLAND

WHAT OTHERS ARE SAYING ABOUT

TRANSFORMATIVE LEADERSHIP

"Re-visioning successful leadership has never been more essential. *Transformative Leadership* reveals the unique, timely blueprint for 'next.'"

~ **Amber Ontiveros**, Author, and Senior Policy Advisor to the Bush and Obama Administrations on Civil Rights Matters

"After reading this book you will have a better understanding of the importance of self-awareness and of recognizing your own strengths and weaknesses as well as those of the people around you. Read *Transformative Leadership* and grow as a leader!"

~ **Dalal Haldeman**, PhD, CEO, Haldeman Marketing, former Johns Hopkins Medicine SVP Marketing and Communications

"This is by far one of the best books I have ever read on leadership! I loved the variety of the stories, the examples of different types of leadership and especially the tools each author contributed, making the book not only an enjoyable read, but also a valuable resource of practical leadership tips and techniques. I highly recommend *Transformative Leadership*!"

~ **Karen Sherwood**, Career, Business & Leadership Consultant, BG5 Solutions-Human Design for Business

"*Transformative Leadership* is a profound compilation of stories from 25 leaders sharing their transformative journeys. From one author to the next, I found the wisdom each story held to be relatable and actionable for new and experienced leaders alike."

~ **Bernie DeSantis III**, CEO of Insignia Training Partners

"I encourage all artists of all genres to dive into this treasure trove of knowledge and inspiration. This book should be required reading for all of those wishing to be involved in the arts no matter what side of the footlights you are on."

~ **Keri Alkema**, International Opera Singer and Founder of ScreamingDivas

"*Transformative Leadership* hit on a relevant topic for anyone with a career—the drive to leave their organizations, their community, and their teams in a better place. I enjoyed the way they shared their unique and lived experiences in 'snackable' ways. The tools they shared will enrich the opportunities for any experienced or emerging leader to create meaningful change."

~ **Patti Winegar**,

Brand Champion, Former CEO & Marketing Business Owner

"Transformative Leadership is engaging and insightful. For anybody who is new to a leadership role or thinks what they are doing is not working, this book is a must-read."

~ **Elaine Heroux**, LCSW, Author, Spiritual and Psychological Counselor

"This book is an absolute gem! The authors' vulnerability makes their stories incredibly relatable, offering a refreshing reminder that my leadership journey—complete with its doubts, challenges, and fears—is not so unique. The insights and tools in this book will undoubtedly be invaluable to aspiring transformational leaders."

~ **Sharon Hickman**,

Co-founder & COO, Adaptient, LLC., Former Healthcare Executive

"The brilliantly insightful blueprint offered by this consortium of courageous and meaningful leaders will leave every reader motivated and challenged to become even more value-driven with warmth, humility, and kindness. This is a beautiful collection of transformative messages which call upon all of us to dig into our deep wells of humanity to serve the greater good with authenticity and compassion."

~ **Rondal Richardson**, Entertainment Philanthropist & Community Activist

"Commit to reading this book: its words will open you to your own world of possibilities."

~ **Jason Watt**, Partner at Smith & Co-Founder of Fishbird

"*Transformative Leadership* is a tremendous contribution to new ways of thinking about leadership in today's complicated world. The insights and tools will be valuable to anyone struggling with their own leadership talent, skill, or the need to know more."

~ **Marilyn Dubree**, MSN, RN, NE-BC, FAAN, Senior Vice President, Vanderbilt University Medical Center

"*Transformative Leadership* is the collective of stories I've been seeking to see how others have challenged themselves to grow and what the catalyst for change was. Each story is written through an authentic lens that shows how we need to challenge ourselves to be at our best. Bravo for a great and inspiring read!"

~ **Lisa Bowman**, CEO, Marketing Mojo, Former CMO at United Way Worldwide and UPS Foundation

"What a resource for readers looking to find their own unique leadership approach and voice in this important time of change!"

~ **Leigh Ann Roberts**, JD, PCC, Executive Coach & Group Facilitator, Circle Center Consulting, LLC

DEDICATION

To Mahatma Gandhi, I dedicate this book to your memory.
Your presence, words, and actions live on and continue to inspire.
Thank you for modeling Transformative Leadership.
Thank you for being the change.

In Memory of Mohandas Karamchand "Mahatma" Gandhi
October 2, 1869 – January 30, 1948

DISCLAIMER

This book is designed to provide competent, reliable, and educational information regarding transformative leadership and other subject matter covered. However, it is sold with the understanding the authors and publisher specifically disclaim all responsibility for any liability, loss, or risk, personal or otherwise, incurred as a consequence, directly or indirectly, of the use and application of any of the contents of this publication.

In order to maintain the anonymity of others, names and identifying characteristics of some people, places, and organizations described in this book have been changed.

This publication contains content that may be potentially triggering or disturbing. Individuals who are sensitive to certain themes are advised to exercise caution while reading.

The opinions, ideas, and recommendations contained in this publication do not necessarily represent those of the Publisher. The use of any information provided in this book is solely at your own risk.

Know that the experts here have shared their tools, practices, and knowledge with you with a sincere and generous intent to assist you on your leadership journey. Please contact them with any questions you may have about the techniques or information they provided. They will be happy to assist you further and be an ongoing resource for your success!

TABLE OF CONTENTS

INTRODUCTION

"Be the change you wish to see in the world."

~ Mahatma Gandhi

It's time for a new voice of leadership to arise.

The formerly dominant voice of command and control suffered a fatal blow by the worldwide pandemic. Covid sent us home, out of routine, out of proximity, out of control, and sometimes even out of sight. As fear flooded our nervous systems, motivation by threats and ultimatums lost its impact due to fear-overload desensitization—an effect known to science.

Leadership struggled when we went home and work still got done. The struggle continues with various attempts to order people back to refill empty offices with few responding to "or else" threats.

At the same time, the abundance of technology became even more prolific creating new horizons, partnerships, and approaches to the market. Companies from Amazon to Zoom swept through our lives, forever changing how we shop, communicate, and live.

The more technology impacts our interface to the world, such as with the rise of Artificial Intelligence (AI), the more a human voice is called for to provide balance, context, and connection.

As another signal for change, we have entered the Chinese year of the Wood Dragon, a rare and unusual occurrence happening only every 60 years. Throughout the ages, the dragon has been viewed as a symbol of power and strength, often depicted as an immense creature that breathes fire and takes to the air with enormous wings.

Combining the fierce nature of the dragon with wood's natural qualities of growth and expansion, the Wood Dragon stands for new, innovative, and unconventional ways to wield our power and leadership. This is a substantial reminder of what will be called for in the times we have entered.

While the symbol of the dragon is shared universally, it takes on different aspects or additional attributes depending on the cultural interpretation. In the Celtic tradition, the dragon is symbolic of the combination of the living elements of fire, air, water, and earth, as embodied by the dragon's ability to fly, breathe fire, swim, and guard the hidden treasures of the universe in its cave. This multi-dimensional dragon can be a protector for good or a force for evil depending on how it uses its power.

The 15th-century story of St. George and the Dragon tells the tale of the courageous hero slaying the fearsome dragon to save the innocent. Ironically, through his act of courage, St. George also saves *himself* by facing and overcoming his inmost fears or *inner* dragons.

As it was for St. George, the act of courage is a source of empowerment for leaders. Those who come face to face with a challenging situation and move through it with courage, become transformed themselves and model it for others.

The concept of leadership, like the symbol of the dragon, has diverse aspects and multiple attributes that differ and adapt according to the larger cultural norms that play out through the family's, community's, or organization's culture.

So, what you're about to read may not look like a conventional book on leadership. Rather you'll find all the elements of transformative leadership present through the multiple voices telling their redemptive stories on becoming the change they want to see in the world.

Find the courageous voice that speaks to you in your situation with your challenges or aspirations. Wander through and discover the tool, framework, or practice that works for you.

CHAPTER 1

THE SELF-EMPOWERED LEADER

A BLUEPRINT TO TURN CHALLENGES INTO CONSCIOUS ACTION

Jill "GiGi" Austin, MBA

*"Until you make the unconscious conscious,
it will direct your life and you will call it fate."*

~ Carl Jung

MY STORY

I wasn't valued or respected for what I did or who I was in my first job. I didn't last long.

Fresh out of college, I landed a highly sought-after position writing commercials for a prominent radio/TV network. My delight in scoring the copywriting role soon morphed into resentment for the ad salespeople.

They draped themselves over my cubicle, waiting for me to produce a brilliant sample ad so they could impress their client and close a lucrative sale.

Your deep sighs while staring at my fingers on the keyboard don't make me write any faster!

I was aware of what they were getting and what I wasn't. While I served up creativity on-demand, unacknowledged in the background, the salespeople were raking in trophies, bonuses, and praise.

Creativity doesn't pay. There's no prestige. No respect. No "front and center" recognition. No power. No money. They're feeding their pocketbooks with my creativity while I barely make enough to eat.

The weighty list of grievances for my deprivation saturated my being. I willed my hands to keep typing and my eyes to stay open.

Is it PJ time yet?

As soon as I escaped home, I dragged myself through dinner and disappeared into a nap, gradually fading into bedtime.

At the time, I knew something was amiss from my complaints, resentments, and exhaustion. But I thought my troubles resulted from what was happening to me externally—things I had no power over or choice about—except to leave.

I danced with that pattern long into my career until I knew something *had to change*, and it had to be *me*.

"Hold plank for one minute," said my pregnant yoga teacher.

One minute. You've got to be kidding me. I rolled my eyes.

"If I can do it, so can you," she play-scolded me with a bemused smile.

I burst into tears and collapsed on the mat, barely restraining myself from pounding the ground like a frustrated toddler.

"Whoa! What's going on?"

Tears rolling down my face, I sobbed, "I'm lonely at work, and I don't have any friends, and something feels missing from my life. I hate to ask the cliché question, 'Is this all there is?' but 'Is this all there is?'"

She straightened up into a cross-legged Madonna-queen pose and made an encouraging sound.

I choked out, "I'm not valued or respected at work for what I know or who I am."

She nodded and eyed me with the patient look a mother gives her tantrumming two-year-old.

Sitting upright, I sighed, "I feel drained and burdened by my team members' feelings. Why can't they get along and live happily ever after? I can't fix them no matter what I do."

Rubbing her large belly, she calmly observed, "From the outside, it looks like you have it all—a loving family, great spouse, healthy kids, a big house, fancy car, travel, nice clothes and jewelry, a big job with a big title in a big place, a big salary, and a big team. You're influential and well-known in your field. And yet, you're not fulfilled."

"I know. I know! I should feel grateful and happy, but I'm not. I may be living a big life on the outside, but inside, I feel small and hollow. I've got to stop complaining about others and how *they* need to change and figure out what *I* need to do differently."

That moment exploded into an intensive period of introspection. What did I discover? I was living Jung's warning, unconsciously allowing fate to have its way with me. I was blind to examples of where I *was* empowered to consciously choose my actions.

When I overlooked warning signals from my inner dialogue, emotions, and actions, I *reacted* to external challenges. When I attuned to those signals, paused, and observed what was happening inside, I pivoted to curiosity and *chose* how to respond.

My knee-jerk instinct in a challenging situation is to internally reject the other person's statement and project my brilliance. *You're stupid, and I'm smart. You don't understand, and I do. You're not valuing me, and I'm valuable.*

When I pause and neither reject nor project, then I become curious and notice what's going on inside me—the flip side of my projection. *You're not stupid; I'm feeling stupid. You're not incapable; I'm feeling incapable. You're not devaluing me; I'm devaluing myself.*

In retrospect, my complaint about the salespeople's behavior was about value. I compared what they got (money, recognition, respect) to what I didn't. Flipping my assessment inside-out, from lack to appreciation, what value *did* I receive? A life-long base of skills and knowledge I drew upon as fundamentals throughout the rest of my career.

I experienced the interplay and interdependence of the sales and marketing functions. I saw how ads help sales. I learned that effective ad content comes from understanding the client's business, what they want to sell to their customers, and how it meets *their* customers' needs.

But I didn't know it then.

So, sales looked like the fix. I jumped from writing radio ads to selling them. The money was good, but I was disappointed. *Something's still missing.* The external rewards and accolades didn't take care of my sense of worth.

I interviewed for marketing positions next but only got offers for sales roles. *How am I supposed to get marketing experience if no one will hire me to get it until I have it?* To solve the experience conundrum, I went back to school for my MBA with a marketing specialty.

The MBA expanded my view to a bigger picture beyond marketing. *Now I see how the organization's business proposition, marketing, sales, and customer needs all dovetail.* Equipped with the confidence of my newly acquired knowledge and degree, I joined a telephone technology company as part of a leadership fast-track program.

The company and its industry underwent massive cultural upheaval, moving from utility order-taking into a competitive marketplace. The shift required system-based marketing and a new view of the customer. *My expertise is just what they need.*

The company was using an old strategy to push products out the door, focusing on the distributor sales reps as our customers and conduit to the broader market. *Can't they see the reps are **gatekeepers** to the customers who use our products in their businesses?*

It was clear to me the gatekeepers were preventing our company from having a full understanding of how products were used and what innovation was required. *We're missing out on a gold mine of market expansion and customer satisfaction a step beyond the rep's gate!*

We needed a new strategy for getting unfiltered input directly from business customers, including how they used the product in interaction with their customers.

I didn't have a way to test these insights until I was put in charge of the annual sales meeting. The typical meeting approach was to host our distributors' sales teams, do a series of presentations with a Q-and-A panel of leaders in front of the room, and hope leadership didn't get asked the hard questions.

I partnered with an innovative business consultant to design a participatory meeting, assembled all the players, and gave them an equal voice at the table. We invited members of the entire value chain, including the often-neglected research and development department, external sales and distribution, and the biggest revenue-producing customers like Walgreens and Bank of America.

At the opening reception, I introduced my boss to our consultant. Turning to her, my boss said, "I've heard about you. A lot is riding on this meeting."

She then abruptly shifted to me, "This is all on your head, so I hope it goes well for your sake." With a dismissive head-jerk and an about-face, she marched off.

A little frisson of fear caught my attention. *This is a big deal. Your job's on the line.*

Fear's warning me. This matters to me. It's a big step into the unknown. I'm up for the risk.

I was conscious of the possibilities, my own exhilaration, my trust in the approach, and the consultant's track record, so I forged ahead.

Everyone got something from the meeting!

We partnered for mutual success, and all participants won—the organization, customers, and their customers. The customers shared their business strategies and info on their customers, which led to new tech solutions and applications for a whopping 30-to-1 return on investment.

Based on our meeting, our customers changed their approach to customers and their organizational structures. Bingo! Instead of getting fired, I got promoted.

Telephone technology kept evolving until it leaped into internet technology, and I climbed another step up the leadership ladder as a VP of Global Marketing and Sales. The market was booming, and sales flooded in until the torrent began to slow down, signaling an impending market bust.

The boom is almost over. Time to leave before marketing becomes devalued and seen as a non-essential expense instead of a crucial investment.

I consulted on growth initiatives in an array of industries. While I loved the freedom and variety of consulting, I missed managing a team and influencing people and systems on a large scale. *Time for my next move.*

I was pumped after several rounds of group interviews for a VP position with a high-profile tech company. When they flew me across the country to meet with the bigwigs at company headquarters, I assumed I was close to being offered the job.

The SVP on my right asked, "How would you describe your leadership style?"

I smiled and answered with the confidence of my deepest convictions, "I believe in understanding team members' strengths and positioning them to actualize those within the organization."

The SVP across from me nodded and said, "Alright. Tell us about *your* strengths."

I've got this! My heartbeat picked up. "My number one strength is strategy. It's the way to accomplish a goal. When I understand the goal and see its feasibility, I can describe multiple paths to accomplishing it."

The room got dead quiet. Not the "what an awesome answer" quiet but the "ah-oh, this can't be good" quiet.

Through narrowed eyes and thinned lips, the SVP on my left replied, "No one does strategy here but the founder, our CEO."

You're kidding me! How short-sighted. How do these SVPs operate if they aren't in on strategy input? Are they highly paid yes-people?

I didn't get the job.

While I was busy judging the company's approach to strategy and criticizing the SVPs as inadequate, I was not present or curious. Turning my judgement of *them* inside-out, *I* was feeling inadequate.

My defensiveness and fear of failure kept me from asking questions like, "How does strategy get interpreted or play out in this division? What is your end-user customer trying to do, and how do you make it easier for them?"

I learned.

When I interviewed for a healthcare Chief Marketing Officer (CMO) position, I asked questions when I received pushback about my lack of experience working in the industry. Because I understood the broad application of marketing principles, I could translate my experience to address the dynamics and challenges they described.

There was almost an audible "click" of my match for the CMO position as I was describing the relevant trends and sound marketing approaches for growing their specialties in a competitive market.

I *did* get the job.

What followed was record-breaking years of growth, matching the external customer needs with the internal specialty offerings.

I became more visible in the organization, fulfilling my early career dream of recognition. I didn't realize how vulnerable I was until I was introduced to the leadership cadre.

The new head of the medical center stood up. "I've challenged Jill to increase our national reputation this year, and we'll see how well she does."

I'd heard this before. It felt like an echo of my first challenge at large-scale innovation. I never lost my composure in the face of his doubt.

Stand back and watch me. I've got this!

I had full confidence and deep knowing of what I brought to the party.

Our marketing team formed an internal coalition whose members stood to benefit from an increase in visibility, reach, and credibility. They were willing to share the risk and reward of venturing into new territory. Because of our in-depth consumer research, we devised a strategy and claimed national leadership in innovation, research, and personalized care. We led the country in successful, unorthodox marketing approaches.

The strategy paid off. I earned the additional title of Assistant Vice Chancellor of Strategic Marketing, and my responsibilities expanded. More specialties were added to the team to support new growth initiatives including those with a focus on digital marketing approaches and websites.

We received enthusiastic external customer feedback on the website redesign and how easy it was for patients to find what they needed. I was anticipating the same enthusiastic response from inside our organization but soon discovered the internal implementation and buy-in hadn't yet caught up with the external view.

My team and I entered the conference room of a prominent department head for a marketing review. As we were taking our seats, he exclaimed, "Our website sucks!"

All heads swiveled to face me. Our excited air of anticipation vanished from the room.

I was devastated and felt the disappointment of the team. We expected praise, not a put-down.

I flashed into a burn.

Oh really? You mean the award-winning website inspiring interactive sites across our industry? My people are good at what they do! You must be stupid if you can't see how good this is.

I knew enough to take a breath, pause, and absorb. *The department head has lobbed a judgment on our work, and I want to defend it with a judgment on him.*

What's another way to look at this?

I turned towards my anger. *I see you. Thanks for showing up to get my attention, reminding me I'm not standing in my power.*

What could I do right now to feel more empowered?

You're feeling like the victim. What is motiving him to persecute? Is he feeling disempowered? Like the website doesn't reflect his identity? What questions could you ask?

The absurdity of the moment caught up with me. I laughed aloud and replied, "Okay, then. Not how I expected to start our meeting. The whole marketing team, including web designers, is here, and we're all ears. Tell us what you miss about the old site, and what isn't working for you with the new one."

As a result of that meeting, the department head became a champion for our work inside and outside of the organization.

Finally, I realized I no longer needed outside approval to feel valued or respected. I learned to value and respect myself. I became my own internal champion, aware of the signals and intentional about my responses.

A self-empowered leader.

You'll find my most effective self-empowerment tool, the POP Quiz (Pause, Observe, Pivot, Question), in the following section. Check it out, and start turning challenges into conscious action.

THE TOOL

POP QUIZ (PAUSE, OBSERVE, PIVOT, QUESTION)

The POP Quiz is a potent empowerment blueprint. It shifts challenging situations into a self-empowered moment for conscious action.

This blueprint applies to inner dialogue, emotions, and actions. The tables below provide ideas for translating signals into helpful messages.

We'll use the emotion of fear as an example. When fear gets your attention:

- **P**ause first and breathe. Breathe. Breathe. Breathe. A full breath in and a full breath out. Repeat. Don't forget to breathe out. I spent half my career holding my breath in!

- **O**bserve. Be present with the emotion. Allow it to be without judgment. Where is this emotion in your body? State, "My body is experiencing fear (or fill in the blank with the emotion you feel). Even though I feel fear, I love and respect myself." It's important not to own the emotion, as in "I am afraid," but rather to observe it as a sensation.

- **P**ivot towards the emotion, acknowledge it, and thank it. "I see you, fear. Thank you for showing up to teach me something I need to know." That's right—bring in gratitude. Gratitude is a high vibration that softens any resistance to having the emotion.

- **Q**uestion. Ask the emotion, "Why are you here? What do you have to tell me? What do you want me to know? Do you (fear) have a message for me? What do I want to protect? What is a step I can take to intentionally address the concern in this moment?"

- Possible translations for emotions:
  - Fear = What matters to me? What do I want to protect?
  - Anger = Where am I not standing in my power?
  - Jealously = What is it I'd like for myself?
  - Anxiety = Where am I out of balance?
  - Grief = What needs to be integrated from my loss?
  - Guilt = Where am I judging myself for my actions?

- ○ Shame = Where do I think I'm a bad person for my actions?

- ○ Resentment = Where am I holding on to what 'should' be?

- ○ Resistance = Where am I uncomfortable? Here's my learning edge.

- • Possible translations for inner dialogue:
  - ○ Complaints = Where am I projecting my emotions onto others?
  - ○ Judgments = Where am I judging myself? What part of me do I find unacceptable?
  - ○ Comparison = Where am I feeling low self-worth?

- • Possible translations for actions:
  - ○ Attacking = Where do I not feel safe?
  - ○ Avoiding (Hiding, sleeping, shrinking, disappearing, leaving) = Where do I not feel safe?

I recommend practicing in low-risk mundane situations to build the self-empowerment "muscle." You'll find additional tips and tools at www.NewVoiceofLeadership.com.

Jill "GiGi" Austin, MBA, CEO and founder of GrowthFlows, and best-selling author, helps visionaries transform their leadership style and move toward self-mastery. She combines her leadership expertise and business acumen with profound energy-shifting practices that unwind limiting patterns, recover sovereignty and joy, and catapult leaders to the next level of success they're dreaming of.

Nationally known as a trendsetter in her industry and field, Jill served as Chief Marketing Officer and Assistant Vice Chancellor of Strategic Marketing at Vanderbilt University Medical Center. She was responsible for brand identity, market positioning and presence, marketing strategies, and growth for Vanderbilt and its affiliated network. Jill also chaired the Association of American Medical Colleges' General Institutional Advancement Council.

Having trained in various energy-shifting practices, Jill is an advanced shamanic practitioner and a certified Feng Shui consultant. Additionally, she has completed formal studies in astrology, the Kabbalah, mindful self-compassion, Google's Search Inside Yourself, tarot, Strength-Finder, chakras, the divine feminine, sound healing, and VortexHealing®.

A classical musician, Jill loves to sing and has been a life-long participant in various settings, from school and church choirs to Nashville Symphony Chorus and circle song groups.

She currently serves as Board Chair of Vox Grata Women's Choir and is an alumni member of Leadership Nashville, Leadership Middle Tennessee, and the Healthcare Executive Forum.

Jill is married to her soulmate, Tracy. She has five adult daughters and sons, including spouses, and is "GiGi" to four grandkids.

Connect with Jill:

Email: info@GrowthFlows.com

LinkedIn: https://www.linkedin.com/in/jilldaustin/

Facebook: https://www.facebook.com/jilldaustin

CHAPTER 2

A RELUCTANT LEADER

EMBRACING UNINTENTIONAL LEADERSHIP

Kathy Divis, MBA

*"A person either hates losing enough to change
or hates changing enough to lose."*

~ Orrin Woodward, Co-founder and Chairman,
Life, New York Times bestselling author on leadership

MY STORY

LABOR DAY WEEKEND 2009

No. No. Nooo! It's not true. It can't be. Can it?

"Sorry. What? I mean, I'm sorry, I misheard you. Pancreatic? It's not possible, is it?"

Sinking into a chair under the weight of what I think I just heard, my brain sputters and then clicks back on, and my hands start to tremble a bit. My mind races and the words don't make sense.

I say, "I don't understand. Pancreatic cancer? You're healthy. You're young. You've only started to feel poorly in the last week, right? Is the doctor sure? There's a chance the tests are wrong, right?"

This isn't happening to John. He's my friend, my mentor, my partner. It's been that way for over 30 years. This can't happen to him. He doesn't deserve this. It can't happen to me.

And with this stark realization, my journey into real leadership reluctantly begins.

The news settles on my soul as I sit quietly in a dark room. The suddenness and depth of this change knock me down as I grapple with what this means for me personally and professionally. I'm bombarded with compounding emotions ranging from surprise to disbelief, sadness to fear and worry, and reluctance—reluctance to accept it, reluctance to move forward, and reluctance to say the words aloud for fear they will make it real.

I've always been a leader, but not the top leader. I'm an excellent Number 2 – making decisions, managing staff, getting stuff done, doing my job well, and doing it efficiently.

But I've just never been *the* leader—never been the one to make the money pitches to the C-suite, never had to execute the toughest of decisions on my own.

John always has my back. And I always have his.

Slowly the fog in my mind starts to lift, and I realize, whether I want it or not, I'm now the leader. It's not my choice nor my decision; it just is. I must step up.

As the sun rises the next morning and with deepening sorrow as reality further sinks in, I pick up my phone and feel its weight in my hand. I find the phone number I need to make for this first of many calls yet to come.

This first one is going to be the hardest.

It's to break the news to Mike, the other executive in our firm.

The message I leave is, "Hey there. It's me, and we need to talk—soon. I've got news. And it's not good; it's going to be hard to hear. Call me."

And with that, the cycle of gently breaking the news starts. In doing so, a plan of what will happen next forms in the back of my head, and I start to lead.

Years later, when I unexpectedly came across the earlier Woodward quote, I realized that this single first phone call was the point in time when I subconsciously decided that I feared losing more than I feared changing.

I had to change. If not, I would've disappointed too many people. And that fear of failure, losing, and disappointing others was a good motivator.

AUGUST 1981

Fresh out of college, with a new marketing degree in hand, I faced a decision between two vastly different marketing career paths: healthcare and banking. With three competing job offers—two from hospitals and one from the bank—I know I must pick one.

What am I doing? Dang, this decision shouldn't be this hard. Banking is my future, isn't it? I've spent all my college years working in the bank as prep for a real job, and I like it. A lot. It's my future. I can't waste those last four years.

Yet, I'm feeling this unexpected and odd pull toward healthcare. It's in my blood.

Is it because I was so sick as a child for so many years?

However, hospital-based marketing is in its infancy. Most have never heard of it, and when they do, I'm always peppered with questions of skepticism or outright disdain.

So, with a mix of trepidation, a lot of parental concern, and the arrogance of youth, I make a pivotal decision. I opt for the job at a smaller, lesser-known community hospital across the river from the name-brand hospital in my hometown of Omaha.

As I start sharing the news of my decision, the response is always the same:

"Why?"

"Why would you do something like that?"

"It's such a bad choice! The other hospital is so much bigger, better known, well respected."

"Um, I thought you were staying at the bank?"

Why? Because of one person. Actually, because one man—brimming with charisma and infectious excitement about the journey he sees ahead of us—extended his hands to me.

His spirit of adventure fills me with excitement, and his absolute belief in the new path he's forging in an established industry captivates me. I dive in, unaware that this single decision would set the course of my life for the next four decades across four cities and five jobs.

Nor do I realize at 22 years old that this choice and the people surrounding me would dramatically help mold me into the person and leader

I would become. This choice laid the foundation for my understanding of the art of leadership and unknowingly filled me with both tangible and intangible lessons about how to lead, and a few ideas of what not to do, too! It jumpstarted a progression to a role I never sought or anticipated yet grew to love.

Over the intervening years from 1981 to 2009, the man I went to work for at the small community hospital became not only my boss but, more importantly, my teacher, mentor, friend, and eventually, my business partner.

We started marketing functions at three academic medical centers (in Birmingham, Philadelphia, and Atlanta) before starting our healthcare marketing firm. We worked together every day for over 30 years until the day he left for a doctor's appointment and never returned to the office. Most of what I learned about leadership can be directly traced back to my experiences working with John and healthcare executives nationwide as we sought to help hospitals and healthcare systems thrive. It was an amazing education.

Many things helped to make me a bit stronger and wiser, and will hopefully help you become a better leader, too.

Woodward also said, "The greatest leaders are reluctant ones who lead because they realize that no one else seems willing to step up. They may not crave leadership, but they're willing to do what they must and accept the charge."

That's my story. And that's not to imply in any way that I'm one of the greatest of leaders, but rather that I realized quickly that I had to step up in a time of need and lead.

SEPTEMBER 2009 AND BEYOND AS THE CHANGE BEGINS

I took the leadership helm at our small, privately owned company.

I struggled with what to do first and how to keep the company stable, then and for the long term. There was so much to do, so many people to talk with, and too many decisions to make.

Sitting in my office, with the door closed, the lights and the music on low, I ponder:

- **How to tell our managers and employees about the change.** What's the best way to share shocking news? How should I comfort them and reassure them about the future of the company and their jobs?

- **How to tell clients and partners.** What do they need to know? How much or how little? How transparent? How do I create new expectations on moving forward together?

- **How to spend my time.** How do I redistribute the work that is pending with one man down? And how do I start to establish relationships with existing clients who were previously managed by my partner?

Adam Grant, a professor specializing in organizational psychology at the Wharton School of the University of Pennsylvania, describes a leader's job like this: "To give people pay and purpose, support their success, and care about their well-being."

As I look back now at those first fleeting days, I struggled to shift my focus off myself and my woes and onto the decisions of where to start. The strain of balancing the needs of clients against the needs of staff and even my own needs was real.

Through my new lens, I realized quickly that job number one was to stabilize the management team and staff. Without a solid, focused workforce willing to stay in place and work hard, we wouldn't survive as a company. Everything depended on that, so ensuring employee purpose and well-being was essential.

I wanted to make sure they shared their sadness, and I hoped I could steer them toward acceptance of the new reality. I had to navigate change in ways that helped retain our workforce, get our jobs done, serve our clients, and grow our business.

It wasn't easy, smooth, or without tears and mistakes, but during a time of immense personal sadness, tremendous company loss, and heavy hearts, it meant:

- **Telling the staff the news at the same time.** I wouldn't risk the news leaking out slowly or catching on fire in ways that would be hard to put out. It was important that there was one source of truth and that I shared news and answered questions openly.

- **Being transparent**, sharing updates when I could—good and bad—while honoring personal privacy. It often wasn't easy to openly talk about what was happening, but I tried to do it as honestly as possible.

- **Spending time with the staff**, individually and as a team, to ease worries and to calm fears. Each person reacted a little differently, needed support in differing ways, and some weren't always ready to hear the news. It was a tough balancing act, knowing what worked with one didn't necessarily work with the next.

- **Keeping the office door wide open** and making rounds to check the temperature of staff psyche. Realistically, I knew there would be private chatter and conversations among the staff. That was okay and expected, but I also wanted them to know they could always come to me with a rumor or a concern.

- **Keeping the work flowing.** The timing of the change wasn't convenient, but it probably never would be. This was just a couple of months ahead of an annual firm-sponsored conference, and we couldn't take our foot off the pedal. It was a challenge to stay focused and motivated and to get the work done.

- **Celebrating the company's successes.** Even in a sad time, it was important to embrace the good and the triumphs and have a little fun. I wanted everyone to know it was okay to continue to live.

- **Recognizing the demands of the work** on the staff, especially those who were going above and beyond to fill the voids. It was important to praise and reward the staff for jobs well done.

- **Accepting that I'd make mistakes**, confessing when I messed up, and asking for forgiveness. Nobody is perfect, and I certainly wasn't.

- **Encouraging work-life balance** and making sure all, including myself, recognized the importance and value of a true balance. Reality hit us all smack in the face. We now knew, beyond any doubt, that life-altering change could happen in the blink of an eye. If it happened to someone as vibrant as John, it could happen to anyone. I had to make sure people were taking care of themselves and their families while protecting their health and well-being.

Sadly, John passed away about 18 months after his diagnosis—far too young—but his memory and his company legacy carry on to this day. And over the years, my appreciation of the leadership and life lessons he taught me has only grown.

I believe the quality of a leader is reflected in the standards they set for themselves and the standards to which they hold others. I expect a lot from myself and my staff, but I also try to give a lot back. For me, an effective leader is:

- Confident yet humble

- Exceedingly clear

- Reasonably courageous.

If you're willing to lead, you can overcome your reluctance. But if you aren't freely willing to step up, then step aside and let someone else do it. There are both leaders and followers in this world; both are important roles. Know which one you are and make your best contribution.

Over time and through trial and error, I learned the qualities of a leader and identified steps that can help anyone, even those with a touch of reluctance, become stronger, wiser leaders.

THE TOOL

Some people are natural-born leaders, but most aren't. If you're in this latter group, like I was, and are reluctant to lead, here are three steps you can use to become a stronger, wiser leader.

Step 1: Understand and Overcome Your Reasons for Reluctance. According to research from the *Harvard Business Review*, reluctance to lead is often traced back to three reasons: being afraid people won't like you, fearing others may label you as overly aggressive or a bully, and worry over being blamed for poor outcomes or business failures.

If you have any of these similar concerns, here are a few tips:

- Don't let the fear of what others may think of you change your goals. As a leader, you will face conflicts. When they arise, and they will, focus on improving the work, not on personalities or personal issues.

- New research suggests that rather than leading with an iron fist, leading others with warmth and kindness is a better way to influence and lead. Practicing kindness can lead to leadership success.

- If you fear failure, seek ways to moderate your risks. Start with less complicated projects to assess your skills. This gives you a chance to experiment with different leadership tactics and hone your own best practices. As you become more confident, take on bigger and more complex projects. Grow into a leader.

Step 2: Correct Your Reluctant Leadership Behavior. Breaking away from the confines of reluctant leadership requires a change in thinking. You must:

- **Shift toward an ownership mindset.** Regardless of your position in the organization, understand where you fit in the big picture and accept ownership of that role and your purpose.

- **Become an avid listener.** Seek out and listen to the opinions of others to improve both your company and leadership skills. You won't agree with or accept everything you hear, and that's okay, but listening to others is a good practice and almost always provides at least one or two useful new insights.

- **Develop negotiation skills.** Focus on solutions rather than problems. A conversation about what's possible rather than arguing about what's wrong is more constructive and more likely to create good results. Remember, securing the optimal outcome is the goal. There is both art and science in providing your opinions in ways that can be actively heard, fairly evaluated, and willingly accepted. Seek out people, resources, and training to help you develop diplomatic-level skills.

Step 3: Build Good Leadership Habits. Through the years, I've observed a set of habits of people I consider to be good leaders. Develop these three skills, and you'll be well on the road to becoming a stronger leader.

- **Be Humble.** A strong leader is a confident but humble leader. Good leaders freely share the limelight and praise and openly solicit feedback, advice, and the opinions of others. Without humility, you risk becoming arrogant or dismissing the perspectives and contributions of others. Build the habit of staying humble!

- **Be Clear.** A strong leader articulates individual and team goals and communicates clearly up and down the management chain. Make sure you create and share a vision that guides your actions and decisions and leads to alignment and focus. Without clarity, you and your team may lose direction. Communicating ineffectively could lead to confusion, wasted efforts, and missed opportunities. Build the habit of practicing clarity!

- **Be Brave.** A strong leader makes tough decisions, takes rational but bold actions, and sees challenges as opportunities. Without bravery, you may become indecisive and may avoid risks. Failing to make tough decisions or confront tricky situations could lead to inaction, slowed progress, and fewer innovations. Build the habit of being courageous!

In *Dare to Lead*, best-selling author Brené Brown concluded that "we need braver leaders and more courageous cultures." She suggested that being unclear is akin to being unkind. Clarity is both helpful and kind. "If you are a leader who is unclear about expectations, fuzzy on what you really need, or skirting around an issue, you are actually being unkind because it sets people up to fail and creates future problems."

Leaders who are humble, clear, and brave don't avoid tough conversations. They provide honest feedback that leads to valuable growth.

So, be brave. Be clear. Be humble. Use these steps and habits to build a leadership style and mindset that moves you away from reluctance. Focus on the collective good. Find a purpose larger than yourself. Boldly take these steps to become an effective, enthusiastic leader.

I wish you only the best in your leadership journey.

Kathy L. Divis, MBA, is President and a founding partner of Greystone.Net, a healthcare web, digital, and access strategy company based in Atlanta, Georgia. Greystone helps hospital and health system clients solve problems and improve performance in areas such as access management, customer relationship management, web and internet strategy, and both traditional and digital healthcare marketing.

Before Greystone, Kathy was the Director of Marketing for Emory Health Care and has held similar positions at the University of Pennsylvania Medical Center in Philadelphia and the UAB Medical Center in Birmingham, Alabama.

A native of Nebraska, Kathy holds a bachelor's degree in marketing from the University of Nebraska-Omaha and secured her MBA from the University of Alabama at Birmingham.

Kathy consults frequently on marketing and digital strategy development, conducts contact center assessments, helps health systems plan new or re-engineer existing call centers, and manages the highly regarded annual Healthcare Internet Conference (HCIC), which is now in its 28th year. She collaborates with clients and partners on many other marketing-related activities.

She is a frequent lecturer and author on healthcare contact centers, traditional and digital marketing, web and internet strategies, and MarTech.

In her downtime, she loves to garden, is a voracious reader, and is an avid sports fan, especially when her favorite teams—the Nebraska Cornhuskers and the Atlanta Braves—are playing. Go Big Red! Go Braves!

If you have questions or comments or want to reach out, connect with her at:

kdivis@greystone.net

770-407-7677

https://www.linkedin.com/in/kathyldivis/

Resources:

- More on Orrin Woodward: https://www.orrinwoodward.com
- More on Brené Brown: https://brenebrown.com/hubs/dare-to-lead/
- More on Adam Grant: https://adamgrant.net/
- *Harvard Business Review*:
  Why Capable People Are Reluctant to Lead –
  https://hbr.org/2020/12/why-capable-people-are-reluctant-to-lead

CHAPTER 3

EMOTIONALLY INTELLIGENT LEADERSHIP

INSPIRE AND MOTIVATE BY PUTTING OTHERS' NEEDS BEFORE YOUR OWN

Mike Milligan

Placing the needs of others first defines the recipe for effective leadership – and emotional intelligence is the key ingredient.

MY STORY

"What in the Hell were you thinking?" shouts a red-faced Dr. Chen, chief medical officer, as he busts the door open.

There are just some days when you'd like to turn back time.

Mine was earlier in my career, as a young hot-shot health system marketing director who had all the answers. Here's my message to my younger self: "Breathe, think, breathe again, then speak."

It all started on a Friday afternoon as I wrapped up the week, head down and door closed, and prepared to inconspicuously slip out a little early to get a head start on the weekend camping trip.

"Come on in, Dr. Chen, oh wait, I guess you already did. How may I help you?" I quipped, not having the awareness to know my sarcasm was making matters worse.

"Listen, smart ass, did you approve this photo?" asked Dr. Chen as he pointed to a stock image of a family accompanying an article in a recently published company community magazine. Although I'm not always the quickest learner, I thought I better cool it. "Yes, Dr. Chen. Is there an issue?"

"Yes, my issue is that we have a marketing director who thinks there's only one race in our society. Do you see how lily white this family is?" shouts Dr. Chen, an Asian-American, as he hovered over my desk.

My moment of self-restraint was short-lived.

"I don't care who you are; you can't speak to me that way!" I retorted as I stood up and pointed to the open doorway, in earshot of all the neighboring offices, including the CEO. "Get out of my office!"

While Dr. Chen's focus on representing diversity in advertising was important, it was his approach and delivery that set me off. But, as I'll address, despite others' behavior, only you are in control of your behavior. In the end, although months later, my inability to control my own emotions eventually led to the organization announcing that I was leaving to "pursue other endeavors."

That life lesson started my journey to becoming a more emotionally intelligent leader.

EMOTIONAL INTELLIGENCE

The concept of emotional intelligence, or EI, was first coined in 1990 by Peter Salovey and John Mayer, and I became more familiar with the concept about a decade later through Daniel Goleman's book *Emotional Intelligence—Why It Can Matter More Than IQ*. In its earlier days, EI focused exclusively on the importance of keeping your emotions in check.

Although managing your emotions is certainly an important element of EI, modern thinking has evolved so that EI also includes being cognizant of how others may view a situation differently than you. Lastly, as we recognize our own emotions, we must also realize how our emotions affect others in both our professional and personal lives.

In fact, in business, in the U.S. and worldwide, companies often place the most emphasis on pre-employment EI scores to determine the cultural fit of prospective employees. According to the World Economic Forum (WEF) 2020 Future of Jobs report, leaders around the globe first seek employees who score high in emotional intelligence. They recognize (as you should) that leaders with strong emotional intelligence are the most successful because of their ability to influence others and behave with composure and professionalism when under pressure.

We've heard the term "born leaders," but I think that's an over-exaggeration. Sure, we might have certain qualities, even in our childhood, developed through positive influences from our parents and others, but leadership is a learned characteristic. Similarly, I believe emotional intelligence is a learned skill developed through success and failure.

In my case, growing in emotional intelligence has been a life-long endeavor. When I shared with colleagues that I was writing a chapter on the subject, they were generous in saying that it's clear that I'm an emotionally intelligent leader, as demonstrated by how I work through a problem or a crisis and how I listen and carefully consider the views of others.

I was flattered by their praise but questioned it. *Do they really know me? Why do I feel like I still don't always have my emotions under control?*

The truth is, while it's fair to say I've improved my EI, I'm still on the journey, and sometimes I get detoured.

RECOVERING EMOTIONALHOLIC

Like an alcoholic, once you're an "emotionalholic," you're always one—you're just in a constant state of recovery.

As I reflect on that infamous Dr. Chen meeting, I realize I was much lower on the EI scale then. First, I certainly wasn't in control of my emotions. My emotions controlled me. I didn't act professionally and demonstrate leadership through composure, and I allowed my leaders and employees to witness my behavior. Furthermore, not until I reflected later did I even consider the situation from Dr. Chen's perspective. *Why was he acting so assertively? Why was he upset?* Upon contemplation and growth, I realized that although he could likely use some EI growth as well, his strong feelings likely came from his life experiences of being an Asian American.

A DEEPER VIEW OF EI – A DR. CHEN FLASHBACK

As a recovering emotionalholic, I've taken every opportunity to learn and develop my skills. Most recently, in completing my master's degree, I conducted even more industry research and incorporated EI concepts into virtually every paper, assignment, or presentation. As important as accounting, finance, statistics, and economics are to one's career, they're all secondary to being an emotionally intelligent leader. If you can't motivate and influence others through positive relationships, your professional growth will be limited.

PRACTICE MAKES (CLOSER TO) PERFECT

As I've shared, although some leadership qualities may be part of your personality, EI growth is a learned behavior, and this constant learning provides tremendous benefits to your work and home life. Let's discuss some basic behaviors that you can work on every day.

Listen First. We likely remember the advice from our childhood of why we were born with two ears and one mouth. Leaders with high emotional intelligence understand the importance of active listening. They create a welcoming environment for their team members to express their ideas and concerns. When we actively listen, we gain valuable insights, build trust, and foster collaboration. I continue to work on this; I'm not perfect.

But the more I truly listen and process what others say, the better the results. EI involves thinking of how others view a problem and considering their unique experiences and perspectives. As eager as we may be to make a point, we need to process what others say, acknowledge them and their comments, and provide a reaction, regardless of whether we agree or not. In the end, you'll be more likely to be received better by them as well.

In my role as a healthcare strategist and planner, I primarily work with CEOs of rural health organizations, helping them build their brands and volumes in their local communities. The process is a collaborative one, utilizing active listening and encouraging dialogue. During the initial engagements with clients, I facilitate a marketing planning process where I'm interviewing various constituents from C-suite leaders to board members, to physicians, to employees, to community members. I insist on conducting these interviews one-on-one to facilitate an environment of openness and candor. This is where active listening takes such a strong role. I may come in with my list of questions regarding brand or patient engagement, but often, other topics emerge through building trust and rapport.

For example, sometimes a cultural issue arises when employees share that the CEO does not encourage new ideas or recognize employees' achievements.

Although my initial task may not have been employee engagement, I know, especially in rural health, that employees are the greatest ambassadors of the organization's message. All the advertising spending in the world will be a poor investment if employees aren't engaged and feeling valued. Another example discovered through active listening could be identifying a customer service issue throughout the organization. We know advertising can't fix an operational problem. Through using proper EI skills, we identify issues and solutions through an empathetic, objective, and non-confrontational approach.

ENCOURAGE DIVERSE OPINIONS.

Effective leaders with high EI focus learn why people feel the way they do. They also communicate the reasoning behind their own decisions, providing clarity and a sense of purpose. When you exercise high EI, you actively engage with your teams, provide feedback, and acknowledge individual and collective achievements. You manage conflicts by fostering open communication, empathizing with different viewpoints, and finding mutually beneficial solutions.

Understand What Motivates Others and Create the Ideal Environment. Foster employee engagement, productivity, and wellness, and prioritize the team's satisfaction and effectiveness. Invest in professional development, provide growth opportunities, and create a culture of continuous learning.

REALIZE HOW YOUR NON-VERBALS AFFECT OTHERS

"Mike, is there an issue with our presentation?" asked a concerned employee sharing her ideas via a virtual meeting.

How does she know I have concerns? I didn't even say anything. Is she a mind reader?

Whether it's in person or on a video chat, our body language speaks volumes.

For me, I'm "follically" challenged, but in times of stress or deep thought, I'm told I tend to rub my bald head as if I'm polishing it. Until I was told by employees, I never realized it.

It's impossible to ignore nonverbal signals to others about what you think and feel. The emotional part of your brain is always on—but you can regulate it.

SELF-REFLECTION – A TOP 8 CHECKLIST

In the true spirit of emotional intelligence, I encourage you to consider the following characteristics in determining your strengths and weaknesses. Considering all the books and articles I've read on the subject, including reflecting on my journey, I've compiled these tenets to stay active in your EI performance:

Do you. . .

1. Hold yourself accountable?
2. Understand you can't surround yourself with "yes people?"
3. Admit you don't know everything?
4. Exercise active listening?
5. Have an awareness of how your non-verbal cues affect others?
6. Respect diverse thoughts?
7. Regularly check in with the emotions of others?
8. Avoid criticizing others for their weaknesses?

THE EMOTIONALLY INTELLIGENT PARENT, SPOUSE, FRIEND

If effective EI is a priority for you in business, it will be in your personal life, too. Or at least it should be. While I've shared that my EI development has been a growth journey, I'm happy to say my commitment has done wonders for me personally—as a dad, husband, friend, and volunteer.

Years ago, my wife and I trained to be Stephen Ministers. In short, Stephen Ministry is a Christian-based ministry that provides counsel and comfort for those enduring any of life's crises, including divorce, death of a loved one, or any number of delicate circumstances. We're not ordained ministers, but rather, we're lay people who provide a lending hand, and often a lending ear, to others. One of the tenets of our training is to practice active listening and not try to solve a care receiver's issue. People want someone to listen to them and to be understood. If they were comfortable, we'd pray with them or share the Bible, but first and foremost to be engaged with their needs and to listen. Listen for cues. Ask open-ended questions to encourage dialogue.

I can't think of a better application of emotional intelligence in my personal life. Whether it's with the Stephen Ministry or how I relate to my wife and grown children, the behavior should be the same.

As I reflect on how my EI journey has affected my personal life, here are some takeaways I know will also apply to you:

OVERCOMING ADVERSITY WITH COMPOSURE

In 2020, I was in my bed, connected to oxygen, afraid to fall asleep. *What if I don't get better? I gotta stay strong. Be cool. Don't show her I'm worried.*

As I learned later, my wife Ann was doing the same, acting strong and pretending she wasn't concerned. *I know if I show I'm stressed, he'll get worked up. Stay positive and wait to cry until I go into the other room.*

I contracted pneumonia from COVID-19, and my oxygen levels weren't improving. I received the oxygen prescription from the emergency room, but local hospitals were so inundated with cases, especially in the rural Wisconsin area where we live, that I couldn't be admitted or even be seen by primary care.

"Call the nurse line for guidance," we were told by the ER staff. But they were so backed up that it often took 48 hours for a return call from an exhausted nurse working around the clock. Fortunately, Ann, a retired pharmacist, had some medical background to guide me physically, spiritually, and of course, emotionally.

The reality was that we weren't sure if I'd survive. Being overweight and having type II diabetes, I was at higher risk, and people my age or younger were dying.

But, to this day, I believe my EI growth, in combination with my Christian faith, gave me comfort and peace to overcome the adversity. Although admittedly, I was anxious, I didn't let my emotions get the better of me. I focused on my wife and her anxiety, and she focused on mine. When we'd get through to the on-call nurse, we'd express our appreciation and empathize with what she was also enduring. *How did these nurses do it? Call after call, with sick and anxious patients, frustrated that they couldn't even see a doctor.*

Don't get me wrong, I'm not saying I was always calm, cool, and collected. But I do know that deliberate efforts to be a more emotionally intelligent person gave me the power to handle what I faced with composure and dignity and by putting the needs of others first.

IMPROVED RELATIONSHIPS

My EI growth enables me to understand and manage my emotions, which allows me to have more positive and fulfilling relationships with immediate family and friends. I'm able to better empathize with others, communicate effectively, and constructively navigate conflict.

GREATER SELF-AWARENESS

Being aware of my EI strengths and vulnerabilities allows me to make better decisions and take appropriate actions. Self-aware individuals can better identify their strengths and weaknesses, set goals, and make meaningful life changes. They can understand their own emotions and how they impact their thoughts, behavior, and decision-making. They also have a better understanding of their values and priorities which helps them to make choices that align with them.

BETTER DECISION-MAKING

As I've improved my EI, I feel better able to evaluate options and make sound decisions. I consider not only the facts and logic but also the emotional impact of my choices.

IMPROVED COMMUNICATOR

As a trained marketer, I always thought I was a competent communicator, but EI development brought me to a whole new level. Although a work in progress, I'm able to read the emotional cues of others, adapt to their communication style, and build trust and understanding with others.

THE TOOL

HOW TO IMPROVE
EMOTIONAL INTELLIGENCE IN 8 STEPS

1. Know Yourself

Being aware of your emotions and responses to those around you can greatly improve your emotional intelligence. Knowing when you feel anxious or angry can help you process and communicate effectively. Consider recording the time you feel a strong emotion and taking notes about what caused that feeling, and how well you did in addressing it constructively.

2. Recognize how others feel

Emotional Intelligence may start with self-reflection, but it's also important to assess how others perceive your behavior. Knowing how to adjust your message, whether verbal or nonverbal, based on how you're received is critical to your EI development. Try to imagine yourself in others' positions and consider how you might feel if in their situation (remember my interaction with Dr. Chen).

3. Practice active listening

As we've discussed, people communicate through their words and body language. It's important to be cognizant of listening and watching for positive and negative reactions. Are others engaged with you, nodding off, making eye contact, or looking at their phones? Taking the time to listen to others indicates a level of respect that forms the foundation for healthy relationships for years to come. Ask open-ended questions to encourage dialogue, repeat back questions to check for understanding (e.g., "So what I hear you saying is. . ."), make eye contact, and even use affirmative head gestures to show you're engaged.

4. Communicate clearly

Understanding what to say or write and when to deliver messages are critical components of effective communication and building relationships. Also, realize that people like to receive information in various ways, depending on their backgrounds, ages, or environments.

5. Stay positive

Use positive, encouraging language in your verbal and written communications. Never be too busy to send an encouraging email, smile, or just recognize an achievement or contribution. By doing so, you're creating an environment more conducive to problem-solving, teamwork, and healthy conflict resolution.

6. Listen to feedback

You must listen to feedback, positive or negative. This means taking accountability for your actions and committing to an action plan for improvement.

7. Stay cool

Approach stressful situations with a sense of calmness, regardless of the scenario. You control the situation; don't let the situation control you. Tensions can easily escalate, especially when people are working on deadlines, so keeping steady can help everyone be successful.

8. Laugh it Up

Humor and laughter are natural remedies to stress. They ease your burdens and help you keep things in perspective. Laughter brings your nervous system into balance, reducing stress, calming you down, sharpening your mind, and making you more empathic toward others.

Mike Milligan, MHA, is senior vice president with BVK. He has dedicated his career to advocating for rural health with specializations in branding, patient acquisition, employee recruitment, and crisis communications. Mike is committed to the industry through his advocacy on Capitol Hill, speaking engagements, ongoing counsel, and his role as a member of the National Rural Health Association (NRHA) Rural Health Congress.

In 2008, Mike founded a healthcare marketing agency. It flourished under his guidance, along with his reputation as a national leader, speaker, and expert in helping health leaders navigate today's evolving demands. In 2022, Mike sold his successful business and continues in the healthcare industry through his leadership role at BVK.

Mike earned his B.A. in Journalism and his Master of Healthcare Administration (MHA). He has served as Director, President, and Chair of dozens of industry associations and for-profit and nonprofit boards throughout his career. In addition to his ongoing counsel at BVK Health, Mike has served in senior communications roles for Advocate Aurora Health, Hospital Sisters Health System (HSHS), and Novant Health.

Mike and his wife Ann enjoy the outdoors in their northern Wisconsin lake house, where they fish, hike, snowshoe, snowmobile, or just relax with a beverage on the dock. They have two adult daughters, two grandsons, and three golden retrievers.

Reach out to Mike at BVK at mike@rhcmarketer.com or via LinkedIn at https://www.linkedin.com/in/m-milligan-mha/ with questions, thoughts, or ideas. Mike and his BVK colleagues offer a variety of leadership workshops available for you and others in your organization.

CHAPTER 4

SURVIVING TO THRIVING

BECOMING A TRAUMA-INFORMED LEADER

Carrie Freshour

"Be the change you want to see in the world."

~ Mohandas Gandhi

MY STORY

It'd been about 50 days since we lost our family home to a devastating fire.

Gandhi's quote about being the change has guided me for years and has long been the tagline of my Facebook bio.

But wait, am I? Am I being the change?

Pulling into the parking lot, I drove to the third level, where the first open spot appeared.

Shutting off the engine, I sat there for a minute. My heart beat fast, and I began to sweat and feel a flush on my cheeks. Calming myself, I took a few deep breaths.

You got this!

Share what you came to share.

Remain calm; breathe!

I missed the previous board meeting because I was utterly hopeless and frozen in action for a moment after the fire.

Going from 100-to-0 in a second was so surreal.

I served as the interim CEO while also serving in my full-time COO role. For nearly 13 months, I averaged at least 79 hours a week.

I entered the building like a bowl of rocks, constantly shifting and churning, leaving a heavy, uneasy sensation in my gut.

The bolder stuck on my chest as the elevator rose. I rounded the hallway and opened the boardroom door.

It was immediately awkward. There was a lack of eye contact, a few superficial glances, and one kind but uncomfortable smile.

In contrast to a few months prior, a significant transformation occurred.

My career path was winding, shaped by personal passions and life's unexpected turns. I began as a clinical therapist, driven by a desire to help children who experienced trauma. However, the demands of that role clashed with my longing to be present for my growing family.

To maintain a better work-life balance, I moved into a leadership role. Yet, an unsettling feeling lingered. The weight of imposter syndrome, coupled with the daily struggle to juggle the roles of wife, mother, professional, volunteer, *and survivor*, eventually took its toll.

See, you are a fraud.

They never wanted you as CEO; that was a pipe dream.

Your voice does not matter.

You will never be enough.

Maybe it's time to quit the field.

A breakdown, marked by tears on my therapist's floor, became an unexpected turning point. My hands clenched, and the familiar tightness in my chest signaled the onset of another panic attack.

How many more times will I have to sit through these hollow platitudes, pretending to absorb their tidy theories while my own trauma screams in the background?

They spoke of resilience and healing, but their words felt like a bandaid on a bullet wound.

It solidified my purpose: to bridge that gap and create meaningful change.

This newfound clarity led me to explore entrepreneurship. Eventually, I landed a contract with an organization whose mission deeply resonated with me. I later transitioned from consultant to COO, embracing the challenge of building a sustainable infrastructure for their vital work as they bridged the gap between grassroots leadership and structured board governance.

Despite my technical expertise, I grappled with the dissonance within the organization—a misalignment between their espoused values and actions.

This internal conflict intensified as I assumed the dual roles of interim CEO and COO during the founder's sabbatical.

Is this the real change I want?

I felt the familiar tug-of-war between ambition and intuition.

The job demands weighed heavily on me, leaving me feeling disconnected from my family and questioning my purpose. The fire that destroyed our family home further amplified these doubts.

While I continued to lead the organization through its recovery, the question remained: *Is this the path I want to continue on?*

BACK TO THE BOARDROOM

Despite my positive reputation and years of dedicated service, tension brewed. The board's recent decisions, made without adequate information or guidance, jeopardized the organization's mission.

I'm ready.

I've seen enough.

I felt defeated in so many ways. Yet, early on, I began to see that fire had a funny way of being a silver lining.

I thoughtfully planned out what I could do.

I'll serve as COO for an interim period and then phase out after the summer when the organization is more sustained.

"We decided to move forward with the other candidate for CEO," she said.

Their victory was never going to be mine.

My heart raced. I'm exhausted from the circular conversations and thinking about so many things at super-speed.

My breathing is labored, and tears come up behind my eyes.

Don't cry!

"I understand your decision. I've been open about my reservations in our past conversations. I, too, believe this isn't the right path for me."

I didn't think they were making the right decision, but not because of me.

With the weight of unspoken words pressing down on my heart, I felt a wave of conflicting emotions wash over me. Relief swept through me, like a cool breeze on a sweltering day, as the weight of the CEO position lifted off my shoulders. But mingled with relief was a raw wound of hurt, a pang of disappointment and anger at the mounting contradictions—a deep sting.

I was ready to step back, pass the torch to someone capable, and return to a role I excelled at while navigating my current challenges. I'd help the organization transition for six months to ensure my successor's success.

The board's choice, seemingly driven by conflicts of interest, felt like a betrayal. Their calculated move prioritized control over the company's well-being and ignited my anger.

The board president's distortion of our private conversation, falsely claiming my commitment against my intentions, set off alarms. I knew I had to take action.

"I'm sick and tired of your go-to-church-on-Sunday and I'm-covered-for-my-bad behavior-for-the-week mentality!" I declared, my voice shaking with suppressed rage.

Packing my things, I realized too late that I let the toll of emotions and pain swoop over me, revealing the tender underbelly of my soul.

I stormed out, a tempest of emotions raging within me, feeling stripped of strength and ***utterly vanquished***.

In the aftermath, no one from the organization reached out to check on me despite the personal trauma I was still recovering from.

This experience highlighted the stark disconnect between words and actions. While the organization championed the values of trauma-informed care and support, their behavior toward me told a different story. It reinforced my belief that change requires more than lip service; it demands authenticity, accountability, and the courage to speak up against injustice.

BEGINNING TO UNDERSTAND:
THE DICHOTOMY OF A PARADIGM SHIFT

When I entered this field, we were trained not to share information about ourselves. From the "it's not about me" and "do-no-harm" ethical and boundary perspectives, it made sense. I could live safely within that boundary.

However, as our field has progressed, we've gained valuable insights from real-world experiences.

By actively listening to people's accounts, we've incorporated new understandings of brain science, specifically neuroplasticity, and various human behavioral theories into our programs, policies, and *practices*.

My understanding of the lifelong impacts of my trauma and the multi-generational trauma I grew up around was critical not only to the field but also to my executive leadership role in developing the internal operating systems to be trauma-informed.

Being trauma-informed means understanding past experiences can leave lasting marks. It's about recognizing when someone's reactions might be rooted in unseen wounds, not just their present circumstances.

Instead of reacting with judgment or dismissal, it's about offering support, understanding, and a safe space for healing. It's about preventing further harm in our words *and* our actions.

The founder and I worked to create the strategy and map the vision with trauma-informed principles, survivors, *and* the staff who served them at the forefront.

I modeled that for over three years. I stood tall and proud in knowing that.

My voice was valued until it wasn't.

In a world where we try to be understanding and supportive, it's disheartening to feel let down. And it's even more painful when it comes from people you trust. It's like they're saying, "Your pain doesn't matter. Only ours does."

But here's the thing: trauma is real. It doesn't just go away. It stays with you, affecting how you see the world and interact with others.

When you experience trauma, you need people who will be there for you, understand what you're going through, be respectful of your boundaries, and listen without judgment.

That's what it means to be trauma-informed. It's about creating a safe and supportive environment for people who have experienced trauma. It's about understanding how trauma can affect people and how to help them heal.

And it's about **recognizing** everyone has a story. Everyone has experienced something that's shaped who they are. It's our job to respect those stories and to learn from them. We've evolved. We're breaking down stigma, shame, and self-blame.

This outward progress sparked an internal conflict, a dichotomy of feelings demanding a new level of vulnerability.

When I brought my whole self to my work—my personal trauma, the self-doubt I wrestled with daily—it felt like exposing a raw nerve. Yet, in that vulnerability, I found an unexpected strength, a resilience born from embracing my humanity rather than denying it.

I uncovered those limiting beliefs I've healed in private my entire life:

It's not about you. It's about those survivors. Why are you so selfish?

They don't want to hear how your survivor experience was counter to everything they say they are doing.

And yet those beliefs were contrary to the evidence I both lived and saw firsthand in my work with others who've also experienced trauma.

It was time for a change.

THE INTERNAL AFTERMATH OF THE BOARDROOM

I sit in such dismay. *I can't breathe.*

How can things move so fast yet feel so unbearably stuck?

My breath hitches, a desperate gasp for air in this suffocating atmosphere.

I spoke my truth and poured my heart out for this organization, for myself, and my words were twisted and turned into a weapon against me.

Confusion swirls around me, a thick fog obscuring my path.

Were these not good relationships?

Where did it all go so terribly wrong?

The answer, though painful, is glaringly obvious: a series of leadership missteps, a mishandled crisis, and the glaring absence of a succession plan.

The foundation we built upon is crumbling, and I'm caught in the crossfire and left to bear the brunt of the blame.

Yet, amidst the ashes of this experience, a spark of defiance still burns within me. I own my mistakes, the moments where a different choice might have altered the course. **But that doesn't negate the truth: I was wounded profoundly and unfairly. And that pain, that righteous anger, fuels my resolve to keep fighting for the cause, for what is right.**

This isn't just a personal wound; it's a gaping hole in the fabric of leadership, a stark reminder of the importance of succession planning and preparing for the inevitable storms. It's a lesson learned through heartache, a lesson I'm determined to share so that others may find a smoother path, a less painful journey.

Here I was at the end of a roller coaster ride through burnout, vicarious trauma, and Complex PTSD. And yet, amid my unraveling, a twisted sort of invitation arrived.

"We want survivor voices," they said. "We value the survivor experience." They claimed to understand how trauma can rear its ugly head and how it manifests in our bodies, minds, and lives.

But here's the kicker: I was already at the table—not as a distant observer, a clinician, or an advocate. This time, I was the survivor—raw, vulnerable, and exhausted from the fight.

BACK TO THE BOARDROOM, KINDA

I was scheduled to meet with the new CEO at a coffee shop a week later.

I was still upset with the board and unsure what came next.

I can do more for the staff and the survivors there. I planned to stay as COO for the summer.

I regained my composure. I wanted the new CEO to come in with a sense of welcome and belonging, not the tension that had been growing between a board and its leaders for years.

This is what I want. Stay true to your values and heart.

It wasn't how you thought it would happen, but you prayed for the answer, and here it is.

Sure, she is their church colleague, and the conflicts of interest are setting my ethical values on fire, but I'm living in a world of ashes. I prayed to let go.

Arriving early, I sat by the window with my favorite cup of coffee.

In walked the new CEO, flanked by two familiar board members. Once allies in shared professional battles, their presence now felt like a betrayal, a stark reminder of the duplicity that shattered our trust.

Something is off.

I awkwardly greet them. They stay stiff and sit at the table.

"I'm sure you've heard there've been some stressful times," I awkwardly stumble over my words, trying to ease the tension and my anxiety as I hand her a gift. *Talk through the hard.*

"We want you to take a two-week break," the new CEO announced. "Paid time off."

Paid time off? My head spun. "Are you firing me?" I blurted out, the words tumbling from my lips before I could catch them. "Or are you pushing me out?"

The shock was palpable, and I felt a bitter taste in my mouth. "I came here to help," I pleaded, the hurt seeping into my voice. "I put my feelings aside, showed up repeatedly, and now you're letting me go?"

Their response was a platitude I heard countless times before. "We prayed about it and think you need time to process."

Process?

Where was my time to process two days after the fire when they needed me to run payroll?

Nine days after, when they expected me to ease back to work?

One month later, when they needed me to lead the fundraiser?

No. I was only offered "time to process" when my disagreement with their decisions became too inconvenient.

I stormed out, tears blurring my vision as I fumbled for my car keys. In a moment of blind panic, I sent my team a cryptic text.

Had I quit? Been fired? I didn't know. The uncertainty fueled a spiraling terror.

As I drove away, I fought to maintain composure, my heart pounding against my ribs, knowing they had a direct line of sight from coffeehouse windows.

Ultimately, it was a familiar story, a painful echo of the past. I took the leave out of sheer necessity, not choice.

Despite being on approved medical leave and continuing to help during their crisis, my reward was a cold email sent while I was on vacation, terminating my employment and demanding the return of company property.

TRAUMA-INFORMED CARE

Trauma doesn't just live in our memories; it embeds itself in our bodies, ready to erupt when triggered by conflict or stress. Whether it's a racing heart, a tightening chest, or a flood of overwhelming emotions, these physical manifestations are our body's way of remembering the past. While time can heal, how we respond to these triggers is crucial.

In this instance, an organization that championed trauma-informed care faltered. While their intentions may have been good, they failed to truly understand the impact of their actions, misinterpreting my distress and exacerbating my trauma.

This highlights the vital importance of recognizing the signs of trauma, responding with empathy and understanding, and creating systems that prioritize the well-being of all involved.

HERE IS WHAT I LEARNED

Through raw vulnerability, I've learned to confront the lies we tell ourselves about our worth. I've found strength in breaking the silence, speaking out when actions contradict values, and doing so with composure. It's okay to stand alone, to extend grace even when it's not reciprocated, and to own our growth without shame.

When leaders face crises, so do their organizations. To navigate these storms, we must embody the very principles we preach. We must *be* the change we seek to create.

My 25-year journey has been filled with similar disconnects between words and actions. As both a leader and a trauma survivor, I've learned to embrace my experiences, using my voice to challenge the status quo and advocate for authenticity.

A relentless pursuit of understanding and meaning fueled this continuous learning and growth path. If my vulnerable story can inspire even one leader to embrace their authentic self and lead with courage, then the pain is worth it. Together, we can dismantle the barriers of shame and stigma, fostering workplaces where everyone feels valued, respected, and empowered to thrive. Through authenticity, we unlock our collective potential and build a world where everyone can flourish.

THE TOOL
THE TRAUMA-INFORMED LEADER'S MINDSET INVENTORY

The crucible of trauma and professional upheaval became my unexpected catalyst for transformation. I discovered both healing and growth are possible and essential for authentic leadership. This tool, born from my journey and informed by trauma-informed practices, gratitude, and mindfulness, helped me navigate the complexities of leadership, heal from deep wounds, and manifest the person I wanted to be.

THE TRAUMA-INFORMED LEADER'S MINDSET INVENTORY: EXCAVATING YOUR AUTHENTIC SELF

This isn't a quick fix but a deliberate, intentional practice requiring time, patience, and a willingness to stumble and rise again. It's a journey of self-discovery; while winding, the path ultimately leads to resilience and empowerment.

STEP ONE: SELF-REFLECTION – DIGGING DEEP

Carve out sacred time for introspection. Dive deep into the depths of your being and ask yourself:

- What truly matters to me? What are the values driving my life and work?
- What obstacles or limiting beliefs are holding me back, like anchors weighing me down?
- How do I envision myself showing up authentically in the world, unburdened by the past?

This is the starting point, the fertile ground for your authentic leadership to blossom. It's about unearthing your true self, acknowledging your wounds, **and reclaiming your power.**

Are you ready to embark on this transformative journey? To cultivate resilience, lead authentically, and create a ripple effect of positive change? If so, let's continue excavating your authentic self together.

To learn more about the Trauma-Informed Leader's Mindset Inventory and access additional resources, visit
www.carriefreshourconsulting.com

Carrie Freshour is the driving force behind Carrie Freshour Consulting, LLC. A seasoned Licensed Clinical Social Worker with over 25 years of experience, her firm is a catalyst for empowering individuals and teams, fostering resilience, and dismantling stigma within the workplace culture. Weaving her lived experience, clinical acumen, and executive leadership, Carrie leads with unwavering purpose.

With a fearless approach to challenges, she initiates difficult conversations that propel toward breakthroughs. Her executive leadership career demonstrates her ability to navigate complex situations, while her trauma-lived experience, clinical training, and resilience attest to her capacity for understanding and transformation.

Her engaging presence and expert facilitation foster a safe space for open dialogue and trust. With unwavering empathy and accountability, Carrie dismantles barriers, fostering a world where every individual feels empowered to speak out against mistreatment and embrace their authentic selves.

Off-hours, when she's not jet-setting, she's whipping up gourmet meals in the kitchen or spending quality time with her hubby, two kids, and their furry family member, Harley. Writing, hiking, soccer, and traveling to soak up new cultures and meet new people are also passions she holds dear!

Connect with Carrie at https://www.carriefreshourconsulting.com/

CHAPTER 5

I KNOW WHY YOU ARE HERE

MAKING MENTORSHIP MEANINGFUL

Karri Morgan

"Live Your Dash: Make Every Moment Matter."

~ Linda Ellis

MY STORY

"I know why you are here."

I wore a poly-cotton blend long skirt and suit jacket with color-coordinated, matching hose and heels, and worked my first big job in a marketing company thinking: *I know why I am here.*

As a 20-something-year-old entry-level coordinator, my newfound career and trajectory reported to Traci, the VP of Business Development. Traci was brilliant, intimidating, and a visionary pioneer at creating partnerships and generating revenue streams. Her brain worked faster than most could comprehend, and Traci's work ethic, direct demeanor, and snippets of kindness seeped from a nature that always presented her as a powerhouse professional. Understanding that she was mentoring me without realizing it was a concept I conceived much later.

Traci traveled extensively for her position, and since she was frequently out of the office, it forced me to forge friendships with many of my colleagues. I treasured being part of a team, especially when it included innovative, insightful, forward-thinking fast movers and shakers.

Many co-workers came from various departments, including the savvy marketing team, the quiet finance hallway, the salespeople when they were in from the field, a cranky graphic designer who loathed last-minute changes, and a spit-fire Italian lady, Joanne, who supported the President.

Every morning, Joanne and I met in the copy room because it was halfway between each of our desks. The copy room was where we'd get down to *real* business, tackling frivolous corporate spending, discussing the latest hire, how much planning stakeholder meetings required, the ridiculous amounts of time spent booking flights, or how much food was ordered for meetings. On the surface, it was the curation of executive logistics, but much more deeply it was talking about life administration (that's what we called it).

Joanne loved to share. A culinarian at heart, her appreciation for Italian cooking often brought in favorite family recipes from her hometown back in New Jersey to where we lived and worked in Tennessee. She spoke so adoringly of her husband, Jeff, a successful operations executive, and gave shopping insights on the best deals from her favorite big box stores. The way she spoke of her four dogs, you'd swear she birthed them.

That copy room became an unofficial standing meeting to download from the night before about sitcoms, her shopping wins, her husband's schedule, and contemplate the direction I wanted to take in my self-proclaimed newfound success at a Fortune 500 company.

It puzzled Joanne that I was so career-focused, and yet I didn't know what I was doing in life except feeling important in my business attire while being a part of a buzzing corporate culture with colleagues who became friends outside of work.

It wasn't long into one of our daily meetings Joanne complained "This mole on my leg is really testing me!" It was constantly covered by a band-aid since she kept shaving over it, and she was miffed that it kept snagging her pantyhose—a 90s version of a much less controversial wardrobe malfunction. Moreover, the HR handbook identified such fashion accessories as essential components of the dress code and compression pantyhose were not cheap. "Get the mole removed and save yourself some money," I remember joking. Joanne made an appointment with the dermatologist.

When Wednesday wielded our usual morning meeting, Joanne wasn't in the copy room when I got there. The expression on her face as she finally rounded the corner was unfamiliar. She pointed to the spot on her leg where the mole once was and blurted out, "I have melanoma. I have a 70% chance I won't make it."

Nothing registered.

Not one thing processed in my head. Not one word was uttered out of my mouth. I wasn't trained to respond to the shocking news of a cancer diagnosis. My life skills weren't polished enough to formulate a single thread of sentiment to express my sadness, fears, or about the friendship we developed, which suddenly felt jeopardized. Joanne's tears started flowing, and that's when my tears water-falled.

At that age, in my mind, cancer's catastrophe besieged other people and was buffered by the distance between a group of human beings I only identified as strangers. Here, it was happening in front of me, and my brain and heart weren't computing what it meant.

The tumor was the size of a softball—stage four, to which the doctors devised a weekly protocol of chemotherapy and radiation. Despite the diagnosis, Joanne kept working. She loved being productive, so much so that she remained full-time, except for the days she had her infusions. Steadfast in spirit, Joanne never complained. Embattled by fatigue, hair loss, and seemingly never-ending nausea, her strength and determination were un-breachable. She found the silver linings and was thrilled to drop 35 pounds off her frame due to the harshness of the treatment. Joanne, bragging and modeling in the copy room, "Look! Another new outfit in a size eight!" while kindly deflecting the reality of her sickness.

My friendship with Joanne evolved. Her family welcomed me. They also needed me as a caregiver, having no immediate family in town to rely on for help with kids, dogs, appointments, carpooling, and grocery runs.

One might not think it, but those times brought so much laughter and unadulterated joy that they mitigated the seriousness of Joanne's prognosis. Nonetheless, she focused on living large (that's 90s speak for living her best life) and welcomed the distractions of work and fulfillment of family as an escape from the burdens of worry and the unimaginable destiny of her fate.

Even Traci, with her busy travel schedule, called regularly to check on Joanne. Jet setting around the states to make the company money and working tirelessly to complete business deals didn't detract from the concern she dedicated to Joanne. I found myself "surrounded by" an executive (and also as my supervisor), determined to impart the importance of employing the head and the heart. Traci encouraged me to "Adjust your schedule and take the time to support Joanne. Don't worry so much about eight to five, okay?" She wanted to make sure Joanne got to appointments, had healthy meals, and was surrounded by a team of colleagues to check on her well-being. Traci became less intimidating and more human to me. Her ability to juggle her corporate leadership role while getting down to the business of humanity made quite an impression on me. Though her role began as my direct supervisor, it was her acumen for living life that she quietly gifted me.

Time was its usual thief. Working in my big job as an entry-level employee, working as a caregiver to a friend who became family, and understanding life balance were skills I developed in real-time. My job was so important to me, and the toggle between friendship, caregiving, and a budding career was all-consuming.

Life was about to change again.

The cancer spread, and Joanne had a stroke. I wasn't prepared for the adjustment, but necessity has an invasive way of instituting the autopilot button for life. The cancer in her brain metastasized and spread like wildfire. She lost her ability to drive or work, and the stroke forced her to walk with partial functionality of one side of her body. The daily meetings in the copy room were relegated into memories and my role as a caregiver exponentiated for Joanne and her family. The demands of work and deadlines were woven with the priorities of transporting Joanne to and from doctor's visits, along with fielding cascades of questions from those concerned about her health. Meanwhile, I desperately tried to maintain my composure while summoning the strength to come to terms with the reality of Joanne's rapid decline. As a family representative, I told everyone, "Joanne will be fine."

The next few months became much of the same. Busy was best for me. Joanne and her family valued my contributions and loved me like family. Work respected my abilities to juggle the unforeseen roles added to my day job. Being busy was a beautiful gift masked in denial. I never heard of gamma knife radiation. I didn't know the acronym for DNR (Do Not Resuscitate) until I notarized the paperwork. Hospice was something I saw in movies and watched on TV. I only knew of older people who experienced it. I was overwhelmed by a crash course in survival, even though it was Joanne who fought to live.

On a Monday morning in November, I arrived at Joanne's through the garage door and entered the kitchen to get the debrief from her husband, Jeff. I took off a few days from work because he needed help. The smell of recently toasted bread permeated the air, and Jeff stood with his back to me, tending to Joanne's breakfast and the myriad of pellets placed in pillboxes. From the living room, I heard Joanne struggling to breathe. It was intense, concerning, and painful. "Can you get her to cough?" I remember asking Jeff. In that moment, he turned around, looked me in the eyes, and said nothing. I recalled the hospice nurse talking about the death rattle, which was just around the corner.

Thanks to the Family Medical Leave Act, Jeff needed to complete his paperwork and fax it to the corporate office to start his leave of absence. I reported in for duty to relieve him so he could tend to this errand along with a list of others while I sat with Joanne. Jeff's demeanor was very deliberate. "Please sit right here and don't leave her side," he instructed. He said I couldn't take the dogs for their walk, couldn't check the mail, couldn't get the kids from the bus stop, and to just stay seated next to Joanne until he returned. And so I sat. The labor of Joanne's breathing was all-consuming, not for the squeamish; the gurgling gasps languished between long lulls were heart-wrenching.

The living room seemed so small, filled with a hospice bed, sofa, TV, and VCR. Watching Joanne's chest expand and contract was my intent obligation. Still, I wondered, *Can I get her to cough it out?* My thoughts were bewildering. Since I arrived, her eyes hadn't opened. I took comfort in being by Joanne's side even if she knew I wasn't there.

Four hours passed of this same up-and-down chest motion and agonizing noises coming from her lungs. The stillness of the room was broken by the clanging bell of her landline ringing. It startled me. A look at the clock showed 12:04 pm, and I assumed it was Jeff, but on the other end was Traci's voice. I wept against the sturdiness of that dated phone. I was so scared. The calmness in Traci's tone reassured me I was in the right place. "Work will still be there when you return." She praised me for using the vacation time I earned for Joanne. She heard Joanne's breathing in the background. She gave what was her last salutation to her co-worker turned friend and the line clicked.

Over the next several minutes, Joanne became restless. Though her eyes remained closed, it seemed she was trying to speak. I thought she was dreaming. Anxious to hear her voice, I leaned in. Her eyes opened, and she took a moment as they focused, and she regained her bearings. "Do you want lunch?" I asked. She didn't answer. For the next few minutes, time seemed to proverbially stand still. Being her caregiver, I asked about lunch again.

Joanne turned her gaze toward me, extended her finger, and softly touched the tip of my nose. In a quiet, coherent voice, she said, "I know why you are here."

Her dogs began howling in the sunroom, and I wept uncontrollably. I couldn't even muster up the words "I love you." With her eyes now closed, I listened to her departing wisdom and she calmy and unequivocally said "I want you to work for a nonprofit, and I want you to be happy." It was simple and profound and the last thing she said.

The hospice nurse arrived, took her vitals, and called Jeff.

I called Traci. She already knew Joanne had transcended, and Traci, never one to be remiss from opportunity, emphatically reminded me, "Joanne's final wish was for you to live your purpose."

In a recent conversation with Traci, I called to ask for forgiveness for writing this chapter without her permission in hopes sharing this journey sufficiently honors what her mentorship has meant in my life. We waded through reliving those intense times with Joanne and in true Traci fashion, she was adamant in expressing her gratitude for the opportunity to still be my mentor. "I was flooded with the thoughts and emotions about Joanne and that time in our lives. I am sitting here in gratitude reading your words."

In 1998, after Joanne's passing, I left that Fortune 500 career, uncertain of the details that would determine my next steps but driven by my mission to heed a new direction into non-profit work. Since that day, I've had the privilege of pursuing my purpose as a fundraiser for cancer care, treatment, and research, embraced by an honorable mentor and the love of my friend Joanne, who reminded me, "I know why you are here."

THE TOOL

MAKING MENTORSHIP MEANINGFUL

Mentors like Traci guide you in setting life and career goals. Their emphasis on the importance of maintaining a healthy work-life balance and building the networks that become your communities of practice are pivotal. We're cooperative creatures who accomplish far more together than we do apart. This is also a lesson Traci gifted me by simply showing up.

In retrospect, Traci empowered me with the agency to become well-rounded in my capacities and prepared me for the hard work and dedication that undergird success. Success, which, most importantly, we learn over time, isn't measured by material wealth but by being able to make positive contributions to our fellow humans, loved ones, and the communities we create.

It's easy to be a mentor. How do you make mentorship meaningful? Ask yourself these questions. Once you do, ask those you're mentoring, leading, supervising, and aspiring these same questions:

What truly matters to us?

How often do we actually (re)claim the time to pursue our dreams?

How often are the passions of our pursuits towards what is truly important to us?

How do you show up for others?

Understand that our purpose and motivations aren't encoded in what we say but in what we do—in the tendencies and inclinations of our nature. Ensure you allocate the time and energy needed to fulfill your purpose. In doing so, mentor someone to help them fulfill theirs.

Karri Morgan is the Executive Director for the Scott Hamilton CARES Foundation, where she raises critical funding for cancer research in immunotherapy. Karri is an experienced nonprofit professional with diverse proven expertise in relationship building, staff supervision, training, and leadership development; program design, start-up, and quality assurance; design and management of volunteer engagement initiatives; communications, corporate sponsorships, and operations management.

Even though always in networking mode, outside of being a fundraiser, Karri is a fan of documentaries, watching *Dateline* on Friday night, Pure Barre and walking her watch dog, Seiko. She enjoys spending time with her circle of fun-loving friends while laughing as often as possible and avoiding anything that involves cooking.

Connect with Karri:

www.scottcares.org

https://www.linkedin.com/in/karri-morgan-a0761360/

https://www.facebook.com/karri.morgan.5

https://www.instagram.com/karrimorgan

CHAPTER 6

SPARK STARTER

IGNITE A CREATIVE CULTURE
TO INSPIRE A MOVEMENT

Chrisie Scott, Marketing Executive

"You can't manage creativity. You need to manage for creativity.
You need to create the space for it to emerge."

~ Arianna Huffington

MY STORY

Dandelions bring me joy.

They're my dream whisperers.

I remember closing my eyes, pursing my lips, and making a wish as white puffs took flight, sprinkling my hopes everywhere.

This whimsical memory inspired our hospital's capital campaign theme. I thought about the lives we'd save and heal in our new, advanced surgery center, and I conjured up "Life.Changing."

To illustrate hope, I chose a child wishing on a dandelion.

I believed the optimistic image would capture the hearts of potential donors eager to fund such a worthy cause.

One board member, however, disputed my approach.

"Young lady, are you really using this despicable weed to promote our sophisticated project? Do you have any idea the money people like me spend eradicating these eyesores?"

Ouch!

Until that moment, I hadn't considered the glitter-spreading wish-maker a weed.

While we proceeded with the campaign, which was quite successful, the encounter became one of multiple tests of resilience my creative spirit would sustain over the years.

SEEING THINGS DIFFERENTLY

I've always seen things differently.

I attribute my unique lens on life to a childhood obsession with headstands.

I was weirdly amazing at it. I mean, I could literally stay upside down for hours with no residual headaches or balance issues. My classmates challenged me during gym, but my reigning title prevailed.

The world looks unique upside down—the same but new.

Originality has always flowed through my being. I radiate a bohemian spirit and enjoy artsy, handcrafted jewelry and clothing that reflect who I am, not who others think I should be. I'm about expressing, not impressing, and being my authentic self. My journey required strength to withstand inevitable criticism of thoughts and ideas that don't fit the norm.

Even prior to my encounter with the weed-worrying trustee, a supervisor cautioned me about infusing lightheartedness into the workplace.

"Healthcare is a serious business," she professed. "There is no room for creativity here."

No room for creativity!? Surely, healthcare could accommodate a spark or two.

CREATIVITY IN MY JEANS

I graduated valedictorian of a competitive Catholic high school. I excelled in whole-brain thinking and had no shortage of opportunities to flex my innovative side.

While in college, I took part in a five-person team that won a national marketing competition. Known as *The Levi 5*, we were challenged with repositioning Levi's button-fly jeans to young adults. We crafted the award-winning campaign tagline: *Live All of Your Lives in Levi's.*

As we revitalized the narrative around this iconic brand, we indulged ideas like sending a pair of jeans into space—yes, we called NASA and asked—and stitching together the world's largest pair of jeans for the Guinness Book of World Records—yes, we did that one! We even donated funds we raised to a hospital serendipitously named Jeanes Hospital. It was too good a tie-in.

My imagination was living its best life.

I knew creativity needed to be part of my future. A gifted writer, I was initially eyeing a career in speech writing until a respected college professor begged me not to "waste my heart" in corporate America. He insisted I belonged in the not-for-profit world.

"They need someone like you," he pleaded.

So, my first copywriter/photographer position at a local teaching hospital was a simple nod to my undergraduate professor—and a spectacular steppingstone to bringing my heart to work.

MY FOOTLOOSE MOMENT

The creativity-dulling comment came while I penned captions for our employee newsletter. My supervisor made me re-write them to be more formal, aka boring. I mean, these were pictures of executives enjoying hobbies like cooking, gardening, golfing, and rollerblading.

Being forbidden to infuse playfulness with photos that were meant to engage readers reminded me of the storyline from the movie *Footloose,* where young people were banned from dancing.

After that "serious business" lecture it was as if someone challenged me.

I dare you to bring creativity to healthcare and make this serious business more human.

I double-dog dare you to dance all over the status quo.

Coincidentally, my first CEO, John, with whom I collaborated for over 30 years, loved to dance. So, I had my first partner. His openness opened doors.

CREATIVITY AS AN ACT OF COURAGE

As the eldest of five in a loving, hard-working Italian Catholic family, I always respected rules and authority. Yet my endless creative spirit was a bit of an instigator.

I didn't just ask *why*. I wanted to know, *why not?*

I discovered early on that creativity requires vulnerability and is often an act of courage. It's an unwillingness to settle if better is possible. This quest for better led me to create safe spaces for my teams to nurture their own aha's. I once even rebranded our team conference room, *The Imagine Nation*.

The amazing thing about sparking creativity in others is that you get to bear witness to their greatness. People shine brightly when they tap into their genius. And when they apply and share their genius, it's like dandelion seeds showering magic.

In the beginning, creativity meant reimagining the mundane. It was having my art director create a giant, life-sized light switch so we could "turn on the lights" in our new health village instead of hosting endless ribbon cuttings.

It was building a sandcastle in the lobby of our children's hospital where we revealed the new name in sand during a spectacular, all-eyes-watching moment.

It was creating a key-passing ceremony for our new pediatric mobile health van so each participant could offer an intention as they passed a decorated key to the driver before they took to the road.

And instead of chest-beating speeches about how big our new organization Virtua Health would be after merging, we invited employees to paint thousands of rocks with kind sayings, placing them throughout the community to signal the collective impact our new organization would make.

Yes, healthcare is a serious business, but even more reason to do everything in our power to make it more uplifting.

HEARTWIRE THE RIGHT THINGS

I confess. I'm a bit of a word nerd.

From the titles I craft for my team—like brand architect and online conversation starter—to the name I gave our first online community for expectant and experienced moms, "momtourage," words fascinate and inspire me.

You see, our words carry more than meaning. They emit energy.

At some point in this serious-business-with-no-room-for-creativity, I decided I wanted to humanize healthcare. I wanted to carefully select words with deep intention and emotive energy.

I recall my executive colleagues discussing the complex concept of high reliability and how we had to hardwire what we did so we could provide consistently safe, quality care.

From my perspective, we wished to *heartwire*, not hardwire, the practices. We needed to connect these actions back to people's hearts because they were the right things to do. We needed our language to appeal to that emotional force that attracted people to healthcare in the first place.

I first introduced the word heartwire in a presentation about high reliability. A confident voice from the back of the room shouted, "You have a typo. You mean hardwire."

As I assured my heckler I had chosen the word to evoke a different feeling, he informed me that heartwire was not a word.

We'll see about that.

That evening, August 4, 2016, I submitted the word to the Urban Dictionary so if ever challenged again, I could suggest the person Google it.

Over the years, I cannot overstate how this word has genuinely resonated with healthcare professionals—this made-up word with the right intention and an abundance of energy.

Who says you can't make up better words?

KINA OLÉ

While helping my organization embrace this high-reliability journey, I stumbled across a masterful Hawaiian word: kina olé. It came from the hospitality industry, and it meant "doing the right thing, in the right way, at the right time, with the right feeling, every time."

Hmmm, sounds a lot like high reliability, only more inviting.

When I offered up this word to my clinical colleagues, they were skeptical but surprisingly open. So, we packaged the education previously labelled something like *Mandatory HRO blah blah blah*, and instead called it *Kina olé: Right Thing. Right Reason. Right Feeling.*

Kina olé became a conversation starter—unexpected, memorable, and even entertaining.

The vibrant word created intrigue and buzz around our health system.

In the months that followed, we presented kina olé at national conferences and to boards of organizations grounded in healthcare experience. An orthopedic surgeon group in Australia even contacted us to exchange ideas on how to build a facility around the concept of kina olé.

Our creative approach to talking about this serious framework became an engagement springboard.

Emboldened by the magic of using the right words, I further reflected on how healthcare could shake its stuffy, tired insider jargon.

GOOD TO GO, ALMOST

I once lobbied my hospital president to get rid of the term "discharge unit."

I pleaded with him that the word discharge was one of the most displeasing words. There is research to support its cringe-worthy status within our language.

"Why would we take such a hopeful and highly awaited moment and liken it to bodily fluid?" He was amused but told me, "That's just what we call it."

So, I created and packaged a "Good to Go Unit" plan and recruited a couple of brave nurses to help me sell it. We almost convinced him, but in the end, he hesitated to be different.

Who are these keepers of healthcare language, and how can I lodge my concerns about the lack of dignity, humanity, and even creativity?

Geesh, even Kevin Bacon in Footloose had a forum in which to make his case for dancing.

CANCER IN OTHER WORDS

I can recall a provocative billboard that read: "She never gave up, so her cancer did."

There was public outcry about how insensitive and out of touch the message was. One blogger wrote: "Are we to believe that surviving cancer was strictly about how hard the person fought? If they died, they must not have fought hard enough?"

The controversy got me thinking about how misguided our cancer conversation had become.

Reports show that the pressure to stay positive and *fight* cancer is one of the biggest barriers to meaningful end-of-life conversations. Yes, people want to *beat* cancer, *overcome* cancer, and especially *survive* cancer, but *fighting* and *battling* are not their preferred words.

How many of your friends and family have *lost their battles* with cancer? *Really?*

Our words matter.

This movement to reduce violent words around cancer sparked a greater mission to re-imagine the language of healthcare. If ever there was a superpower to lift people up, to help them be more resilient, it's our words.

HUMANIZING OUR LANGUAGE

When doctors diagnosed my 17-year-old son Austin with type 1 diabetes, I made a mother's pledge to never refer to him as a diabetic. I wanted to avoid the stigma and self-limiting power of labeling him with his disease. Yes, he'd face serious challenges, but he's neither a victim nor a warrior. He's a young person filled with possibilities.

Research confirms that insensitive language can lead to a lack of engagement, satisfaction, and outcomes. Using negative terms like *uncontrolled* or *non-compliant* can disconnect people from their doctors.

With a desire to be more purposeful, I recently asked my team to set their intention for the upcoming year. I encouraged them to think about what impact they wanted to create and choose one word that reflected how they wanted to show up for themselves and others.

They chose words like *curious, empower, connect,* and *present.*

It was a simple but meaningful exercise to remind us to take accountability for our thoughts, which become our words and actions.

I chose the word *spark.*

I knew I wanted to embrace my creativity while also activating difference-making in my team.

I've seen firsthand how bringing others along for this work and igniting their creativity can build their confidence in endless ways. Rituals like setting intentions reinforce beliefs and behaviors they can carry with them.

START WHERE YOU ARE

My team works under the *Fishbird* premise: "No one is coming."

No one is coming to do this work around language. There are no "serious business" police or creative license granters.

It starts with us, and it's up to us. It's what we *get* to do.

Who says we can't ban the word discharge, borrow the word kina olé, or invent the word heartwire?

Our language was on full display during the pandemic. We knew we needed to inform, but we especially wanted to connect with empathy.

The standard signs that appeared to be yelling felt very off-brand.

Stand six feet back! Stop! Do not enter without a mask!

We chose to reimagine these messages to signal this was a human moment we were in together.

Yes, these were serious times, and we had rules intended to keep people safe. But our community was going through a collective trauma. Didn't this call for empathy and hope?

This was a pivotal opportunity for us to live our brand, and we seized it with creativity and an approach our CEO Dennis likes to call "by design."

Shortly after the first waves of the pandemic, unsettling aggression against healthcare workers, once hailed as heroes, reached a fever pitch. As other organizations erected bold signs acknowledging zero tolerance for rude and threatening behavior, we raised our creative voice.

We believed that kindness and respect were as much a part of the solution to uncivil behavior as vaccines and masks were to the spread of Covid.

So, we flanked our entrances with signs that read:

Kindness and patience are good for your health.

Other signs reminded people that everyone deserved respect.

This is a caring organization and a place of healing. Inappropriate language, loud and demanding behavior, or threats of violence have no place here and will not be tolerated. So, take a deep breath or take it outside; just don't take it out on our staff.

How we speak to, listen to, and treat each other in anxious and uncertain moments matters. Giving respect is an opportunity to earn respect. If we want to be part of a bigger solution, we need to take a higher road.

Bringing optimism and resilience to this serious business is also how we become a better part of someone's day.

WE'VE ALWAYS HAD THE POWER

This brings me back to the dandelion. Whether we choose to see a weed or wonder is within our control.

My wish for healthcare is that we stand in our power—that we recognize no one is coming to fix or save us from this serious business with its dated and uninspiring words and ways.

Creativity is a mindset. It's about turning our view upside down to see another way forward.

It's more than playful thinking and colorful ideas just for fun. True trailblazing business strategies are born from sparks—insightful connections around seeing things differently to create more meaning.

Creative design thinking inspires me to consider who benefits from each new idea or action. What do they need? How will they feel?

It's for 14-year-old Hannah who was not afraid to die but afraid to be forgotten that my team created the end-of-life planning campaign *Your Life, Your Wishes.*

It's for the underrepresented, overlooked, or taken for granted that we crafted the heart-centering theme *Everybody Always* to always see the good in each person, patient, or colleague.

And it's the words of focus group Barbara that often come to mind as I craft marketing messages. She asked, "Why does healthcare brag so much about themselves and their awards? Isn't healthcare supposed to be about me?"

Yes, Barbara, it is!

Creativity is not careless. On the contrary, it is a profound act of caring.

Like making a wish on a dandelion, creativity allows us to release what no longer serves us and spread new possibilities instead.

THE TOOL

Get your team's creativity popping like popcorn at a movie premier using these fun, simple exercises that make up the acronym **SPARK**.

SONG TITLE SWAP

- Create a presentation and substitute each topic or heading with a familiar song title. You'll be amazed by how your team's points sing with engagement.

PURPOSEFUL PRAISE

- Have your team randomly draw names. Then, have them create an award along with a short speech describing what they value about this colleague. They can draw the award, make it from clay, or repurpose something. We're never more creative than when we're shining a light on others.

ALTERNATIVE WORDS

- Create a list of words that need makeovers. Now, instill new meaning and energy by substituting, combining, or conceiving new vocabulary. *Word play is how I came up with heartwire.* Or play buzzword bingo to highlight just how entrenched the least human words are.

REIMAGINE THE ROUTINE

- Renovate an upcoming event of its cliché moments. How could you reinvent employee orientation or modernize a ribbon-cutting ceremony? Find one of your organization's form letters and reimagine it. It's like playing dress-up and seeing how fashionable the ordinary looks in more colorful outfits!

KINDSTORMING

- Enjoy a creative, feel-good ideation session focused on generating ideas that spread joy and enact positive change. When *kindstorming,* allow the heart to fuel your thoughts and let that kindness confetti rain down.

Remember: Small acts of creativity can lead to the more organic generation of big ideas. And big ideas can spark a movement.

Chrisie Scott is the senior vice president and chief marketing officer for Virtua Health in New Jersey, where she focuses on turning stakeholder insights into compelling human-centric strategies. Throughout her 30+-year career, she has empowered impactful and engaged teams, aligned brands and cultures, amplified the consumer's voice, and humanized healthcare language.

Under Chrisie's leadership, Virtua underwent a transformative rebranding, introducing an exciting positioning of *Here for Good*. Chrisie initiated a host of digital capabilities, a unique segmentation model, an online consumer feedback panel, and a robust reputation management practice. She championed a podcast hosted by her CEO and a systemwide movement in human understanding to support relationship building and connection back to purpose.

Prior to joining Virtua, Chrisie led the development and launch of the inaugural brand strategy for Hackensack Meridian Health where she served as chief marketing officer. She spent her early career building the brand of Meridian Health, one of the first integrated health system brands in the state.

Chrisie blends purpose with possibility and is passionate about *heartwiring* what matters. She's a *lightmaker* for type 1 diabetes, serving on the NJ Breakthrough T1D Board (formerly JDRF) and championing cures in her son's lifetime. She has been honored as a *Top Women in Business* and a *Brand Builder*. She holds an MBA from Fairleigh Dickinson University and a bachelor's from Rowan University. Industry colleagues respect her creativity and enthusiasm around personalizing brands and experience.

An authentic Jersey girl, Chrisie is a country music fan, mom to Austin, Haley and fur baby Piper, and Nonna to grandson Holden. She and her husband Greg host a family "Pizza Friday" every week at their home in Colts Neck, NJ.

Connect with Chrisie:

LinkedIn: https://www.linkedin.com/in/chrisiescott/

Email: cscott3@virtua.org

Check out her ideas in print and podcasts:

https://bit.ly/3Vk5Grz

https://apple.co/4aPrmk0

https://bit.ly/3wWHJgu

CHAPTER 7

FINDING THE SPRING AND CREATING TRIBUTARIES

DREAMWORK AS BOTH CREATIVE SPARK AND MAGNET OF OPPORTUNITY

Kiran Lakshman, M.T.

*". . . Whatever inspiration you find within you
is capable of magnetizing support for itself
if you find the courage to stay the course."*

MY STORY

Although scientific research could categorize my mother's experiences into symptoms of schizophrenia, and it could chemically sedate those, it couldn't describe anything redeeming about her experiences. In my process of finding a place in this world for me, I re-categorized some of my mother's symptoms into characteristics we shared. Because I found tools to shed light on those, I could continue to feel the momentum of ancestral support fueling my future opportunities.

From the time I was born, my mother's point of view, only half-informed by the common sense of reality, engulfed each of my developmental stages. By the time I was eighteen, more than one drop of my mother's ocean filled my sea of consciousness. As I sought a strainer for the swamp water,

I arrived at the original spring itself in my work with dreams, visions, and journeys of the spirit.

If all my experiences were an ocean, in one trench of the ocean floor, we could visit the following memory:

> As the long night loomed ahead, my mother roamed the rooms of the house, checking and rechecking safety bolts on windows and triple locks on doors. She put on every light. She checked the seals of the plastic over the air vents. As the troops of darkness surrounded the house, she would protect her domain with the force of an army. "Send it back on them ten times as powerful," she crooned, brows furrowed and fists tightly clenched. "Make them keel over."

There are scientific terms to classify and categorize the thoughts I remember my mother having, however, somewhere on Earth, someone is feeling defensive and antagonistic in a similar way by circumstances that science would label "reality." Now that news of people, places, and events is more accessible, "realities" like genocide, political imprisonment, and violations of human rights surface regularly. Perhaps my mother did not have a false experience, as science would say; rather, she had someone else's experience. Perhaps she slipped unaware through the solid basin of her pond into a flow of underground tributaries.

I can pick up the pieces from there. The capacity to move between versions of reality requires awareness and values. Of course, that was a mouthful. However, in that mouthful is the flow of clear spring water that I discovered while wading in the bog. A series of three related dreams facilitated my discovery process.

Around my early forties, I dreamt of a tan horse. It was raring to go, but with front limbs half-amputated and bandaged and with eyes bandaged too. I implemented personal practices and sought new teachings, and in a year's time, I dreamt of watching an enormous, honey-colored horse emerge from behind a barn and run unbridled with a flying mane alongside the barn. I saw it at a distance. I kept on improving my connections and professional activities, and about a decade after the dream of the handicapped horse, I dreamt of standing on a battlefield while a female knight on a gigantic horse came up behind me and waved to me to join her in her position of empowerment.

A decade passed from the first to the third dream. I invite you into the pool of life around the dream of the bandaged horse. It was a crisis point. In this crisis, I awakened from parasitic relationships with agents, tradesmen, accountants, employers, religious organizations, and more. In the dynamics of these relationships, people fulfilled their goals at my expense. They prospered, and I lost.

Although I could hardly afford it, I put together a trip to New York City to engage my inner wisdom more deeply. I journeyed by train, and stayed in a hotel where doors were slamming all night long and the rooms were the size of the beds. I brought cornflakes, powdered milk, and apples from home to mitigate the cost of food in the city. During my stay, I attended a Bluebeard presentation at the C.G. Jung Institute, and I conducted a vision quest at the southern tip of the city. The latter was where the dream of the bandaged horse was given to me.

The legend of Bluebeard, dating back to real individuals in fifteenth-century France, tells of a wealthy sorcerer named Bluebeard, and his ill-fated wives. Bluebeard marries women, and when they follow their own curiosity instead of Bluebeard's own rules (they open a forbidden room with a key when Bluebeard is away), he kills them. Then, he hangs their bodies in the aforementioned forbidden room with all the other wives who came before. As the legend's cycle repeats for the last time, Bluebeard's wife summons help and defeats Bluebeard when the hour of demise is upon her.

Awareness of feeling surrounded by Bluebeard prompted me to awaken my survival instinct. It became silent during my upbringing when I couldn't bring in support for my own well-being. Just as Bluebeard killed one wife after another, I set up a world of one-way relationships. I had to find another spring to water the riverbed of my life in order to save myself.

Thus, I turned to powerful waters: the confluence of the Hudson River and the East River at the southern tip of Manhattan. My shamanic studies teachers, Jose and Lena Stevens, had once discussed the productive, creative qualities of this masculine vortex, where New York City's financial district trades an immense amount of wealth daily. The Statue of Liberty herself also stands tall in that watery confluence.

The day of my vision quest was sunny, and the sparkling water reflected the scintillating charge in the air as I approached the vortex. I walked several miles south on the Manhattan peninsula along the Hudson River. Like a traffic circle, the powerful vortex ahead was managing massive river currents. Each river brought a load of dissimilar charges to the spot from its origin. By circling together in a vortex, they could harmonize at will instead of colliding in one cacophonous, destructive mess. The new symphony brought new life to lower Manhattan. I hoped it would bring me new life, too.

At a public leisure area on the edge of the river, I sat on a low concrete wall and began invoking my vision quest. I had already covertly distributed offerings—pieces of homemade banana bread—when I walked among tourists waiting for river shuttles and visitors of the fallen Twin Towers site. I had sought consent from the spirits of that place and had sung blessings under my breath, making sacred space as I offered the banana bread. Sitting on the wall, I watched a father walking nearby with a young son riding a small bicycle on the sidewalk, and beyond them, gulls and pigeons fluttering over crumbs at the edge of the river flowing by. I pulled my hood over my head and closed my eyes, relaxing into slumber.

I did drift in and out of sitting-up-sleep, and when I could no longer drift back in, I knew I had completed the quest. I'll admit I was expecting to be clobbered with a blinding premonition of the future. Instead, the dream of the blindfolded, bandaged horse rearing to leap forward intermingled with the sounds of the child on the bicycle and the flapping of wings. The dream was so subtle that it felt ordinary, like any of the many thoughts I had each day, except that I had intended to quest for "a vision."

Perplexing as it was, I guided myself to observe the creature I saw and relate to it. I felt the horse's bandages covering my eyes.

I pray that I see what has the most value in me.

I felt the horse's rearing-up motions like restlessness in my heart.

I pray that I offer my gifts in ways that improve the world.

I felt the horse's amputated, bandaged arms like an inability to use tools and techniques.

I pray for opportunities to recover and apply the skills that seem severed and lost.

My compassion for the bandaged horse insisted that I "Do something! Do it now!" I closed the vision quest with gratitude, and took leave of New York City.

In the past, I didn't know that I needed to repair a broken link with my mother's lineage—my ancestry—nor could I have fathomed how to do so anyway. Instead, I strove to do the antithesis of my mother's experience, which was to acquire professional degrees that fit into job descriptions. I thought I would "look straight ahead" and steer clear of the ditch my mother fell into beside the road. The dream of the bandaged horse begged to differ from my beliefs. It informed me that the life I was building was inherently harmful and that I had to take wholeness and healing more seriously.

After my vision quest, I reshuffled my priorities to bring new skill sets into my life. I decided to dive more deeply into programs with my shamanic studies teachers. In the process of quitting a job, selling a house, and finding flexible work as a food and beverage server to accommodate this intention, I certainly had doubts about my decisions. Guidance again came from the realm of dreaming. One night, when there was a new moon, I dreamt of the second horse in the sequence. In the dream, a honey-colored horse thrice the normal size came bounding in slow motion from behind a barn and rounded the left corner. Still in slow motion, without saddle and reins and also without sound, it galloped along the long barn side. From my point of view, I saw the unblemished horse's silky mane and tail riding the wind as it ran.

I took heart that the same source that had admonished me to go in a new direction now shone a positive light on my reshuffling efforts and, furthermore, oversaw my steps from an unobtrusive vantage point. It updated the warning about the bandaged horse with an image of a healthy, robust horse running free. I vicariously visited and revisited that free feeling in the horse's flying mane and tail.

I pray for courage to run freely toward my own health and happiness.

Soon after this dream, words of specific guidance carried me further down the same stream. While studying pictures of constellations of the zodiac, I heard, "I want to sleep out under the stars." I imagined myself just so, asleep in an open field under the stars. My body felt the stars gazing at me as one of their own. It felt expansive, free, and mysterious. I wrote about it, talked about it, and felt open to it. I kept to my plan of working in food and beverage and going to shamanic studies trainings. It came to pass that through those, I slept under the stars for three consecutive nights in a nature solo, and I spent entire nights under the stars in ceremonies led by native shamans in a sacred desert.

Unknowingly manifesting opportunities to sleep out under the stars like an unfettered horse was not the only way I found myself dumbstruck. I was also dumbfounded that shamans practicing their ancient ways moved between their own reservoir and larger tributaries—the same quicksand of shifting realities that swallowed my mother!

I pray to know the difference between the experiences of a healer and my mother's experiences.

As I stayed the course, my prayers were answered. The crack in my childhood foundation found a rare filler as if by luck. Although I did not plan the endpoint of the journey, it connected very directly with finding a life-giving spring of inspiration to resolve a crisis.

I now invite you, dear reader, into the pool of the third dream in the horse sequence. It occurred a decade after the first. The spring of inspiration made me embrace new opportunities, and I was halfway through a course of certification in experiential embodied dream work, as compiled by Dr. Leslie Ellis, Ph.D. In this third horse dream, I'm on a battlefield in India. Troops on each side are ineffectively hurling wooden cannon balls at the opposite side with their bare hands. On my side, a horse the size of a large elephant strides forward from the rear. It seems to be the solution to the stalemate. I move aside to get out of the way. However, the horse also moves that way, and I'm still blocking him/her. So, I move to the other side to clear the horse's path. Oddly, the horse moves that way, too. Determined to clear the way, I move aside several more times, side to side, repeatedly, only to have the horse shadow my moves. I'm confused about where to go. A female knight appears atop the horse. She motions with her hand as if to guide me.

As I relive the dream, I learn that the hand motion invites me to unite myself with the female knight and the horse. I feel in my hips the alignment between my side-to-side movements and the horse's, like a dance. I feel the tenderness of moving in sync with this large presence I cared for, trusted, and grew with over time. It feels like a glow in my heart.

I pray that the origins of inspiration and manifestation in me unite to create a path of growth and service.

In the four years since the third horse dream, I continue to experience new rivers of opportunity. The supportive resources flow down the river just as naturally to cover what I need when I need it. A path of serving others— its time and place, continues to unfold step by step. I'm grateful to be an outlet for the wisdom of my ancestor's experiences. I'm grateful to help others fill the cracks in their foundations, discover what they value most, and embark on the river of opportunities that support their inspirations.

THE TOOL

Dear reader, the origin of dreams and opportunities is the same. The same spring of inspiration that mobilizes a creative process in you also clears your vision, gives you a new vantage point to see from, and mobilizes the opportunities around you. This means that whatever inspiration you find within you is capable of magnetizing support for itself if you find the courage to stay the course.

In the context of leadership, inspiration around global problems leads to discoveries in clean energy, health care, justice and equity, environmental preservation and restoration, education, organizational restructuring and more. It is not that inspirations lack resources, it's that the will to live by inspiration lacks training.

The path of dreaming is not like a man-made system of education that leads to participation in man-made social structures. Worldly ways of acquiring knowledge and social networks may be used in service of true inspiration. However, dreaming comes from a deeper source, the way that spring water comes from aquifers within the earth. It responds to the needs of humanity while responding to your own greatest needs.

It would be my pleasure to offer you a discovery session here, now, and also live in the near future. Members of my private practice generally use dreamwork, quantum structure teachings, and shamanic energy work for several months on the way to strengthening their connection to dreaming. I invite you to choose one of the two dreamwork starting points below and try the other point whenever you wish! I also invite you to make contact through my website, www.OpenPortalWorks.com

STARTING POINT ONE, WITH A DREAM SCENE FROM YOUR DREAM LIFE:

I invite you to relax, feel comfortable, and breathe long breaths through your nose, pausing after inhaling, pausing after exhaling. You may enjoy lighting a candle and gazing into the flame as you breathe. When you're ready, enter the dream scene. Narrate it to yourself slowly, in the first person. Narrate where you are and what you see around you, with any sounds, smells, temperatures, or climates. What is your sense of what is happening? Put into words what is happening and your reaction. You may react anew in ways you did not in the dream. You may log all this in a journal to stay focused or not. Notice and note the feelings in your body around the most important parts of the dream.

Come out when you're ready.

Use the physical sensations you noted to generate a spring of inspiration, as follows. Choose one to expand. Focus on the sensation. Feel the sensation. Breathe in and out seven times, pausing as before. On each inhale, intensify the sensation. Feel it more, and add awe, gratitude, love, or compassion to it to make it bigger. Hold the seventh level for a full minute (breathe, but hold the intensity). After one minute, relax the intensity through several exhales. Plan a small step to take or stone to turn over in the "real world" to crystalize the inspiration you chose to intensify.

STARTING POINT TWO, WHERE YOU WILL INVOKE A DREAM-LIKE SCENE:

I invite you to relax, feel comfortable, and breathe long breaths through your nose, pausing after inhaling, pausing after exhaling. Close your eyes and imagine being in a small canoe on a narrow river in the jungle. Go forward, and feel the movement in your body as you drift. Intend to enter a meaningful scene. Drift forward. Accept what comes. Capture an image or experience you are drawn to, and return with it.

Begin at starting point one above with the image or experience. Repeat these journeys until you feel you're connecting to a source of wisdom. Give the process time to awaken to your call.

Kiran Lakshman is a healing artist, a teacher, and a writer. Members of her private practice enjoy finding clarity about their ideal path and conviction about their inspirations sooner than they thought possible. They also enjoy integrating shamanic ceremony experiences, healing trauma, confronting addictions, generating life according to their greatest gifts, updating their approach to accomplishing goals, and living with an active exchange with the natural environment. Kiran's healing arts practice combines dream work, shamanic practices, and quantum structure meditations. She enjoys giving shamanic ceremonies to small groups on request.

Kiran earned her experiential embodied dreamwork certification from Dr. Leslie Ellis, Ph.D, and her advanced training in shamanic practices from the Power Path School of Shamanism founded by Jose Luis Stevens, Ph.D., and his partner Lena Stevens. She has traveled to 14 countries, including parts of the Sierra Madre Mountains and the Amazon basin, where she attended ceremonies conducted by different lineages of shamans. She has completed three years of study of the quantum structure teachings and practices of Marina Jacobi.

Kiran holds a Master of Teaching degree from the University of Virginia. She majored in the Dramatic Arts at the University of California, Davis, where she was also recognized for her outstanding leadership skills in the Dramatic Arts. In addition to her private practice activities in Charlottesville, Virginia she also teaches school-aged children at a learning center in the private sector.

Kiran enjoys tending her cat companions, her garden, and her health through hiking and finding superfood recipes to spruce up her healthy diet. She welcomes your contact and offers a free introductory session of dreamwork, healing or manifesting. Please visit her website at www.OpenPortalWorks.com. Until then, may you enjoy health and prosperity!

CHAPTER 8

UNMASKING YOUR POTENTIAL

HOW TO OVERCOME IMPOSTER SYNDROME AS A FIRST-TIME LEADER

Ely Jones

"There's power in allowing yourself to be known and heard, in owning your unique story, in using your authentic voice. And there's grace in being willing to know and hear others."

~ Michelle Obama

MY STORY

We are all imposters in one way or another. How you leverage your internally perceived shortcomings will determine how you learn to lead with authenticity and purpose.

It's a day like any other to the outside world, but not for me. As my heart beats out of my chest, I push instead of pull open the large wooden door.

Read the sign, Ely.

Crisp, cool air blasts across my face, offset by warm, soothing lighting. An eerily quiet yet comforting ambiance, except for the muffled sniffles from a man in his mid-50s walking out the door. This is my first time here, but certainly won't be my last. I'm anxious. A mild feeling of dread creeps over me. Life's unrelenting ups and downs have led me to a crossroads where I don't know how to proceed.

People count on me, but can I count on myself?

"Come on back."

Staring back at me was a pleasant, smiling face with jet-black hair in braids sitting in a bun on the top of her head. I got up, and we walked back down the dimly lit hallway to her office for what felt like an eternity. Then I spot it—an oversized brown couch with a dozen lightly colored throw pillows.

"Take a seat."

Am I supposed to sit or lay down? In the movies, everyone lies down. Isn't this couch supposed to be red? No way I'm lying down. That's too awkward. I'll sit.

I plop down and grab the closest largest pillow I could find.

"Congratulate yourself for taking the first step. So what brings you in here today?"

Well, ma'am, I have a multitude of reasons for being here.

- *I'm having a quarter-life crisis.*
- *I never processed grief and resentment from my childhood.*
- *I feel like I'm just going through the motions with no path forward.*
- *People count on me and expect me to be this joyful, fun, smart, strong black man when, deep down, I don't know what I'm doing.*
- *I don't think I understand myself enough to be an effective leader in a role that I find myself thrust into.*
- *I feel like I'm just faking it till I make it, but I don't know what 'it' is.*
- *I feel like an imposter.*

"I just want to talk to someone."

"Well, let's start at the beginning."

Growing up was relatively okay, except for my father not being involved in my life. We millennials are fortunate enough to know a world of pre-internet and cell phones and to also have lived through the tech boom firsthand. A world where you only knew where your friends were because you walked over to their house, making sure you came back home before the streetlights and fireflies shined their bright orange glow. I was a happy kid, scraping my knees, riding my bike, picking strawberries and pecans off trees with my friend Bob, discovering my love for Saturday morning cartoons and video games—just being a kid.

That all changed one fateful night in November 2002. My mother battled stomach and colon cancer for a while. No one should have to deal with a loved one going through this terrible disease, let alone a fifteen-year-old kid. In some ways, I felt like the primary caretaker. I dealt with the nurses who came to visit and administer drip medications through a tube in her chest. I dealt with the daily pains, the frequent smells of bile, and changing colostomy bags. I sat with her and watched *The Price is Right* and *Young and The Restless* while she tried to keep down her daily cup of chicken broth or a handful of Frosted Mini-Wheats (her favorite snack). This day was no different than any other.

"Ely, come in here, I need help," my mother said as loud as she could muster from her bathroom late at night.

Helping wasn't new, but something felt off this time. Panic ensued.

"We need to get you to the hospital. I can try to drive you."

No one was home at the time but us. I didn't have my driving permit yet. Her navy blue diesel Mercedes Benz wasn't something I wanted to drive even if I legally could. It was so loud. Anyone would hear us pulling up from miles away.

Bad idea.

"I'll be right back."

Track and field was my high school sport of choice, and what ensued was a personal record 100-yard dash to the soft orange sherbet-looking neighbor's house on the left. Awoken by frantic knocking, an older couple answered the door.

"Something's wrong. We need to take her to the hospital."

Intentionally or not, I blocked out much of the time between that night and when my mom gained her angel wings. Ever since then, I've been somewhat of a nomad in my head. I'm fortunate enough to be surrounded by friends and family I love but I'm often mentally checked out and separated from reality—not having any sort of path, going through the motions, being an imposter.

"That's all the time we have for today. Let's pick this back up in a few weeks. I recommend every two weeks for the first few months. We have a lot to unpack here."

Ugh great. I thought we were just getting somewhere, but I'm dreading what else we're going to unpack.

Mildly annoyed but slightly relieved to be done spilling my guts for the first time, I walk down the seemingly mile-long hallway towards the exit.

SECRET #1: UNDERSTANDING YOURSELF IS A STEPPING STONE TO UNDERSTANDING HOW EXPERIENCES SHAPE YOUR WAYS OF LEADERSHIP.

Over the next few months, I learned not only how to manage grief but also the importance of learning oneself. No one can truly realize their potential without knowing one's strengths and weaknesses, environments you thrive in and the energy drainers (or energy vampires, as I call them), your triggers, and mechanisms to work through adversity.

Post graduation, I made a slight detour to work in Michigan, but after a year or so, ended up in the music capital of the world—Nashville, Tennessee. Nashville is a vibrant city with live music on every corner and a bustling food scene. It booms with possibility. It's a city with a grim but rich history, making its mark and growing exponentially. It's a city that isn't equitable for all but, in its heart of hearts, wants to be.

Blistering summer southern sun drives locals to either stay indoors or find the nearest watering hole with ample amounts of shade to weather the cloudless sky. I opted for the latter and sat there enjoying whatever local craft beer was on happy hour. But then, a sudden wave of guilt and anxiety crept up the back of my neck.

I did the same thing every week—I worked during the day and then lay on my beat-up leather couch most nights, staring at my phone with the ambient glow of a TV in the background. Weekends were a blur of stepping over homeless bodies to take in bright neon lights and honky tonks loud enough to cause minor hearing loss.

Is this what I'm going to be doing for the rest of my life? I feel like doing more. I want to and should be doing more.

I stumbled across a young professional organization during a quick Google search later that evening that, outside of therapy, changed the trajectory of my life.

I found purpose.

SECRET #2: FIND A COMMUNITY OR NETWORK THAT WILL ALLOW YOU TO FAIL WITH PURPOSE AND COMMIT TO SHOWING UP.

Hesitant to sign up for something I knew very little about (other than what was on the website), I paid my membership dues before the introvert in me could slap me out of it.

This organization seems like the right fit for me, but I'm already dreading this commitment. Something isn't going to work out. Did I make a mistake? What if no one likes me? Or is this also a group of imposters? Searching for their place in the world outwardly portraying happiness when in reality they're also resembling ducks treading water?

Commit to a year, Ely. See where it takes you.

Properly networking, engaging civically, fundraising—all unknown ways of adulting. Over that next year, learning to fail or not meet expectations became a part of life. And guess what? Life moves on. The organization didn't implode. You learn. You regroup. You have a foundation of peers and alumni who pick you back up and push you forward.

This community of peers helped me understand the power of leaning on others. We were all imposters simply trying to be better young professionals and make any impact change to the city we call home.

Suddenly, I came to. It's been a couple of years since I started my membership and grew into board service. A room of roughly twenty-five 20 to 30-year-olds is staring at me like I have food smeared on my face.

SECRET #3: ACKNOWLEDGE THAT YOU WON'T HAVE THE ANSWERS, AND SOMETIMES THOSE ANSWERS (OR ACTIONS) WILL BE WRONG.

'Visibility and Value: Ely's Presidential Platform' read the navy and crimson handouts passed out to this group of my peers. Buzzwords littered this half-page-size platform flier:

- Tangible results
- Emphasis on value and benefits
- Unique offerings
- Pipeline to growth

Maybe if I can distract them with visuals, they won't catch on to the rambling words coming out of my mouth.

In my heart of hearts, I don't believe the majority of the population truly understands half the business slang and buzzwords we use daily— vague language to mask true intent, knowledge, or purpose. They sure do sound good.

The next 60-minute peer interrogation seemed like it lasted an eternity. I ran opposed but still feared I'd be exposed for not knowing what being President would entail.

"How do you manage stress?"

"What is your leadership style?"

"What level is your financial acumen?"

"How do you handle conflict, and how will you reconcile between two opposing views?"

"What do you want your legacy to be?"

"How are you going to be any different than any other past President and going to grow our organization?"

Cotton-mouthed, broad enough answers were my reply. My blazer felt tighter and sweatier with each question.

"Congrats to the 101st President, Ely Jones," our current President exclaimed, and my journey to leave an impact on this city began.

There were two unforeseen hiccups to my plan before my term began: the COVID-19 pandemic and the murder of George Floyd. My plan had to be drastically altered: 1) How to guide our organization back to and exceed pre-pandemic membership levels that dropped significantly (for obvious reasons) during a time of quarantine, and 2) How to implement diversity, equity, and inclusion practices authentically in our organization to drive purpose and value.

"What's causing your hesitation? Why don't you think you'll succeed?" questions my therapist, this time over a video chat (we were on lockdown, after all).

Beads of sweat form on my forehead. Hands clammy. Heartbeat elevating.

Merriam-Webster defines imposter syndrome as "a psychological condition that is characterized by persistent doubt concerning one's abilities or accomplishments accompanied by the fear of being exposed as a fraud despite evidence of one's ongoing success."

My non-scientific and simplified take on imposter syndrome is one or more of the following:

- An overwhelming feeling that you will fail and be exposed for your failure
- Not living up to your own or society's expectations
- Afraid society won't like you anymore once they know the real you
- Professional insecurity when you feel under-qualified to be in the room

"I've never been a front-line kind of guy. I operate more in the shadows—a solid wingman or VP type. I'm never the one taking charge, and this is my first time doing something of this nature. I'm afraid of doing or saying the wrong thing. Scared of failure. Terrified of being a phony and being perceived differently than intended," I replied, shaking.

"People respect you and believe in your ability. Otherwise, they wouldn't have selected you to lead," she says reassuringly.

I had two distinct experiences in which I was reassured that my ability to lead and be considered a leader was validated, and my feelings of being an imposter were minimized.

Each spring, the hopefuls run for organization president, and those hopeful candidates usually (if they're smart) set time to gather crucial insight and feedback from current and past presidents before being interrogated by their peers. The first such experience was this exact situation.

"Thanks for taking the time to chat with me," a cautiously optimistic board member of mine said while sipping a freshly brewed medium vanilla latte with oat milk and an extra shot of espresso.

"I just want to say you've been a wonderful president this year, and if I'm elected, I hope I'm half of the leader you were. How did you do it, and what should I prepare myself for?" they continued.

This flattery is nice. Never really considered myself that good at this role. Just thought I'd done fine enough to keep the organization afloat.

"Honestly, you should want to forge your own path. Don't just follow in my footsteps. I haven't thought about it, but I guess what has helped me tremendously is just being my authentic self. People will want to work with you if you give them the freedom to work within parameters and encourage their creativity to get the job done. There are so many things I wish I could've accomplished during my term but didn't have the time to. I consider that a failure, and I've been open and vulnerable with our entire board about that."

The other time, a group of myself and other community leaders shared experiences and soaked in the mountain views on an autumn Saturday. We were forty-four, mostly strangers, selected to an executive leadership program.

These people were way more advanced in their careers. Searching for any reason to excuse myself from awkward small talk, my feelings of imposter syndrome started to overtake my brain.

No way I'm qualified enough to be in the room with them. There has to be some mistake in being selected for this program.

Working my way around an elaborately decorated covered patio outside of the mountain view home, I slowly learned that these highly coveted and successful community leaders were equally as nervous as I was. They were nervous about putting forth a good first impression and saying the right thing, nervous about remembering everyone's name, and nervous about fitting in. However, in this space, we weren't what our professional titles were. We were just community leaders carefully selected for our diverse experiences, ages, and backgrounds to get to know one another on a human level and form authentic bonds to impact our community.

SECRET #4: SHOW UP AND BRING YOUR AUTHENTIC SELF TO LEADERSHIP.

"I guess so, but. . ." I say before my therapist abruptly cuts me off.

"That's all the time we have for today. Let's pick this up next time."

THE TOOL

Throughout this chapter, I've provided my own experiences to better understand what imposter syndrome feels like. Included were my four secrets to overcome. I think there will always be a sense of this feeling now and then, especially when starting something new. These secrets or tools are not the answer to resolving, but they will hopefully guide you on your own quest to unmask your potential when imposter syndrome-like feelings arise. To recap, these four items were:

1. Understanding yourself is a stepping stone to understanding how experiences shape your ways of leadership.

I'm a major advocate of therapy and think everyone should have access to affordable mental health services. While stigmas still exist (especially in black and brown communities), talking about mental health and asking for help is becoming a normal part of our lives. However, I understand that therapy can be scary to start and/or isn't within the budgetary means for everyone. Some other self-discovery tools I highly recommend are the Enneagram and Strengths Finder. Both are online tests that are cheap and offer great insights into your personality, what triggers you, and what energizes you. I was shocked at how spot-on both tests were and how they helped me understand how to be a better leader and surround myself with others to supplement my shortcomings.

2. Find a community or network that will allow you to fail with purpose and commit to showing up.

The best thing that ever happened to me was seeking out ways to get plugged into Nashville. This helped me battle severe bouts of depression and gave me a sense of purpose. Friends and family are great, but having another group that strives to impact your place of living and are sounding boards for failure is a gift that most people miss out on. My only regret is I wish I figured this out sooner in my post-graduate career.

3. Acknowledge that you won't have the answers, and sometimes those answers (or actions) will be wrong.

This is probably the most difficult thing to grasp. It's okay not to be the most perfect leader who has the answers to everything. No one does. Life is constantly evolving, and we're all learning as we go. Being vulnerable, asking for help, and owning up to your failures are important qualities that all leaders (especially new ones) must learn.

4. Show up and bring your authentic self to leadership.

Be you. Simple as that. Imposter syndrome feeds on the idea that you have to fit someone else's narrative of who you should be. Who you are and what you've accomplished got you into leadership. Being authentic can be daunting, but you'll be a better leader because of it.

Ely Jones is a community leader serving and supporting various young professional organizations, most prominently the Nashville Junior Chamber. A member since 2017, board member, and President, Ely has implemented various long-lasting initiatives for the organization such as Network Nashville, Social at Six, defining organization values, and implementing DE&I practices. Originally from Birmingham, Alabama, Ely has a Bachelor of Science in Operations Management and a Master of Business Administration, both from the University of Alabama. Having lived in Nashville since 2014, he was a graduate of the Young Leaders Council in 2020 and 2023 ambassador of Men Wear Pink.

Most prominently, Ely was selected to the 46th class of Leadership Nashville. Leadership Nashville is an independent executive program that strengthens Nashville through deep connections formed among diverse leaders while experiencing a three-dimensional view of the city. He served as part of the leadership team for the following class. His most recent accomplishment was being honored as the Nashville Business Journal's 40 Under 40 for 2024 which has been a culmination of his community impact thus far, while also springboarding him into his next chapter.

To learn more about the organization that set his life on a different course, the Nashville Junior Chamber, visit https://www.nashvillejuniorchamber.org/. A champion for the Nashville Junior Chamber and supporting young professionals, he's always eager to chat with young people to help them get plugged into the city.

Follow or reach out to Ely on Linkedin at https://www.linkedin.com/in/ely-jones-43343430/

CHAPTER 9

THE POWER OF SACRED RELATIONSHIPS

BECOMING A TRANSFORMATIONAL PHILANTHROPY LEADER

Susan S. Holt

"Truth and courage aren't always comfortable, but they're never weakness."

~ Brené Brown

MY STORY

"Does the doctor have anything to say?"

Those seven words revolutionized my work and life. They were the start of a remarkable relationship. And, they were the beginning of a path to a $16 million charitable gift that, to this day, changes lives.

How often do relationships, sacred relationships, change everything?

I can name several in my work and personal life. I'm talking about the relationships that change trajectories, change lives, change our work, and even our world.

How? Because they're built on deep and abiding connections. Connections our brains crave. Connections our hearts yearn for. And, more and more, they're the trusted, precious, and even sacred connections our world so desperately needs.

How do we create powerful, sacred relationships that change the way we lead and maybe even transform our world?

Let me tell you about my friend Frances.

The first time I met Frances Preston I was with several leaders from the University Medical Center where I was a major gift officer, the fundraisers responsible for raising large gifts. At the very heart of major gift fundraising lies meaningful relationships, and I was young in a career that required exquisite self-mastery. I had a lot to learn.

Sitting behind a desk where only leaders who know how to lead dare to sit, Frances' office towered over Music Row. She was immaculately dressed in a black pantsuit—her signature. Her jewelry was big and elegant, and her commandingly powerful voice was laced with a touch of deep southern silk without a trace of accent.

To say I was in awe, even intimidated, is a wild understatement! I felt way out of my league, yet intrigued. Eager to cement my work, I immediately sensed this was the kind of woman I wanted to get to know. I was drawn to her and wanted to learn from her. Little did I know the force she would become in my life's work and life itself.

With little ceremony, Frances shared her vision for the large charitable gift she planned to direct to her hometown, Nashville, where our institution was located. It was clear that whatever Frances set her mind to happened. This was a woman who never heard no. But, there were many unknowns about how this gift would unfurl. Big ones. Nonetheless, we were elated at the prospect of a significant new investment in our cancer research that could change the curve of our work! We were ready to do whatever it took to work with Frances to make sure this gift happened. Clearly, Frances understood how to navigate the music industry. What we didn't know was how she would walk the perilous and ego-fraught road that one day would grow a $1 million commitment to a $16 million-plus gift from that industry.

I was nervous as we drove back a few blocks to the Medical Center. Everyone was quiet. We knew the next steps in developing this important relationship with our new friend on Music Row could be a game changer.

Later, Frances confided, "Susan, I'm not good at fundraising. I don't like it. I can't ask for money. But I'm very good at making friends." Indeed, she was. Truth be told, she was an excellent fundraiser! She excelled at touching her friends' hearts and inviting them to participate in our shared cause.

I was new to transformational giving, gifts that can change the trajectory of an organization, an institution, and even the donor. I had little idea what I was in for: the gratification, the learning conversations, the deep connections, and the sacred relationships that oftentimes stretched across decades.

Professor Elizabeth Dunn, who studies happiness and generosity, explains, "People we are giving to because of a relationship have a deeper experience and a deeper connection. It's a fundamentally different zone, where the 'magic of humanity exists'."[1]

There was a lot of magic that occurred in the humanity of the special relationship with Frances. We also needed everyone at the Music Industry Foundation to feel that same magic. Ultimately, we needed them to fall in love with us, with the work, and with our powerfully bold vision.

The Medical Center research laboratories were just a few blocks from the music industry offices. Culturally, they couldn't have been farther apart. To make matters worse, we had no shared history. There was a lot of territory to traverse, and it could only happen with one person leading the charge: Frances.

The next time the Cancer Center Director and I met, Frances was following a charity golf event. Our fundraising program shied away from event fundraising. But, lo and behold, this was the Foundation's fundraising bread and butter. Again, we were completely out of our element!

The Director and I practiced our scripts for this second meeting. We knew exactly what we wanted Frances to know about cancer research, down to minute details! We wanted to describe the challenges, opportunities, and ways the Foundation could elevate the Center's programs. It was a lot of information. And, in the way that academic programs tend to do, our scripts were peppered with way too many details.

We arrived at the small room set aside for our meeting at the golf club, anxious to begin. It was Nashville, and the humidity lay in drops down our backs. We found Frances as she was finishing another business meeting. She never stopped. Then, suddenly, we were left together, just the three of us. The Director, a humble, soft-spoken, and brilliant physician-scientist, was brand new to the fundraising business. It was a somewhat terrifying

---

[1] *Happy Money. The Science of Happier Spending*, Elizabeth Dunn and Michael Norton, Simon and Schuster, 2014.

moment. I was "glowing," as we say in the South, and determined not to miss a beat, I leaped into our script.

Time with this woman is precious, after all!

I managed to share all of our plans without the Director ever uttering a word. The next thing we knew, Frances smiled, looked squarely at us, and said,

"Does the doctor have anything to say? Does he talk?"

I was horrified! What a horrible mistake I'd made.

In my haste to make sure all the material was covered, I stepped all over this renowned scientist's message. And Frances called me on it. I think she was also a little amused.

I talked as fast as I could to fill the void, not listening. We all took a deep breath. The pre-eminent scientist smiled and said that, yes, he had a few things to add.

Of course, he was brilliant, and Frances beamed. I appreciated her generosity and sense of humor. She was in the entertainment industry. She knew how to tell not just a good story but a great one, all while leveraging influence and power.

Our sacred relationship was just beginning. And in that moment I began to learn about leadership, trust, bold listening, and becoming vulnerable enough to build the deep, meaningful, and even transformative relationships that nurture philanthropy.

Soon afterward, we invited Frances to tour some of the research laboratories that would eventually bear her name. We began to develop transparent, comfortable conversations built on trust and honesty. And, although we weren't the bold listeners we eventually became, Frances was. She asked an abundance of deep questions, and new worlds began to open for all of us.

Gradually we became comfortable refining our stories while learning about the complex business she spent her life in. It was a two-way street. She helped us tell our pioneering stories in ways that resonated with the average person who didn't know a nucleus from a cell to a protein. Conversely, we helped her become proficient, even compelling, at telling our stories, too. I think she almost surprised herself at how adept she became at sharing the profound stories of cancer research. In time, we developed shared languages.

That was the beginning of what became a unique and sacred relationship that existed between us and Frances until her death. She opened doors to some of the most influential people in the industry. With humor and grace, she held our feet to the fire, pointing out when we slipped up.

Eventually, the centerpiece of the Vanderbilt-Ingram Cancer Center was named in her honor. It was made possible by an anonymous donor who challenged the music industry Foundation to give another transformative gift that honored this great lady and named the building for her that anchors a great Cancer Center.

What made it possible to reach out, build new friendships, and create this transformational gift?

Shared passions, values, beliefs, impact, and gratitude are the bedrock of transformational giving. Without them, transformative generosity simply does not occur. But, even the best leader will be challenged to navigate transformational gifts without the qualities that build and sustain sacred relationships. These were central to my self-mastery as a successful leader in transformational philanthropy.

You'll find these qualities described in The Tool at the end of the chapter. But first, I want to share another story with you, one that again shook me and tested our relationship.

I was given the job of asking Frances to serve on our prestigious Campaign Leadership Committee for the Medical Center's half-billion-dollar campaign. It was a mighty ask. A bold ask.

We knew this would be a heavy lift for Frances, requiring a significant commitment of time. Truth be told, I wasn't quite prepared for the conversation. I picked Frances up for lunch, as was my custom, at the lobby of the imposing BMI offices. She got in the car looking a bit distracted. It was another hot, sticky Nashville summer day and we were in a rush to one of her favorite restaurants. Glancing down, I noticed a stain on the arm of my otherwise crisp suit.

Oh, man, not looking very polished today, are we?

We settled into our table without our usual friendly greetings.

Why am I doing this? She's got a ton of other stuff going on, and my heart's not into it. Oh, man, here we go.

I opened with a stark, impersonal description of our expectations for the committee, punctuating her influence on other members and donors. I was hiding behind words.

Slam! I could feel the door closing.

I'm so grateful this conversation occurred well into our relationship. Otherwise, no doubt it would've gone differently.

Suddenly, Frances interrupted me in mid-sentence, "Susan, this is ME, Frances. You know me. I know you. You can just talk turkey and cut out the bull, okay!? Just tell me what you need, okay?"

She leaned right at me and called me on my inauthenticity.

I stopped. She was right. I was shocked. I realized I wasn't being faithful to our relationship, to the trust, transparency, and honesty we had built over nearly a decade.

"Frances," I said, "You're right. I've got a tall ask of you. To succeed in this campaign, we need your leadership and passion. We need your power. We need your influence," I bravely explained.

"Well, you're not asking too much, are you?!" She chided me with that Frances look we came to love.

My stomach turned. *Maybe I've finally blown it.*

I screwed up all my courage, and my stomach still turning said,

"Yeah, Frances, we're asking a lot. I know it. But I'll make this responsibility as simple and rewarding as possible for you as I can. I'll be there every step of the way, I promise."

She smiled that all-knowing smile again, and we discussed what was required and the terms of this commitment.

I'd been phoning-in this ask. Distracted and unprepared, I wasn't being open, transparent, honest, and, yes, vulnerable. In the end, we reached an agreement. Our relationship was even stronger, but only after a few uncomfortable moments!

One of the things I've learned is how much we can learn from our friends and colleagues who come from the most unsuspecting places. But this only happens if we take the time to be present, listen deeply, ask bold questions, listen more deeply, and be honest. Only then can we understand clearly and know how to act on passions, visions, beliefs, and dreams. And, in the case of philanthropy fulfill theirs' and our institution's bold visions.

Frances taught me so much, much more than business and philanthropy. She was intensely loyal. She took care of people. She would go to the ends of the Earth for her staff and friends, and they for her. She asked deep questions. She listened, but most of all, she cared.

Frances possessed many sacred relationships. This came back in spades when it came time to bring together all the people needed to create the transformative gift in her honor. People wanted to join her and support her cause. Undoubtedly, some of this was a part of doing business with her. Most of it was simply heart.

Years later, our journey came full circle as I walked through those Cancer Center doors. I no longer worked there. Instead, I was a scared patient. My eyes welled up with tears as I walked through the door, and looking up saw Frances' name on the building. There was a huge rush in my heart. It nearly knocked me over. I stopped for a minute. Then, just as suddenly, a calm came over me as I took in that sight. I knew everything would be okay. Together with other visionary donors, something special and meaningful had been created in that building that changed lives and continues to change lives to this day.

I said a prayer of thanks for her, for her life and friendship, for the sacred relationship we had shared, and indeed everything was okay.

THE TOOL

This is a tool to help you explore the qualities I've found time and again are central to creating sacred relationships and becoming a transformative leader, whether in business, fundraising or even in life.

I invite you to visit my website, www.visionphilanthropy.com, to download a series of exercises, including "Creating Sacred Relationships," "Bold Listening," and "Signature Language." These will guide you and your team as you discuss and hone these qualities individually and as a team for your transformative work!

1. **Deep Trust.** Trust that is courageous and daring that may be tested but will be stronger in the end. Trust that says, "I know you for who you are. You can count on me. I can count on you."

2. **Honesty.** Honesty comes from a place of trust and willingness to be vulnerable, even when it's uncomfortable. Honesty permits (even invites) and perseveres through difficult conversations.

3. **Vulnerability.** Sometimes, this is the scariest of all. If we're going to truly connect in meaningful ways, we have to be ready to be vulnerable. Indeed, this is where some of the magic happens, where relationships flourish through true, deep, and authentic connections. Vulnerability becomes a strength as partners share their true selves and create authentic bonds. Be ready, though, because vulnerability does not come without discomfort.

4. **Respect.** Knowing the other person genuinely for who they are and being willing to hear them. In major gift fundraising, we talk about being donor-centric, honoring the donor's interests. But this kind of respect goes beyond even the concept of "donor-centric."

5. **Bold listening.** Listening to understand by being present, by asking learning questions—not on your phone, not checking emails, social media, or text messages. Phones have no place here. Bury them. Be present and ready to ask bold questions and listen deeply to understand by reflecting and reaffirming.

6. **Transparent communication and shared learning.** How often do we hedge even a bit in conversations with colleagues or donors? Not in transparent communications. There are no smoke and mirrors here but, instead, a willingness to lean into learning conversations that listen and understand experiences.

7. **Willingness to go the extra mile.** Being ready to be open to another's point of view. To truly ask, seek, explore, and consider their thoughts, advice, hopes, and dreams. Be ready to listen and receive them. Indeed, oftentimes, transformational gifts or business decisions must percolate. Sometimes, for a long time! It may be a million-mile journey. It's the strength and even sacredness of the relationship that is what, in large part, makes this journey possible. Going the extra mile is not a duty but a choice. It's a demonstration of commitment out of respect.

8. **Genuine appreciation.** When it comes right down to it, we have to appreciate each other if we're going to create even a simple relationship. We have to be eager for and *value* deep connection. In the fundraising world, it means appreciating these friends for what they bring well beyond financial resources and treasures, valuing the friendship and joy of being a part of the dreams and reality that together we are creating. Ultimately, the relationship is nurtured by a mutual appreciation that shares gratitude and an acknowledgment for the sacredness of this connection.

9. **Finally, Connection.** Ultimately, all these qualities roll up into what Dr. Michael Lieberman writes about in his book *Social: Why Our Brains Are Wired to Connect*. That is the need and power of deep human connection. Indeed, connection is at the very core of the fabric of our humanity. In his book, Dr. Lieberman talks about the overwhelming drive that we humans have, deep in our brains' wiring, to connect.[2] Indeed, in sacred relationships lie deep, honest connections!

Thank you for taking the time to read my story. I hope you'll join me in discovering the sacred relationships essential to transformative leadership that can change our work, our lives, and even our world!

---

[2] *Social: Why Our Brains Are Wired to Connect*, Michael D. Lieberman, Crown Publishing Group 2014.

Susan Holt is a recognized philanthropy leader with over 40 years of experience in leadership positions and as a senior advisor to leading higher education, health care, global health institutions, and non-profit organizations. She founded Vision Philanthropy Group (VPG) in 2009.

Recognizing the universal need for a deeper understanding of and confidence in major gift fundraising and philanthropy by boards, executive leaders, and fundraising staff, she created Bold Asking®, a transformational gift coaching and training program. Susan de-mystifies and even creates joy in major gift fundraising! This is now the focus of her work, where she delights in helping clients raise gifts they never before thought possible.

One fundraiser who recently attended a Bold Asking® training wrote, *"This week, I secured my first transformational gift! I have no doubt that you influenced my ability to make the bold ask in these donors closing out a campaign and giving almost 10x more than they had to us before! Thank you for equipping and inspiring me to have these impactful conversations with donors!"*

Before founding VPG, Susan led the development programs at the Vanderbilt University School of Nursing, Vanderbilt-Ingram Cancer Center, Case Western Reserve University Medical School, Weill Cornell Medical College of Cornell University, and National Jewish Health. She's managed and advised numerous successful campaigns from $10 million to $1.3 billion, partnering with institutional leaders in securing *single* gifts ranging from $1 million to $250 million for capital, operating, and endowed projects.

Susan's undergraduate and graduate degrees in music and vocal performance, bring a unique perspective from her formal performing arts training to her philanthropy training and coaching. She and her husband reside in Nashville, Tennessee where she also loves hanging out with her four grandkids, studying voice, singing in her church choir, and regularly heading off to Pilates and spin classes!

Questions? Write her: susan@visionphilanthropy. She'll answer!

CHAPTER 10

BEING A PROMISE KEEPER

A FOUNDATION FOR SUCCESS AND SATISFACTION

Joel English

You and I can choose to be an anchor point in a time of chaos.

MY STORY

"I think we should get divorced while we're still friends."

She had to see the shock on my face. I didn't see this coming. Our marriage wasn't perfect, but this was extreme.

I know things are hard, but do you care so little for me and us that you're ready to quit so soon? What about the promise we made to stay together regardless of the circumstances?

Debbie and I met in college our freshman year and spent three years getting to know each other. I knew in the first few months of our relationship that I wanted to spend the rest of my life with her. It took her just a bit longer to get to the same place.

We had a beautiful, traditional church wedding witnessed by 300 of our family and friends. *And now, 18 months later, we're talking divorce?*

Was I consistently the husband I wanted to be and that she deserved? No.

I thought I had time to work on it.

I was wrong.

The tipping point was the shocking news that her mother wanted a divorce from her father after 28 years of marriage. This came on the heels of one of her brothers having divorced his wife after six months and the other on the way to divorce as well. The sad list extended to a favorite aunt and uncle and Debbie's grandmother.

"I think my family is congenitally incapable of staying married. I want to end ours before it gets too painful."

I didn't know whether to laugh or cry.

Debbie was contending with an immature, often selfish husband, as well as the crumbling of her entire family structure and sense of what was possible in marriage.

She left her pronouncement as an open invitation, one that couldn't be ignored. I went for a run late one night, resolved to decide what to do. Being in limbo wasn't an option for me. Many thoughts ran through my mind.

Maybe I should just do what she wants. She doesn't seem committed to me or us and her family situation is not going to get better any time soon.

Or is she just getting overwhelmed by the stresses all around her? Maybe if I helped to stabilize things, we could get through this.

The stress isn't helping me either. But my stress doesn't even come close to what she is dealing with.

And if I leave her, where will she turn for help to get through this? What she seems to want could be disastrous for her.

I made a promise to her. This is no time to turn away. But it is hard to stay together when it seems she doesn't want to.

As I ran, the phrase "I made a promise" repeated over and over in my mind, soon matching my running pace. The closer I got to home, the more my resolve solidified.

I MADE A PROMISE. AND PROMISES SHOULDN'T BE BROKEN.

What seems like such an obvious truth isn't obvious anymore in our culture. In America, half of all marriages end in divorce, with the rate of divorce in second and third marriages even higher. *Don't we promise "till death do us part?"*

Bankruptcy rates continue to rise. *What about paying what we promised to pay?*

Unlimited warranties are sprouting fine print. *Can you put limits on unlimited?*

Health insurance plans seem to spend as much time telling us about the care that we can't have as what we can. *I thought you enabled care, not excluded it.*

The examples go on and on.

We live in a world that relishes pushing back against absolutes. We seek "our truth," a truth that can easily change tomorrow, next week, or next year. There are "absolutely no absolutes."

No wonder we're seeing a growing hunger for people and promises we can believe in and anchor to in a world clouded by chaos and uncertainty. We search for concrete anchor points that will not change based on the whims of personal desire or self-interest. We search for companies we can count on to be there for us as we contend with an increasingly unfriendly world.

HEREIN LIES THE POWER OF PROMISES KEPT.

You and I can choose to be an anchor point in the chaos.

We can be promise makers and keepers that will attract engagement and loyalty because our commitment doesn't sway with wind or whim.

We can choose to make non-negotiable and absolute promises as family members, employees, and companies.

When we do so personally, we become known as people who can be counted on regardless of circumstances

As employees, we become known as someone who will always deliver.

And as a company we become known as a brand people want to support and advocate.

Where do non-negotiables come from?

My absolutes come from the timeless promises and statutes of God. Some fall back on legacy beliefs from family or clan, others look to the laws of science or nature. Regardless of where they come from, they need to be anchor points that don't change. They must truly be non-negotiable.

Here are some examples.

Debbie and I didn't divorce because she also believes in the power of a promise made and kept, even though circumstances early in our marriage obscured her view for a time.

God blessed us with three wonderful children. As they grew older, they felt the pain of friends whose families were torn apart by divorce. Even though they didn't voice it, when Debbie and I disagreed, we saw fear in their eyes.

"Are you going to divorce and split us apart too?"

"No. We made a promise before God to stay together until we are in heaven, and that promise means we will never divorce. You never have to worry about that happening to our family."

Before Debbie and I had that conversation, we recommitted to our mutual promise so we could do so with our children.

Their fear went away and never returned.

Your coworkers want the same kind of promises from you. It's the basis for respect, commitment, and loyalty.

They wonder things like:

- "When the bullets fly, where will you be? Standing alongside us or running for the hills?"

- "When we must admit failure to the bosses, will you blame others or accept responsibility?"

As a senior leader in a consulting and communications firm, one of my responsibilities is to head up teams seeking to win new clients. It involves complex and carefully orchestrated presentations. I'm known (and not very fondly) for being inflexible about rehearsals. The conversation usually goes like this:

"Rehearsal tonight at 6:00. We need to do a time check, work through the overall narrative and handoffs."

"Really? I'm tired. I had a long flight, and I still have a lot to do on our other accounts. The other pitch leaders don't expect their teams to rehearse like you do. Why can't you be like them?!"

If this sounds like trying to get your teens to cut the lawn or clean their rooms, you get the feel of the conversation.

Yes, my teammates are busy, and travel takes it out of each of us. They're some of the best presenters in the business. We could do fine with a light talk-through. But good enough should never be good enough. After all the work attracting a new client, we owe it to ourselves and them to give our best effort.

After all the harumphing is done, we put our best foot forward resulting in more and better relationships and more rewards for everyone involved.

And, critically, my teammates know I'm just as inflexible with myself in applying that same high standard to everything I do. They should expect nothing less. That is my promise to them.

While we think of promises as made by people, they're also made by companies. The company I work for helps organizations discern their brand promises and the human values they support and customers experience. My area of focus is healthcare. If there's ever a category where promises should be made and kept, it's healthcare, where we're dealing with the greatest aspirations (like bringing a new human into the world) and fears (unnecessary death and disability) in life.

While a company's values are commonly outlined in Mission/Vision/ Values statements, in my experience, they can be more aspirational than real. A promise must be achievable and non-negotiable, so corporate values are a starting point for discerning promises.

My company (BVK) has an overarching imperative concerning long-term relationships. As a result, we have a non-negotiable promise:

- We will always place integrity and long-term relationships over ethical compromises and short-term profits.

I worked on developing a relationship with one of the nation's largest healthcare systems for several years. I became acquainted with the Chief Marketing Officer (CMO) but hadn't broken through to an actual business relationship when I got the call.

"We just acquired a new health system that will be merging with an existing system member. The new CEO has a brand construct in mind for the new merged entity, and he wants to do some market research to validate his approach."

I said, "Excellent! I am very familiar with both systems and recently reviewed research on marketplace perceptions. That will give us a head start on fielding a study that will lead to the best way to portray the combined entity."

His response: "As long as the research creates a foundation for his approach."

"What if it doesn't?"

"That would be a problem."

As much as I wanted to cement this new relationship, it couldn't be based upon us providing an inaccurate representation of the strengths and weaknesses of the proposed branding approach simply to mollify the CEO. I declined to put in a proposal for the project; we couldn't support him the way he suggested. I explained my reasons in an awkward conversation. It was disappointing, but the only way for us to go was for us to stay true to our promise.

Fast forward a decade.

The CMO was now at a large multinational health system. We participated in a national search for their business and prevailed. When he debriefed us on the reason for our selection, he mentioned he never encountered a consultant who passed on a project the way we did or for the reason we did. It earned his respect and stayed with him. He became a valued client, a good friend, and one of our best references.

Another testing moment came when one of our existing clients learned that their biggest competitor with a much larger budget was looking for a new agency.

Another awkward call, this time from the client.

"I am sure you heard they're looking for an agency."

I could hear some anxiety in his voice.

"Yup, they've already called us."

"Did they tell you the budget? It's no doubt much larger than ours."

Anxiety mixed with fear.

"We never got that far. We told them we weren't interested. They asked why. We told them that we work with you. I suspected they knew but thought we might be willing to trade relationships. The sharing stopped right then."

"Is Michael (BVK's CEO) okay with that?"

Guarded hope.

"It was actually his idea."

A few years later, a project didn't go as we both planned. It was the kind of miss that usually causes relationships to end. Instead, we worked through it. They never told us so, but I believe they stayed with us because we showed them our commitment years earlier.

We're still working with them 25 years later.

Promises also should be made between companies and the people they serve.

One of our clients is a prominent cancer center with a stellar reputation. Despite being one of the top cancer centers in the country, it wasn't attracting the number of patients its reputation warranted. We determined that the center's brand promise should focus on the value of courage. This courage was reflected in how patients and their families wanted to feel when confronting cancer, as well as the passion and excellence in the care they needed to battle courageously.

We launched a comprehensive communications effort that engaged people in new and encouraging ways. In the first year after the launch, they experienced a double-digit patient volume increase. And pride within the cancer center skyrocketed because we also gave voice to their aspirations and motivations.

No new programs, procedures, or processes were shared—simply a clear and insightful promise that compassionately addressed our fears related to cancer and our desires for the people we need to trust on the journey. The growth came solely from a promise made and kept.

THE TOOL

THE PROMISE KEEPER'S PLAN

A fellow author of this book, David, asked me a question. "When did you become a promise keeper?"

Great question.

We aren't born one. It's a choice.

After reflection, I believe it was on my midnight run.

So, if you haven't yet had your promise keeper challenge moment, make this your "midnight run," sans the sweat and lost sleep. When confronted with a promise challenge (and you will be), you can be well prepared!

Begin by asking yourself:

In my life, what are the things I must do where I can't fail to positively impact the lives of the people I love, those who trust me at work and in other important relationships?

Write down your answers. List them for your personal life, your professional life, and, if a leader within a team or company, for your organization as well.

For each of these imperatives fully articulate:

- What is it, and why this promise? Where did the imperative come from?

- What happens when you hold fast? What would happen if you compromised?

Don't worry if you don't have many. This is not a numbers game. It's a faithfulness plan.

Next, take some time to find inspiration in your sacred writings, family history, or observations on nature and the universe for additional possibilities.

If you're tempted to say of any of your initial promises: "I will try to do that/be that way," then I want to ask you to do something.

Try to stand up.

Are you standing? If so, you didn't try to stand up; you stood up.

The "T" word is what people (me included) use to hedge our bets with promises we don't think we'll be able to keep. If you have one or more of these on your list, move them to an "aspirations" parking lot. Don't give them up; just set them aside for further reflection on how to make it without equivocation.

Now, put everything on one sheet of paper. Write your promises on the front side and your aspirations on the back.

Again, don't worry if you have just two or three promises. These should be high-bar statements. Remember, must do, can't fail!

Now, for each promise, write down how you'll stand behind it and what people or resources you need to support you and hold you accountable.

If you write in a journal, spend two weeks with your initial thinking. Read it each day, capture your excitement and your fears, and use them for a final read and editing before sharing.

Now, share the product with the people who know you best. What rings true? What could use some help? Will they stand beside you to uphold them?

Then put the resulting promises in a form that can be reviewed during a daily reflection or devotion, on your desk, or wherever you go to be inspired and sustained. And make sure to keep your aspiration list handy as you may be moved in the future to elevate them to promises.

Throughout, think about how a chaotic and struggling world will respond when they know that in these ways, you're becoming an anchor they can count on—a person who carefully makes and keeps promises.

Yes, it will be hard, very hard sometimes. But the rewards you get in return will eclipse the effort. Your efforts will impact lives, companies, and destinies.

At Thanksgiving, our family pauses at the dinner table to thank God for blessings during the year. When it was her turn, our daughter Erika, reflecting on a singularly challenging year, looked down at our four-year-old grandson Leo and said, "I am grateful that as a family, we do the hard things and keep our promises."

Leo chimed in, "Yes, Mommy, we do."

Tears of joy flowed from two proud grandparents.

Joel is a Senior Vice President with BVK, a business and brand consultancy and communications company. Joel has been there for 35 years and worked with over 150 clients in the health and healthcare fields. He has a passion for finding the intersection point between the greatest aspirations and fears of people and the greatest passions and accomplishments of those who care for them. He has spoken at several national and regional conferences on healthcare branding and business issues. He has contributed numerous articles to industry publications, and his thinking has been featured on NPR's *All Things Considered*. Joel has received the prestigious Leadership Excellence Award from the Society for Healthcare Strategy and Market Development.

He is a trained Biblical counselor and mentor and has been married to his wife Debbie for 45 years. They have been blessed with three children: Andy (deceased), Erika, and Andria joined by their husbands Nate and Keith, and grandson Leo. They are also joined by their fur, fins, and feather collection of dogs, fish, and a parrot.

Joel can be reached at joel.english@bvk.com with questions, thoughts, or ideas. Joel and his BVK colleagues offer a variety of leadership workshops available for you and others in your organization.

CHAPTER 11

CHANGE THE PROCESS, NOT THE PEOPLE

HOW TO BE A PROCEDURE FANATIC

Laura Lee Jones

"Excellence is never an accident. It is always the result of high intention, sincere effort, and intelligent execution."

~ Aristotle

MY STORY

BAD NEWS: Communication is the problem. GOOD NEWS: Communication is the fix!

As I sit across my desk from Josie, the president of my firm, I ask, "Do we need to fire someone or move them to a different role? You know I loathe errors on client work. How many times has this mistake happened? Who made the mistake?"

"No, we do not need to replace anyone. You always jump to the conclusion that someone did something wrong. A debrief will occur and we will identify why this error happened. Most likely, it is related to processes, not our people."

"But how did it happen? Was it Bob? We've covered this type of error multiple times!"

I listened a bit defensively as Josie told me very directly, "Laura Lee, for years, I have watched you make others cringe when you question them about a mistake. You have a right to be upset or disappointed, but your tone seems angry. I know you don't intend to hurt them, but you do."

She continued, "It is a process issue. Not a people issue. Our people are amazing. So, no, we do not need to replace anyone. They need better processes. You need to remember that in the absence of specific guidelines, they're using their best judgment. Maybe their judgment isn't as good as yours or mine, but as their leaders, we're setting them up for failure by not having well-defined procedures. The pressure you apply when there is a gap shuts them down."

"What pressure? I'm not angry. I just want it done right the first time. Why did the same mistake happen again?"

Josie lowered her voice and responded very calmly, "Again, you need to put the pressure on the process, not the people. Every person that works here wants to get an A on their work. They want to do it right. They want to please the client, and even more importantly, they want to please you. The common denominator is you. When you hear of a mistake or gap, you immediately think someone did something wrong. You need to change your perspective."

She was so kind and truthful with me. She spoke softly, but her words were super heavy to hear. I'm fortunate to have a colleague willing to speak to her CEO with such clear words on desperately needed changes. Processes, procedures, and me!

Could this be the answer to fixing gaps and errors? Even when I think I'm communicating clearly, mistakes still happen. Do I make people feel bad, pressure them? Sound angry? Ouch, that hurt to hear.

I sat in my office quietly, not moving, just thinking. I thought about the last time I spoke to a colleague about an error. I felt his reaction in the pit of my stomach. I remembered the hurt in his eyes when I repeated the same question to him for the third time.

"Why did this happen again? Why?" I asked more loudly the second time. "Please tell me how this went to the client without proper proofing again?" He seemed frozen in place. He didn't answer me. He was focused on the feelings I created in him, not the process. After the third time I asked, he answered, "I just forgot to do the final proofing; it was an honest mistake."

Josie is right and courageous to speak the truth to me. I need to learn more about this process stuff. Equally important, why is my behavior causing others to feel bad?

Why do I behave that way? I like to think I am a kind and benevolent leader. As a company we have won *Best Places to Work* several times. That must count for something.

Why do I get so stressed when things are less than perfect? One fear for me is others won't deliver on the promises I give regarding LionShare when they hire us. I want my delivery to be a 1:1 ratio. I say it, then do it. No excuses. I needed that from others, too. I had to resolve this as quickly as possible.

Soul searching, I knew it was rooted in my childhood. That is where we all get programmed. I was raised in a family where we were always expected to do better, go faster, and do more.

Even when I ran the mile in high school and broke the school record, my dad said, "You had about three more seconds you could have shaved off if you had come out of turn four differently."

"But Dad, I broke the record and threw up at the end of the race. I didn't have anything left."

I sat back in my chair and forced myself to think about it. Ahh, there it was. I felt all the pressure on me. I heard it so loudly in my head.

YOU HAVE TO BE BETTER! Those words are what I learned in childhood, so as a leader, that is how I lead. I applied pressure on people. They must be better.

Dad was right; I could've "shaved off" those three seconds. What I realized now as I examined my leadership skills is that his intent was good when he said those words. It was his delivery about what was wrong with me that hurt.

In hindsight, what I needed to hear from my dad was about the process of getting better at running the mile. The way he made me feel was exactly how I was making others feel at work. I just wasn't good enough.

Sitting alone and examining it again I can see he wasn't mad at me at all. I was mad at myself for disappointing him. I was sad I didn't understand what he was yelling at me from the sidelines. He was so proud of me and happy. He saw me finish strong and win. Most importantly, he wanted me to understand the process of running and where I could close some gaps in my next race.

He saw how hard I worked at track and wanted me to get what I deserved for those efforts. He wasn't disappointed at all. He did see three more seconds, and he wanted me to take them off my time. He communicated it in a way that hurt. It was not intentional, but the pain was still there.

"Don't try and pass on the corner. Stay tucked in behind the leader until you hit the straight. Then finish fast. Now! Go now!" These were the words I wished he told me.

"Do the best you can until you know better. Then, when you know better, do better." This is one of my favorite quotes from Maya Angelou. It was time I became a better leader. A better communicator.

I know better now. I figured out the importance of processes and procedures. I learned a long time ago that *communication is the problem and communication is the fix*. At the core, though, I just didn't understand what it meant. I put the pressure on the people, not the process. It became very clear to me. I will be better!

How can I be better? How can the team help me make it better?

For years I tried to train everyone the "right way" to do things. What things? Everything! I'm very particular!

"Please don't let the phone ring more than three times, and if it does ring a fourth time, someone should break a leg getting to the phone for the client," I said those words, always with a laugh, but everyone who worked with me knew I meant it.

"If you're sending a follow-up email after an hour-long client strategy call, it must be done exactly this way."

"When is it the right time to remind a client they owe us money? What should it sound like when we do ask them to pay us because they are late on the payment? Why the correspondence must be just so every time we communicate, both internally and externally."

"What is the difference between a bill and an invoice? We all need to know this so we communicate effectively and consistently."

I'm good at direct and honest conversations. That was easy for me. What I wasn't good at was leaving people whole at the end of those conversations. I needed to "be the change I wanted to see in the world." That world was our office. We needed a new communication style, and it had to start at the top.

It was me. I had to change. Thankfully I was surrounded by team leaders who were comfortable speaking honestly to me about me. They were also all on board for becoming fanatics regarding procedures and processes at the company. We would write a standard operating procedure (SOP) for everything and then continue to improve them as needed.

A high-performance company requires high-performance processes. To adapt to ever-changing business needs, the team needs to use the processes and procedures in place.

As the company grows and our services and products grow, so should our processes. We will continue to improve them, and it must be the expectation of every team member to follow them. They must be trained and explained to every new hire during onboarding. We will keep searching for ways to add new processes and improve the current processes and procedures.

Our battle cry will become "At LionShare, we put the pressure on the process, not the people." This is how we continue to grow. This is how we will go faster and be scalable, and more profitable.

Wow, this is a new way of thinking for me. Can I do it?

Yes, I could, but first, I needed to be honest with myself on how I managed gaps and errors. I am a high D on the DiSC© scale. I don't like rules or procedures, and I like to go fast—fast all the time, with a hammer in my hand as my favorite tool.

Years earlier, my mentor Carl helped me understand how to do a DiSC Profile on each employee, but more importantly, how to help understand the natural tendencies of each person to ensure we had them in the best position and doing what comes naturally to them.

The DiSC model describes four main styles: D, I, S, and C. D is for Dominance, I is for Influence, S is for Steadiness, and C is for Conscientiousness. Everyone can have a bit of each behavioral style. The DiSC is not a measurement tool for intelligence, aptitude, mental health, or values.

The use of the tool is to help understand human behavior in different situations. For example, when you are challenged, how do you respond? What is your preferred pace at work? When you're working with others, how do you try to influence them? Lastly, how do you respond to rules and regulations? At LionShare we use this instrument to place colleagues in the right position.

I heard my former mentor Carl in my head: *Every strength over extended can become a weakness.* Somewhere in his teachings, I realized that my high D nature isn't always the best, and no matter how difficult to do or how unlikely it seemed, I needed to temper it. I can't always be a hammer.

I would need to engage someone else on the team to manage all the standard operating procedures and get them in writing. This would also mean keeping them updated and constantly scrutinizing them for improvement. This person is going to have to have a lot of S in their profile. Those S's really like rules and order.

This knowledge about team members is key to setting up an organizational chart and understanding how we will use processes with each of those individuals. We'll all have different needs. Some processes and procedures will need extreme detail, while others could be more of a guideline.

I needed to consider how big this shift would be for the whole organization. I knew it would be good and eliminate more of those yucky feelings I caused. It would require a lot of discipline to make a change every time there's a gap. It needed to be the standard for me first, and then all the team leaders, and every person on the team.

It will be fun, right? We will become a process-driven machine—fanatical. I have always had a need for speed. If we do this process thing right, we really can go fast and be repeatable, which will allow us to be more profitable.

The team leaders were all on board. We decided to write an SOP for just about every task and procedure. In the beginning, we did go over the top. We even wrote a process for where to find the toilet paper in the warehouse and how many rolls go into each bathroom. I, not the others, almost went as far as to insist the paper rolls came over the top on the holder. Someone on the team stopped me.

My mindset changed. I needed this new way to look at errors and gaps in the office. Josie's suggestion of focusing on the processes, and less pressure on the people is now the foundation of examining our mistakes at the company.

THE TOOL

We have built a successful company by putting the pressure in the right places. It's almost always about the procedure or process, especially if you have people in the right positions that best suit their behavior and natural style.

Having a simple framework for dealing with errors makes it much easier to have difficult conversations in the office. This tool is instrumental in making the workspace feel better. It helps keep everyone calm and gives us all a tool to use when things aren't perfect. It's simple and functional.

Everyone is trained (and conditioned) to think this way and ask these four questions when a gap is identified:

1. **Is there a process or procedure?**

2. **Is there a gap in the process or procedure?**

3. **Was the process or procedure properly trained?**

4. **Was it followed?**

In addition to asking the questions above, I also learned to start every conversation with an apology. It felt funny at first, but now I see the necessity of an apology.

"I'm sorry. I wasn't clear, and I apologize for not putting the pressure on the process. Please let me start again."

This allows all parties involved to settle into an honest conversation that isn't about them but about the process. It also allows me to slow down and focus on what matters, keeping people whole and asking them to help solve any problems or gaps without personal pain.

It's rare, but on occasion, we do find ourselves saying, "The process is great, there are no gaps, and we have a team member that is just not a fit for us because they don't understand the value of process and procedure." We set them free if we can't convince them of the need to *pressure the process*.

I'm a very passionate person—passionate about everything in life. Becoming a fanatic about process has been life-altering for me and the whole team.

Is it challenging? Yes. Old programming from childhood doesn't go willingly. As a leader, I get it wrong sometimes. Now, I always know when

I'm putting the pressure where it doesn't belong. I feel it immediately. If I slip back into my old ways of pressuring someone on the team, one of my colleagues will smile and ask, "Did you ask about the process first, Jones?"

A native of Wisconsin, **Laura Lee Jones** graduated with a BA in Social Work/Psychology from the University of Wisconsin-Madison. After college, Boston was home for several years. While there she worked at a nonprofit organization where she assisted developmentally disabled adults, and then she trained dogs with the police Canine Academy before moving to Kansas City to start a company.

An entrepreneur at heart, she is passionate about growing companies and building teams. As Founder and CEO of LionShare Marketing, Inc., for 30 years she has focused on internal team communications first. With her team, she has become an industry expert on building complex healthcare databases and using data to drive successful healthcare marketing campaigns with high return on investment.

She takes pride in team culture. Her desire to lead with honesty, transparency, with a work hard/play hard attitude has led to exceptional retention of colleagues and clients.

Laura Lee is the Mentor Chair for the nonprofit *Helzberg Entrepreneurial Mentoring Program* and has been involved since 2006. She gets great joy in encouraging young entrepreneurs to lead with process, transparency, and life balance. She is also a member of *Women Who Mean Business*.

A sports fanatic, she loves cheering on the Kansas City Chiefs, Royals, and both pro soccer teams. She enjoys Pilates, weight training, and boxing. In 2019, she trained, then entered a cage for an amateur kickboxing match. She won by knock-out in Round 3.

A lifelong learner, she loves the front row of any event she attends. Her love of animals led to raising and training award-winning Dobermans. Travel is a fond hobby, especially if near an ocean. When relaxing, you will find her by the pool mixing a fruity cocktail (without a process or recipe).

Her very favorite pastime? Any activity with her daughter Eden.

Connect with Laura Lee:

Email: lauraleejones@lionsharemarketing.com

LinkedIn: https://www.linkedin.com/in/laura-lee-jones-a917153

Resources:

Process! by Mike Paton and Lisa Gonzalez

EQ Applied by Justin Bariso

DISCprofile.com

CHAPTER 12

FINDING THE LEADER WITHIN

ARTICULATE AND MANIFEST
YOUR GREATEST DESIRE

Mary Kipp, MSW

*"The test of leadership is not to put greatness into humanity,
but to elicit it, for greatness is already there."*

~ James Buchanan

MY STORY

Despite over ten years of experience, I trained my future male bosses to do a job I was better equipped to do. My undergraduate degree wasn't enough.

I arranged a loan, entered Syracuse University's two-year Master's program, followed two areas of concentration (individuals and organizations), worked full-time, completed two separate field placements, and fulfilled all requirements. I needed the credentials.

Finally! Two years well spent. Almost time for graduation.

Not so fast.

Right before finals, my grandmother died. She lived with us forever and called everyone "Love." She was Nanny to us and Love to everyone else. Never Mrs. or Mary.

It was time for goodbye.

By the time I returned to Syracuse, all ceremonies and celebrations were over. I made arrangements to meet with each professor and met all class and exam requirements. I landed a social work position in North Syracuse's School System with perfect hours. It covered the entire district. It was an upgrade in responsibility, visibility, and status.

Three months later, we left Syracuse for Albany, New York.

I needed to progress—gain position, at least on paper. I obtained a college teaching appointment that covered theory, practice, field placements, and oversight for 30 students.

And I had a therapy practice partnership.

Ahh. An ideal position with flexibility and proximity. I can provide parental supervision.

It lasted less than three years.

We moved again—this time, we really moved—from Upstate New York to Nashville, Tennessee. Our three kids were thirteen, twelve, and eleven— all boys. The catalyst was the usual: my husband's job was eliminated. Each time that happened, we pulled up stakes and adapted. There were seven moves in 16 years of marriage.

It was 1981. The economy was bad, and prospects were dismal, except in Tennessee. Healthcare providers created nationwide networks, and HCA hired my husband.

I needed to work. My requirements: no travel, no emergencies, regular hours, and progression for the resume.

Five possibilities showed up. Four produced offers. I had one more to go.

I walked up the stairs to an office that showed all the earmarks of an under-financed social service organization: Big Brothers Big Sisters (BB/BS) of Nashville. I met with the staff and, finally, the Program Director.

His office was tucked around the corner in back. It was comfortable enough, although my chair was wedged into a too-small space.

His name was Dwayne. His style was casual and relaxed. He had a Southern accent.

"The Program Director's job kinda' takes care of itself. The staff are very skilled. All women." He reached into a desk drawer and pulled out a file.

"Here's an example of the screening we do for a match. We interview the parent and child. Mostly at-risk kids in single-parent homes."

"I'm lost. What's a match?"

He showed me two files, one inside the other. A volunteer's and child's records were combined.

"We do an orientation, then a screening interview with potential volunteers. We get three references. Check criminal records. With parents and children, we ask about medical issues."

I was used to a therapy framework. "How many times do you see them?"

"One interview until we're ready to make a match. We choose on a needs basis, then share info with the volunteer after the parent's initial go ahead. If the volunteer says yes, we speak with the parent. Finally, if the adults are in agreement, we arrange an in-person match with all three."

"How do you establish standards?"

This all seemed so pat, like a recipe. Follow directions, get the right mix, set the right temperature, and create a perfect cake every time. I knew nothing about BB/BS. It was foreign territory. Seemed low-key. I was used to more hard-driving environments. This one seemed free of emergencies and pressure.

I began to ask questions. *Maybe all this is a waste of time.*

"What skills do you look for?"

"How do you screen?"

"Where does funding come from?"

"What's volunteer training?"

Finally, "What is your biggest challenge?"

"Pedophiles." The tone never changed.

"You mustn't know anything about them." My impression of the agency moved to a downgrade. Its culture and practices fell to a "no go" status. I had four offers waiting.

"We are considered an authority on pedophile characteristics and screening protocols. We continually gather the latest and most accurate information. Other organizations, including law enforcement, see us as up-to-date and well-informed."

"Why don't you do something about it?" *Are they sitting on their laurels? Glad to be a passive authority of sorts?*

His answer was as unadorned as his office.

"Because we don't know what happens to the child." He took a deep breath.

"It's an unknown for all of us in children's services." He glanced over my shoulder and looked out the window to some horizon only he could see. "We have minimal understanding. It's random."

"We can profile volunteers. Pedophiles have some identifiable patterns. We can screen. There isn't a source for recognizing kids' signals. We don't know what happens to the child. There's no way to gather or provide intelligence through a child's eyes. We can't deepen our understanding."

In that moment, my other four options evaporated.

"If you think you're interested, the director would like to meet with you."

"I am." My mouth was dry. My palms were wet. I pretended to wipe some imaginary specs off my slacks.

He picked up the phone. "Hi Mike, it's Dwayne. Do you still have time for a candidate conversation?" It was a connection between colleagues. Casual. "Great. We'll meet in the lobby."

The rest of the process was a breeze and a blur.

* * *

As I drove home from that interview, an old conversation played in my head like a needle stuck in the deep groove of a too-often-played record.

Part of me felt ten years old again. I was the fourth of six kids, five born within seven years—a five-year gap—then a baby girl. An infant boy came two years after that. He never came home.

I was lost in the subtle disarray of a large family.

That changed with a random ride to church. My sister was eight. My dad's oversized black umbrella kept us protected from the pelting rain as we waited for the bus. A green convertible pulled up with Dr. H, the family dentist, and his wife. "Going to the children's Mass?" A reluctant head nod. "Hop in. You'll be soaked."

They waited for us after church, took us for pancakes, and brought us home. It was past our time restrictions.

My parents invited them in.

A pattern developed. Short outings eventually turned into overnights. Finally, I was special. Everyone said so.

Eventually, I was lost.

Drowning.

* * *

I was fourteen when my dad died.

I was naive. Starting to date. There were lots of injunctions.

Something was wrong. I was confused. I searched. Decided.

I called Dr. H on our upstairs phone.

I wrote every word down so I'd remember even if my voice and hands shook.

His wife answered. They had company. I asked for him.

"It's me..." I choked. "I asked a priest. I told him what's going on between us. It has to stop."

"Is that the way you want it, Mary?" His voice was steady.

"Yes."

"Okay then." *Why didn't I do that a long time ago? This was my own fault. He didn't care. He said it would stop.*

Fifteen minutes later. "Get down these stairs!" Mother's strained voice.

I sat between them in the front seat.

Dr. H was driving.

"Mary, you're making it up." He looked straight ahead. "None of that ever happened."

"I'm not lying." Between sobs. "I'm not."

"Mary, you're missing your father." Her voice declared an irrefutable truth. I felt invisible.

"You are flattering yourself to think someone would find you attractive." Mother was placating. Paving the way.

The abuse stopped. Dr. H stayed in my family's life until he died decades after that night. He claimed credit for my accomplishments. I carried the guilt. No one ever spoke of that night or any of it ever again.

* * *

Two weeks after my BB/BS interviews and a job offer, Mike, the agency's Executive Director, met me at the lower entrance. He climbed the stairs ahead of me.

"Let's start you off right." He held the door open. "Coffee?"

"Black, please."

"Here you go. They're waiting in the conference room."

And they were. Four women. Two mid-twenties, one early thirties and one like me—thirty-eight.

We began.

"What do you like about working here?' I set my coffee aside. There were bottles of water in front of each of us. I uncapped mine and took a sip.

They were dedicated, enthusiastic, trained, and mutually supportive.

The groundwork was set. Strengths were exhibited. The twenty-somethings loved interviewing kids. The thirty-year-olds liked parents and kids. One identified single-parent challenges and possible supports.

Everyone admired the volunteers and provided consistent oversight and contact.

"Where do you get standards, protocols, and training?" They slid a couple of manuals my way.

"At National's annual meetings and intermittent training. We modify for regional differences. Nothing on abuse besides volunteer screening."

Finally, "Would each of you write down your wishes on these slips of paper? If you had your druthers, what would you like to see?"

They passed me their notes:

- Better minority and volunteer recruitment
- Adolescent prep. Girls 11-13. "Climbers Club."
- Something on sex abuse.

We spent three more hours. I shared my background. I worked in recreation with kids from three to eighteen, foster care, group home development, and oversight, counseling with various agencies and programs, and taught college courses in Human Services.

We spent the next six weeks listing things we had in place: what talents, longings, what worked, and what needed modification. We identified and assessed resources and points of leverage.

Most of the areas had something. All sex abuse had was worry.

Historically, it was early days for the question of sex abuse and any research. It was looming and illusive.

The worry and desire were palpable.

"We need to gather whatever information we can. Like picking up pawpaws, something difficult to track and find but not impossible." I was the secret weapon.

We scoured for any information within medical, social, and educational resources. It was scattered and inadequate:

- Medical personnel were beginning to recognize physical, and some emotional, signs.
- Videos went the full gamut from explicit to vague and lacked a clear target audience.
- No methods. No emotional, physical, intellectual, or intuitive signals for parents, victims, social or therapeutic services.
- Perpetrator indicators were vague.

We split into teams. The two who were good at interviewing children studied norms for ages five to mid-teens. Two workers studied parent vulnerabilities and roadblocks: guilt, denial, ignorance, relationship to the perpetrator (friend, relative, volunteer, parent, spouse).

I stitched the patches and parts together.

Information and training came from random sources:

- First, "flooding" to become saturated with information, move past denial, overwhelm, shame, blame, and disgust into professional understanding.

- We researched everything.

- Eventually, objectivity was reached. Each area's lens became focused.

- Roles and relationships were defined and understood.

Unlike today, where labels such as 'grooming' have become commonplace, at the time, there were no comprehensive models, programs, or labels.

We created a two-part program that covered all dimensions. We, in our late thirties, worked with parents, and two others dealt with the kids. Mid-way, the parents and children were brought together to view a stylized video, then returned to their groups to practice conversations and appropriate responses. It helped communication. In the end, parents and kids were brought together. That pre-match training uncovered abuse in 10% of kids' situations every time.

Six months later, four of us were at national BB/BS's annual conference in front of a packed ballroom. This level of intervention training was unheard of. The blank faces and crossed-arm postures spoke volumes.

It was ragged at first. My staff was nervous. Someone handed me the microphone. My staff joked about who I became in that moment in spite of any audience judgments or criticisms. It was redemptive. The program was adopted by all BB/BS across the country.

Today, the national BB/BS's website states:

"More than 230 agencies in over 5,000 communities in all 50 states inspire and engage youth from age five through young adulthood...more than 400,000 Littles, their families, and Bigs are part of the evidence-based program each year."

"Everyone associated with the Big Brothers Big Sisters program, including professional staff, parents, volunteers, children, and board members, is required to be trained in recognizing and responding to suspected child abuse."

That day, 40 years ago, BB/BS programs across the country changed, but so did I. I found my voice. Tragedy shifted into triumph. Denial shifted into dignity. I felt validated. That fragile ten-year-old sheltering under that oversized umbrella found a way to expand that protection, to recognize and embrace others.

It was early days.

I did not know it then, but the tectonic plates of my life were shifting.

I began BB/BS board retreats. A female volunteer wanted to change careers from a Procter & Gamble rep to a professional advertising executive.

"How's it going, Nancy?"

"I'm nowhere." She spent what today would be $5000 on prep but was losing ground.

Because of my husband's and my many job changes, I was well-versed and practiced in job searches and positioning.

"It's not that hard, Nancy."

"If I paid you, would you work with me?" In that moment, my life as a career coach began, although there was no such label at the time. Coaching took on a life of its own. The hours and client flow were erratic. Word of mouth was my marketing. Nancy was a great networker and supporter.

A Chicago advertising firm hired Nancy. "My fiancé needs to be up here too." Eight weeks later, with coaching and networking, her fiancé's engineering firm decided to open a Chicago office. He got a promotion.

BB/BS of Nashville's programs and national influence became well established. The professional staff had expanded. A new location was built. Policies and procedures were in place. I decided to coach full-time.

The job market was shifting and volatile. Within months, I got a call from an outplacement agency's owner. I'd met him at a networking breakfast. "Would you be willing to help revise and expand our business across the country?" My coaching morphed into consulting and program design.

That request came from a leader in a large church. "Our church has a problem. We're overcome with out-of-work middle managers. It's the economy. Could you come up with something?" I designed a 12-segment program. Its framework endures. I continued as a volunteer speaker/facilitator for 20+ years, and my coaching grew.

At one point, a colleague who specialized in grief and loss therapy asked for my business card. Six months later, the director of Alive Hospice called me. My brother, age 47, died the summer before. "Hospice needs consulting; would you consider it?" The criteria: be familiar with death and medical protocols (I had two years of nurses training), understand social work, groups, systems, therapy, loss and separation (my graduate work), and live in Nashville. Within three years of that call, Alive Hospice expanded its services and geographic reach.

The last week of my husband's life was spent in Alive Hospice's residence. The plans for that residence were envisioned years earlier in that strategic plan.

I met Scott Peck at a community-building workshop in Knoxville, Tennessee in 1989. His process model, experienced through weekend programs, was purely experiential with four stages, but it didn't incorporate content. "Could you translate community principles from a process model into organization and systems work?"

The concept of "community" was part of my volunteer, board, and founder's work with L'Arche in Syracuse and Albany.

"I think I could." The enhanced model kept its integrity and impacted a variety of organizations and major change initiatives. My consulting work became international.

And...

I still use a microphone.

Use the following tool to articulate *your* desire.

THE TOOL

STEP 1

Imagine you are talking to a good friend who is supportive and good listener:

Write a story and include:

- What do you desire?

- What values are exhibited or supported?

- What action does it call for or lend itself to?

- What supports that action?

- What fears overshadow? (Failure? "If it's to be, it's up to me" syndrome?)

- What supports are available or need to be built?

STEP 2

Desire x Value x Action >Fear of Failure (It'll never happen. False beliefs).

Example:

Desire	Foundational values	Possible Options
A career and family	Stability, Integrity	Move to large area
Friends, spiritual retreats	Learning/growth Adventure Intact Family	Position with reach Trips, camping Medical services Financial security

STEP 3

Today's ingredients, tomorrow's promise

Current Picture	Bridge to Future	Future Picture

First - First, fill in the *Current Picture*. Include all parts and details.

Second - Create the elements of the *Future Picture*. What do you hope to achieve? Create a robust picture and all requirements.

Third - *Build a bridge to the future*. Look at current situation. Classify what shifts:

- **Keep what supports the future.** Draw an arrow from current to future
- **Eliminate** - X those things out.
- **Modify** - Draw an arrow with an M.
- **Add** - Create an addendum to the future picture.

Example:

Current	Bridge	Future
Good schools	Keep	Strong education
Small house	Modify	Large home
Moderate commute	Keep	Moderate commute
Gas guzzler	Replace	Smaller car
Job of convenience	Replace	Reward/promote talent

Plan and prioritize:

- Create priorities.
- Select time frames.
- Resources involved.
- Criteria to declare success?

Sit with that good friend. Paint the picture of the leader you've become.

Mary Kipp is a consultant, author, and executive coach with a track record for creating sustainable change. She has a talent for understanding complex structures and systems, generating encounters that enable organizations to gain focus and achieve enduring results. Her experience is international with clients such as Unilever Holland, PolyGram, British Airways, Banana Republic, and NATO. She designed and facilitated projects with Harvard Business School's Clayton Christensen, author of *The Innovator's Dilemma*.

As a content expert, she developed the innovative desktop program for the functionality of virtual teams, *Working Remotely, Virtual Teams, and Beyond*, and simultaneously revamped the product development process within Ninth House Network itself. The program was required for the Silicon Valley Executive Business and the US Navy's leadership programs.

She presented *Five Ways Leaders Sabotage Their Careers at American Management Association's Peter Drucker Forum. Mediatation™*, a method for incorporating analog and digital technologies to enhance the impact of facilitated interventions, was showcased at the Organization Development Network. Ms. Kipp presented at the Association for Quality Preservation and Association for Manufacturing Excellence.

In Human Services senior roles, she designed mentoring and national training initiatives that endure to this day. She authored Family Business for McGraw Hill's *Handbook of Management Consulting*.

In the mid-eighties, Ms. Kipp began coaching executives, was featured in American Demographics' *Job Shift*, was an advisor to Right Management, and was a founder of the Career Transition program.

She holds a BA from St. Anselm College and her Master's from Syracuse University. She redesigned Community in the Workplace initiative for M. Scott Peck's Foundation for Community Encouragement, and she presented similar programs at the Center for Creative Leadership.

Adjunct faculty positions included the College of St Rose's Business Division and Vanderbilt University's Human and Organization Development program.

Contact: Marykipp43@gmail.com

CHAPTER 13

THE POWER OF REACHING FOR WHAT YOU WANT

BREAKING THROUGH LIMITING PERCEPTIONS OF WHO YOU ARE AND WHAT YOU OFFER

Don Stanziano

"Ask for what you want and be prepared to get it."

~ Maya Angelou

MY STORY

As we boarded the plane, I began to feel anxious, knowing I'd spend the next few hours seated next to the president and CEO of the company. After two exhausting weeks in the thick Texas heat and humidity, it was time to go home.

The Scripps Medical Response Team completed two weeks at the George R. Brown Convention Center in Houston. It was October 2005, and a few weeks earlier, Hurricane Katrina destroyed New Orleans, sending thousands of newly homeless Louisianans to Houston, where the city set up a temporary shelter in the expansive space.

I worked for Scripps Health at the time, and the U.S. Surgeon General invited us to staff a medical clinic at the convention center to care for this traumatized population. I was there to chronicle our efforts, share information with our San Diego colleagues about what our team was doing there, and manage the local and national media onsite.

Although I wasn't in an executive position, my role as director of public relations gave me a lot of access to senior leadership, especially the CEO. On this trip, he and I were interacting throughout the day. But as a still relatively young professional, the idea of having a few hours of unstructured time created both opportunity and risk. We had a good rapport, and I know he appreciated what I did. But still, the power differential was not lost on me.

We were about 30 minutes into the flight to San Diego talking about the work we had just completed together when he asked an unexpected question.

"What do you want to do, Don?"

"What do you mean?" I asked.

"What do you ultimately want to do with your career? Where do you want to end up?"

Wow. Was not expecting our plane conversation to go there. Of course, I had ambitions, but I hadn't really felt comfortable sharing them.

I paused for a second.

Do I say it? Do I just say it?

"I want the VP job," I said. "If and when the time comes." Exhale.

There, it's out there. I said it.

"Really?" he replied, somewhat surprised. "Okay. That's good. I think you can do it. Of course, you'll have to learn the elements of the role you don't have responsibility for now."

I nodded. "Yes, for sure."

Do you have your master's?"

"No"

"Well, you'll need to get that."

"Understood."

With that, the conversation ended, and we each turned back to our reading materials and were mostly silent for the rest of the flight.

That was 2005. Over the next four years, without sharing that conversation with anyone else, I started to fill the blank spaces in my resume. I sought the mentorship of the CEO, meeting with him once a month. I completed an external leadership fellowship and an internal leadership development program. I looked for every opportunity to stretch my work beyond the common boundaries of public relations and communications. And I started to pursue a master's degree in healthcare administration – intentionally avoiding marketing and communications programs to better round out my knowledge base.

In January 2010 my boss announced she was leaving. The next day, I'm summoned to the CEO's office. The door closes and he looks at me and says, "You still want that VP role?"

"Yes, I do."

"In that case, we don't need to do a search. You're ready. The job is yours."

Did I hear that right? Just like that? Not a word for four years, and then bam. Is this for real? No interview process? No search committee? No interim appointment?

"Um. Wow. Okay. Thank you," I stammered to reply. "Is there a process?"

"No process. We know you," he said, with a smile that demonstrated confidence in his decision. "We know your work. HR will prepare an offer, and we'll make an announcement."

"Oh, and you'll need to finish your master's," he added.

"Understood."

I didn't appreciate it at the time, but getting the job was the easy part. I was not prepared for the transition that followed.

First, taking on a much bigger role—three times larger—while midway through a master's program was more than enough. For the next year, I had no time for anything but work and graduate school.

But the biggest challenge was taking on a team that didn't understand how in the heck this guy who they'd worked alongside the past five years was now suddenly their boss.

The team's reaction was mixed. Before an announcement to the organization, my new boss, the chief strategy officer, assembled and informed my new team without me in the room. She took questions and then left the room as I came in to speak to them.

The reception was chilly. Cool stares and looks of shock from the group of seven. Two of them started with me in the company during another department leadership transition a decade earlier. The rest were brought in by the outgoing leader.

I made some comments about knowing them well, appreciating their talents, and that nothing would change in the near term.

"We all want a smooth transition," I said.

Hey, I was as surprised as they were at the suddenness of this change. Did I have ideas for the department? Yes. But I wasn't prepared to discuss any of that. This was a time to listen and assess.

The body language and chilly reception made it clear this wouldn't be smooth for me. In hindsight, this is where a more formal selection process would've helped. Being chosen from among other qualified candidates and allowing others on the team the opportunity to raise their hands would've helped.

"How did this happen?" one of them asked, suggesting something untoward was going on even though our current boss was leaving for a much bigger job in a larger organization.

In that one skeptical question, it became clear that some of them didn't see me as someone who could or should lead them. After all, I was the PR guy. The press release and memo guy. What did I know about marketing? Branding? Creative campaigns? Much less digital marketing, websites, and social media? Who did I think I was?

Well, to be clear, I was the new executive marketing leader for a $3 billion nationally recognized health system. And it was time to own it.

Once the shock of my appointment wore off, most were supportive, and we were able to develop a good working relationship. But two members of the team felt differently. The first made it clear that he was not on board with the reporting structure change and left quickly. The second began a months-long passive-aggressive campaign of career sabotage that required performance management. He found another job before I had to do anything more.

Dealing with these early tests quickly and decisively sent an important message that I was filling the new shoes and bad behavior wouldn't be tolerated. But more importantly, my proactive efforts to engage and build bridges with my former peers paid bigger dividends.

First, I went on a listening tour, meeting with every single department member. I wanted to know where they spent their time and what they enjoyed and didn't enjoy about their work. I wanted to know if they had ideas for how we could improve the department and what their career aspirations were. What had they done before joining our team?

This gave me a sense of who had ambition, what needed to be fixed, and, more importantly, who I could turn to for advice, especially in new areas of the portfolio where I didn't have deep—if any—experience. Through these conversations and those that followed, I learned how things worked. And in some cases, what wasn't working.

I also met with stakeholders across the organization to learn how the department was perceived. Were we meeting expectations? This gave me a sense of where to improve and helped answer questions about our structure.

Second, I asked questions of my leadership team that weren't easy to answer. Why do we do it *this* way? Can we track and measure? How do we know if what we're doing is working? Mostly, the responses were unsatisfying because we hadn't invested in the tools or developed the skills on the team to allow us to answer these questions. That set up the case to invest in new tools and refocus the team on delivering results versus responding to requests.

A department restructure followed, which changed roles and responsibilities for some of my direct reports and new opportunities for some next-level staff. It also changed the level of support we offered some of our key stakeholders. I was fortunate that timing lined up nicely with an enterprise-wide push to centralize administrative functions and with my plan already built, the CEO asked me to go first and lead by example. That gave the air cover needed to tear up the current model and transform the function.

Within two years, with a newly configured team structure and shift in focus, old doubts about whether the PR guy could lead marketing subsided.

After eight years of leading the function, I was recruited away to take on a similar functional makeover at a much larger health system on the other side of the country. Stepping into that role from the outside was a completely different experience. Expertise was assumed and expected. Change was anticipated and desired. Early successes resulted in more responsibilities being offered. The portfolio expanded.

And with each new challenge presented, the lessons learned from taking on that first executive role have carried through as new functions, new lines of business, and new responsibilities were added to the next position. Leaning in, listening, assessing, deciding—these have all been applied to career transitions big and small and have served me well.

Now, I sit in a seat that affords me the opportunity to pass along this lesson and be that talent scout and coach to my team. Each new hire gets an introductory meeting with me. As new functions have been added to the portfolio, I set up individual meetings with each new team member. And I reach down into the org chart and randomly set up skip-level meetings with staff at all levels of the department.

Standard questions are:

- "What do you like most (and least) about this work?"
- "What would you want to do next?"

Often, and surprisingly, most can't answer the "what's next" question. This is fine. We're all on our own journeys. But for those who can express a desire for something more or those who have an idea of what they want the next stop on their career journey to be, I file that away. Sometimes, I'll share it with their managers. But more often, it becomes a reference when needs arise and we're looking for someone to take on a new project or lead something we've never done before.

A companywide downsizing focused on reducing leadership roles left gaps in the org chart. Who would take on some of these functions that were now suddenly without a leader?

A conversation with one of my VPs went something like this:

"By eliminating that position, all those staff will report to me. I don't have the bandwidth to manage six more people," he fairly pointed out.

"What about Josh?" I asked.

Josh reported to someone else, had lost half his team in the downsizing, and was now under-leveraged.

"Josh? Can he do this?" he responded.

I knew Josh was interested in exactly this kind of work. What he didn't have in direct experience, I knew he'd make up for in motivation and tenacity.

"I believe he can, with your mentorship," I said. "You won't let him fail."

We made the change. Josh is thriving in his new role, and his team is as well.

Similarly, a big website rebuild project was stretching our digital customer engagement team beyond its limits, and although we had a strong agency engaged to lead the work, we needed someone to manage the project. Hiring was not an option.

Our VP of digital expressed concerns about team capacity.

"What about Liz?" I asked.

"Liz?" she asked.

"Yes, she's already demonstrated she can lead big technology projects and manage stakeholders well. I bet you can find someone on her team to take on most of her current work so she can move over and do this."

That's what we did. The project is going well. And Liz is fully engaged.

I often push my team to take chances on ambitious staff, even those who lack some of the specific experience the work requires. Knowing who is ready for more or who wants to do something new and different can be enough to give them a shot. Hey, it worked for me.

By giving Josh and Liz new responsibilities, we showed them we have confidence in their abilities, we want them to succeed, and that they have a career path here. We're retaining talent and building loyalty. But more importantly, we're giving Liz and Josh new skills and deeper experiences so they can fulfill their career aspirations.

I often reflect on that 2005 airplane conversation as a defining and pivotal moment in my career, but more importantly, my life. As a natural introvert, it would've been easy for me to give a more timid answer to the CEO's question. Had I set my sights smaller, had I chickened out, I'm confident I wouldn't have been considered for my boss's job when the opportunity came. Without that role, the next role wouldn't have been possible. But to get to the next role, success in that first position was essential.

It was transformative for me, for sure. But that conversation set in motion a series of downstream relationships and reactions that have allowed me to truly pay it forward. Without those roles and the lessons learned, I wouldn't be helping the people I've had the good fortune to help over the past 15 years. Knowing that and seeing careers and lives changed by simply giving someone a chance has been the greatest reward of my career. I hope that by setting that example, others will pay it forward, too.

THE TOOL

1. Prepare yourself for success by having a vision for the future. You don't need to look out all the way into the farthest horizon to retirement. But have a sense of what the next rung on your career ladder is.

   - Visualize it. Write it down.

   - Practice saying it out loud.

   - This will prepare you for the question. Don't be caught off guard as I was. Know your next move and be prepared to say it.

2. When you achieve the next level of success, know it is just that, the next level. You have much to learn. The hard part is demonstrating you belong there.

   - Expect to be challenged, especially by those closest to you.

   - Expect to be surprised—positively and negatively—by how others react to your success.

   - Be fearless. Fill the new shoes.

   - Take smart risks. Seek new challenges.

3. When taking on new responsibilities, humbly listen.

   - Talk to everyone you can about your new responsibilities.

   - Prioritize those who are unfamiliar and those who have the information you need to succeed.

   - Seek out the ambitious members of your team; they will be among your greatest assets.

4. Be exhaustingly curious about anything new to you.

- Ask why a lot. Why do we do it this way?

- Ask how a lot. How is this done? How do we know what we're doing is working?

- What needs fixing? Your early wins can be removing a barrier for staff or improving service to a stakeholder/client/customer.

5. Make quick and clear decisions.

- Once you have the information you need, act quickly.

- Learn from mistakes and course correct quickly.

- Hesitation is not your friend.

6. And when you're no longer seen as someone who can offer more than you currently are, it's probably time to move on.

- If, despite your best efforts and accomplishments, you find yourself stuck in a pigeonhole, you may just need to find a new place to grow your career.

Don Stanziano, MHA, APR, has nearly 30 years of experience in marketing and communications and has been leading teams since his 20s. Don joined Phoenix-based Banner Health in July 2024 as senior vice president of marketing, brand, and public relations. From 2018 to 2024, he led a 115-person team responsible for marketing, communications, and customer digital engagement as chief marketing and communications officer for the Geisinger health system. His prior experience includes 16 years at Scripps Health in San Diego, serving in a variety of communications and marketing roles. In 2010, he became vice president of marketing and communications, a role he held for eight years. During his career, Don was communications director and press secretary to US Congressman Bob Filner, D-California, ran a communications consultancy, and spent ten years as an award-winning print and broadcast journalist where he covered national stories like the Heaven's Gate mass suicides and the 1996 Republican National Convention. He earned a BS in journalism from Bowling Green State University and a Masters in Healthcare Administration (MHA) from Ohio University. He is accredited in public relations (APR) and has received numerous awards and recognitions for his work. Don is a frequent podcast guest and national conference speaker. A native of Lorain, Ohio, he and his partner Michael divide their time between Phoenix, Arizona, and Camden, Maine.

Connect with Don:

email: donstanziano@gmail.com

LinkedIn: www.linkedin.com/in/don-stanziano-mha-apr-1960787

CHAPTER 14

AUTHENTIC TRANSFORMATION

IMPACT THE WORLD;
LET YOUR SOUL OUT TO PLAY

Mitsy Andrews, Author, Creative Guide, Developmental Editor

"Love is remembered in the hearts of all human beings."

~ Spoken by Panache Desai in Call to Calm Free Daily Meditation
I dedicate this essay to you, Dear One!

MY STORY

I. BE STILL:

My mind is haunted. Raised by television, my show playlist—*New Zoo Revue, Popeye, Adam—12, Emergency!*, and my favorites, *The Waltons, Wonder Woman*, and *Space 1999*, engrained patterns in my mind. Fantasies in 60-minute chunks where I speak the right words at the right time. A world where I change lives. Where I am loved.

My mind—it's haunted. It creates death. Tragic accidents or sudden illness, and I lay beautifully motionless in a hospital bed and listen to the ventilator's hiss and wheeze as it breathes through me. The sound of the ground made hallow. Gage from *Emergency* screams, "Lactated Ringers!" His partner, DeSoto, pops open a syringe and plunges it into my heart.

There's a sharp electric pain; my chest expands and breaks open. I watch my heart fall further and further into the hollow below me. I flat line. Forget myself on purpose.

It's haunted—my mind. Haunted because even in fantasy, I'm unable to find the love I desire. Unable to imagine my one true love who crawls in bed next to me and pleads, "Breathe for me." The one I wake to, who cradles my eyes in his and says, "I'm with you. We'll stand together."

What haunts me is the idea there *has to be* a reason to be loved. And sickness is the only one I could find.

Illness is a powerful ally. Death a potent leader. Illness offers a sense of safety, an inner reunion back into your soul. When courageous enough to be vulnerable, to be still and receive, illness illuminates the pieces within who want to die, who need to die for stillness to expand and embody harmony. A thought projected early in life develops a belief, develops a behavior, develops an identity. It's a protection not against the world, against the knowledge of your divinity. In stillness, answers rise into faith.

Stillness taught me where my strength lies. My choice to love deeply is my superpower!

I sit with my mother and caress her hand's thin skin, more bone than flesh. Afraid to lose the silent grace between us, I whisper our never-ending story. Moments crafted from abandonment, perseverance, and forgiveness.

Our story opens with my mouth suckling her breast, feeding from both nipples. Eager to lay in her arms and drink her in. She loved it! How easy I latched on and let greed take us both. She rocked us in Great Grandma's wooden rocker and memorized every detail, sharing with me the dust floating in the sun's warm shine through the cracked window. In her mind, a moment everlasting lived over and over and over.

"You loved my boobies. You'd start at one nipple, and when you finished, you'd cry till I gave you the other one. Back and forth. Back and forth you'd go." The moment forms in her eyes. "I rocked you till you fell into sleep. Held you till you woke and wanted more." Her dreamy complexion focuses as her eyes find mine. "Your brother was too sick and never latched on." Her smile widens. "But you—you loved me!"

Even as an infant, I gave my mother what she was unable to give to herself: Acceptance. My role as her caregiver came intuitively without understanding there *was* any other role. I knew simply it was the reason I was born.

Throughout my life, I was still. I watched and listened and noticed how her words seldom aligned with her actions. I felt in between them and saw how hard the child in her played and acted at being an adult, how foreign it was for her to be anything other than childlike. And when she embraced herself fully, she glowed alive and free.

All she wanted was to have a good time.

Now in my late 50s, Mom in her late 70s, I want the same, a good time. Not hers, mine. I felt in-between her and me, mother and daughter, female to female, and gave myself permission to be a child, to let go of any responsibility beyond caring for anyone other than myself.

Through my mother, I searched myself and found a heart in sync with a haunted mind; through Mother, I found purpose, path, and privilege.

I found purpose in self-love to accept and be unapologetically all I am.

A path into a more enriched understanding of how to love and be loved in unison.

Privilege to live delicate and wild.

II. LISTEN DEEPLY WITHIN:

I wiggle. I wiggle every day but Sunday. Outside in the world, among people I don't know, out in the neighborhood as if everyone is watching, I dance and lip sync.

Music streams into my hearing aids heard by me alone, and I move across the sidewalk, between streets, down roads, through front yards, and among trees and raindrops. Song after song after song, I move as the music beckons.

Sometimes slow jazz and soul. Sometimes upbeat disco. Sometimes folk or blues. Sometimes hard rock and nasty rap. Sometimes piano. Sometimes Barbra Streisand! Each day is a bit different reliant on how my soul wants to play and the weather.

I put myself out in the world to be seen at my best, which isn't to say I'm a good dancer. In my haunted mind, my movements appear disjointed and floppy. In my mind, I look like a valley girl spazzing out and not the elegant dancer I fantasize I am. This is why I do it. I challenge myself to do what I've believed is impossible, to be wild and free in the open for others to witness the pure, sensual nature of my being.

When I started, people were confused. They fell silent except for a few who tried to persuade me to stop.

"That's not ladylike."

"Don't be a fool."

"You need to stop that right now! You're asking for it."

"Are you okay, Lady? You need help?"

"You crazy! Why you do'n that here?"

Each stung. And each stung a bit less as I leaned into each rejection and asked, *Do you believe in their idea of you; their projection of who they are onto you? Are you okay with disappointing people and not giving them what they want and how they want it? What do you want?*

My answer was always, *keep dancing!*

Gradually, the comments changed, and so did I. I expressed more. Moved with greater ease, even tried new moves. I pondered my writing and starting an editing business as a side gig. I grew more fully into who I always wanted to be—kind, independent, loving, and supportive.

Then, I experienced something altogether different. A young man tapped my shoulder. I turned and his eyes captured mine. In earnest he spoke. I smiled, reached for my phone in my back pocket. "Let me turn off the music. I can't hear you." I smelled the liquor on his skin. The sour scent of hard drinking. I paused the song. "I'm sorry. What were you saying?"

"My friend and I drove by, saw you, and I had to meet you. I told him, Stop the car. Stop the car! I *have* to talk to her."

"Why?"

"What are you listening to?"

This question I was prepared for. Many inquiring minds asked what I listen to as they already know the affect different music has on my body. I laughed. "Today it's disco, Bee Gees, and Donna Summers."

"Who told you you could move like that—that you could?"

I know what he was asking, what he needed. I saw underneath the sour in him and knew exactly what he was asking. "God told me I was worth it, and I believed her."

He fell silent. Thinking. Beginning to believe. He looked directly into my right eye. "Like a raindrop in the ocean becomes the ocean."

"Yes. Exactly." I whisper through my widening smile.

"What's it like for you?"

"Harmony. Peace. Love."

"It's so hard. Everything is so hard."

"The first forward step is movement. Not a thought."

"You'll never see me again. I had to stop and tell you how special you are."

I shook my head. "I'm nobod…"

"I know you think you're no one. But you are. You do this, and you give people joy."

I stepped toward him and placed my hand over his heart. "So do you. We are the same drop."

He nodded. "I want to. I really do."

"I know. And you will. I know you will."

I stepped closer, held his face in my hands, and wiped his tears with my thumbs. "You are. Right now. Sharing yourself with me gives me joy."

"You'll never see me again."

"I hope I will."

"I just had to stop."

"I'm glad you did. Thank you."

Our eyes held on to each other longing to be closer, to touch, to hold each other. We stepped closer and embraced. He cried hard on my shoulder. Cried from the belly up through his heart. I stood strong for us both.

"You remind me of my sister. Everyone's watching us."

"Let them. It's just us. You and I. This is our moment."

I squeezed him closer, gathered him up till he was able to stand firm on both feet. He wiped his face dry. I kissed his cheek. We smiled and said goodbye. And truth be told, I hold him still in my heart. We never exchanged names. And I truly hope to meet him again, to see for myself the seed we planted in him and how he nurtures it, allows it to root alive inside him, and grow.

Never underestimate your impact in the world when you let your soul out to play. Nor how it comes back to you tenfold.

III. RECEIVE:

It's hard to resist a little boy who's going to be a good man!

I have a crush on my neighbor Zander, who is four years old and already believes he's a monster.

I knew very young I wouldn't be a mother. I chose it. I didn't want to teach another human being sickness when it was all I knew.

Zander and I met shortly after he and his brother moved in with his aunt and uncle. To say he started hard is to say the ground is wet when it rains. Already at four, he knows abandonment and self-reliance, and I hope to teach him forgiveness. It's a different kind of love you give yourself. And once it's in you, you remember it in times when you need it most.

We share play dates at least once a week. And more than anything, when we're together, I want him to experience what it feels like to be a child, to be innocent and free of responsibility. Free from making another adult happy just so he feels safe and loved. I want him to know deep within himself he is loved because he's alive, and because he's alive, he's unique. Only he can be Zander.

One of the first traditions we started was ice cream on the couch. We don't use spoons. We use our fingers. We make a mess and laugh at the faces we make when our minds freeze from too much ice cream. We walk holding hands, and he tells me he got a star at school for listening. We crush shelled peanuts with a hammer. We make bubble juice and blow bubbles large enough to fit our whole bodies into their transparent universes. We run in the rain and stomp in puddles up to our ankles. We splash each other and scream and laugh. We buy lottery scratchers and plan a life of luxury. We search for robin eggs high up in the trees. His feet on my shoulders, I lift him as he walks his hands up the trunk of a pine tree. We go to the movies, run up and down stairs, hang from guardrails, and chase each other around chairs. Everything but watch the movie. We listen to music and dance. We share the *us* we are when together with each other.

For his birthday, he wanted a purple cake with his face on it. We searched through pictures of him in my phone, and he chose the one he wanted. I ordered the cake.

His aunt planned several events for him, which she included me in as well. We started his special day with ice cream breakfast and copious amounts of sprinkles and chocolate syrup. I woke early, gathered everything, and took it next door. When I arrived, he screamed my name and ran to me, hugged my legs, and with the biggest smile and wiggly body proudly stated, "It's my birthday!"

I ran my fingers through his hair and patted him on his back. "I know. Let's celebrate your special day. The day my best friend was born. How lucky I am to know you and be your friend." He ran to the table and climbed into his chair. "It's my birthday! No spoons today."

I will never forget the joy I received watching him put more and more sprinkles over his ice cream, repeating over and over, "It's my birthday."

"Yup. All day. Your special day, all *days* today. The whole day, your birthday." I pulled his first present out of the bag and watched him open it. He told me about his big party on Saturday and asked if I'd come.

"Yes, little man. I would be honored to share your birthday party with you. Thank you for asking."

After his party, his aunt invited me to a private birthday party dinner where we could share his cake. I was beyond excited and proud to present it to him. I brought party hats for all of us to wear. They quickly became unicorn horns, and he wanted two. When I placed the cake in front of him, his eyes widened. He clenched his fists and shook. "That's me."

"You said you wanted a purple cake with your face on it, so I wanted it for you too." I gave him his candles and told him he could put them anywhere he wanted.

"Can I put them in my eyes?"

"Oh no, don't..." I froze mid-sentence. *Mitsy no... you just told him he could put the candles anywhere he wanted. Don't confuse him. Be true to your words. It's his cake. Let him do what he wants.* "You know what. Yes, absolutely you can. Put the candles in your eyes and we'll set them on fire. Make them glow."

A month later, his aunt let me know both Zander and his brother would be moving to live with another aunt and uncle permanently. The original date was August 2024. Their case worker accelerated the timeline, and they left Memorial Day 2024.

When she told me, I was shocked at the visceral response inside me. All of me clenched and cried out *NO! I… I thought this was forever. I thought he would always be here next door for us to play together.* Tears immediately filled my eyes, and I leaned against her, needing her support to hold me up.

"You've made such a difference in his life," she whispered.

My God the difference he's made in mine. What I wanted for him I received from him. I wanted him to thrive, to be the very best he could be and believe it within himself. I wasn't aware he was doing the same for me. I wasn't conscious of how we were leading each other.

My four-year-old crush showed me we're always receiving. In every single moment, there *is* only receiving more and more of who we are back to ourselves.

THE TOOL

You are the tool! You are the medicine. Your body inside your soul is *your* path to self-leadership, and so being, *your* life, *your* freedom, *your* harmony, *your* love… heals the world, evolves the cosmos. Make Love Real, again!

Be Still – You are an individual. Each experience is unique to you. Each feeling is yours and yours alone. Only you know what stillness is in you. For me stillness is music and dance full of outward movement. Yet inside I am still. I am with myself, enjoying who I am, making myself laugh. Find your individual path into what brings you peace. Your stillness is within.

Listen – Do not seek enlightenment. Listen to how *your* mind wants to play. How *your* body wants to play. How *your* soul wants to play. And just play!

Receive – Each relationship, each encounter no matter how brief, we experience it as a reflection of who we are now in the moment as we experience it. There is no sin– no wrong decisions. As you receive more and more love and compassion for yourself, you lean into life differently. Know who you are, love *all* of who you are. Everything you experienced in the past, everything you experience now in each new moment, each situation you find yourself in, *is for you*. Every experience leads you to a deeper and deeper understanding of what it means to be human—what it means to love.

Be the change you seek within yourself. Give yourself permission to be human, to love fully, to hate fully, to experience the full essence of your humanness. Don't let another's experiences determine your experience of love. Let your soul out to play. Be delicate and wild every day from this moment on!

Mitsy Andrews lives in Columbus, Ohio with her three cats and her mother. A graduate of The Ohio State University in 2003 with a Master's in Poetry, she is a budding author and developmental editor.

Visit her site

https://mitsyandrews.com

Say hello!

Introduce yourself.

She is always excited to make new friends who quickly become family. Live long and prosper!

CHAPTER 15

THE SACRED GEOMETRY OF CIRCLES

WELCOMING INTUITION BACK INTO THE BOARDROOM

Dasha Allred Bond

*"The power of the World always works in circles.
Everything tries to be round. The sky is round and the earth
is round like a ball, and so are all the stars. The wind in its
greatest power whirls, birds make their nest in circles,
for theirs is the same religion as ours. The sun comes forth
and goes down again in a circle. The moon does the same,
and both are round. Even the seasons form a great circle in
their changing, and always come back again to where they were."*

~ Chief Black Elk

MY STORY

My finger frantically scrolled through the various open tabs on my phone screen. *What do I have next? Crap! Only five minutes before the Administrative Leadership TEAMS meeting. It's almost 2:30. I haven't had breakfast, much less lunch. And I still haven't peed! Arghh! I can't hold it any longer.*

I raced into the restroom and found the first empty stall. I closed my eyes briefly to try and center myself before charging back into the rat race.

But even behind closed eyelids, my mind was already moving on to the next meeting, skimming through the agenda and PowerPoint slides.

Did I update the new staffing projections? Did I include the chart outlining our most recent Employee and Patient Engagement scores? I must remember to email all directors requesting their action plans for our Back to Budget presentation, due tomorrow...

I heard the door to the restroom open. Footsteps raced across the floor. Someone tested the door to my stall before settling into the stall next to mine. Soft sniffles quickly turned to heaving sobs.

Should I say something? Should I stay as quiet as a mouse and wait for them to leave? Phone check. Meeting starts in three minutes.

Still crying, the female slid hard to the floor; the thin metal walls around both of us began to shake, mirroring her panicked breathing. The edge of her foot jutted awkwardly along the floor and over into my side of the stall—classic red-patent leather, peep-toe, kitten heels.

I know those shoes.

I was new to the hospital but still recognized the shoes. *This is one of my employees — Alice!*

"Alice? Is that you?" I quickly washed my hands and tried the handle of the stall door. "Can you let me in? What's happened? What's going on? What can I do?"

The latch flipped up, allowing the door to swing open. There, I found Alice crumpled on the floor, dry-heaving and trembling. She was in the throws of a full-blown panic attack.

I worked to help her stand and catch her breath. My phone was illuminated with text messages and pings from my CFO. *Shit! I'm late! The presentation!*

I walked Alice to my office and closed the door. I chose to stay. I chose to stay because I knew what happened before she began to explain herself. I knew because I witnessed it. An entire boardroom of executive-level employees witnessed the occurrence. We all sat watching and shrinking back into our chairs.

Sadly, this wasn't the first time. Not the second or even third time. It wasn't always Alice. Sometimes, it was Parker. Or Sarah. A few times, it was me. I handed Alice the box of Kleenex and sat down beside her. I waited for her to speak.

"I can't take it anymore. Nothing is ever good enough. Damned if I do provide the data. Damned if I don't. It's too little. It's not enough. The chart colors are too bright and distracting. The chart colors aren't bold enough. They are boring. He wants the data breakdown in volume counts this week. Last week, it was percentages. I can't win! I'm so sick of being made to look and feel like an absolute idiot. Why isn't anyone doing something about his behavior?"

I felt the weight of her question. *Why isn't someone doing something about this? About him? What could I possibly do? I just started here only a few months ago. He's the head of the entire program. He could ruin my career.*

I owed it to Alice, all my other employees, peers, and myself to at least try to speak up and do something. We filed into the conference room the next week and settled into the cold leather seats around the large rectangle table. The room's energy was unsettling and anxious as the 20-plus team members waited for the program leader to arrive and sit at the table's end.

I decided to tune into this meeting as an observer. I watched and listened and used my intuition to better understand the dynamics of what was happening. This group often met with other leaders and had no issues navigating conversations and problem-solving to help effectively grow our programs and better support patient outcomes.

The program leader walked in and sat down. I noticed the employees averting their eyes, hoping they wouldn't be the target of his endless, berating questions and negative public forum feedback. Heads were all turned down. *Please don't notice me.*

"Dasha—do you and your team have anything relevant to share today? Or will this be more of the usual waste of my time? These numbers don't mean anything if my template slots are still not getting filled."

I found myself suddenly standing and walking towards the front of the room. I stopped directly beside the program leader and looked him straight in the eyes. *No more cowering.*

"You know what, Dr. (he who shall not be named). You're right. You're absolutely right. Everyone in the room would agree. This is an utter waste of everyone's time. We have come to this meeting for weeks and have zero results to show. I would like to instead meet with you one-on-one right now. Your office or mine?"

He was surprised, even taken aback a little, but he agreed to meet with me in his office. My heart felt like it was lodged hard in the base of my throat, but I knew at that moment I at least had to get him away from the other employees.

I followed him into his office. My eyes scanned the classic navy blue walls, mostly covered with countless framed degrees from all the best academic centers of excellence: awards and more awards. I wanted to back out of there.

Who am I to try and negotiate with someone so well-educated? So well received by the medical community.

He sat down across from me and, for the first several minutes, just stared at me in that super awkward space of calculated silence and testing.

My voice must've cracked a little, but I found my nerve and calmly explained to him that the week prior, I saw one of our employees on the floor in the bathroom, very upset following the meeting. He seemed interested, even a little concerned by this news. *Is he actually listening to me?*

"We do not feel like we have a voice in the decision-making. We're afraid and even humiliated by how you speak to us in front of the group. I know you're frustrated, but we must figure out how to communicate during these meetings."

I was surprised to see him take all this in and not get defensive. "I think it might be helpful if, in the future, you have a concern about one of my team members; please bring it directly to me to manage."

I scheduled one-on-one meetings with him every week the day before we met with the group. We reviewed the agenda in advance and the data and supporting resources, allowing him to talk through it with me first. I received his feedback and ensured that the team arrived at the meeting better prepared. He would also feel like he had a say in what was presented.

Noting that we could have calm debates over concerns and suggestions, another idea came to me. *Could this be more about the environment for the meetings versus his personality?*

I remember my time in graduate school studying conflict management. There was a fantastic group of mediators that came and spoke about the power of meeting in circles, so I arranged a meeting with the program leader's boss and asked him to please begin coming to the meetings, arriving early, and seating himself at the head of the table, but not participate, just observe. This forced the program leader to sit towards the middle of the table. This small change made a huge difference in shifting the power dynamics of the team, allowing for a more fluid exchange of information and subsequent problem-solving. Even when the program leader's boss stopped coming to the meetings, the program leader continued to sit in the middle, and meetings ran smoothly.

Over the years, I continued to ensure seating arrangements were in circles to encourage collaboration. If we can't sit in a circle, I ensure the person leading the discussion is seated in the middle, not at one end.

Native American and indigenous cultures and the ancient mystery schools of the gnostics and other spiritual elders understood the sacred power of the circle. When we sit in a circle, no one is ahead or behind us. It's an equal playing field of connection—no end, no beginning, and limitless possibilities.

"There is a voice that doesn't use words. Listen."

~ Rumi

If you've been in the business world for a while, regardless of the industry, you have probably sat through meetings where only one or two folks were doing all the talking. You know the ones. Or maybe you're one of those people yourself. Ideas come to you quickly, on the fly. Thinking aloud is easy for you.

Or perhaps you're more like me. You don't like to be called out without warning. If asked to troubleshoot an issue on the spot, everything seems to go blank. *Please don't call on me!*

Historically, research has shown a bias towards extroverts being more promotable. They have more "air time" during meetings, so their ideas are brought forward and adopted more quickly. However, studies have also shown that the fastest solutions are only sometimes the best solutions when looking for sustainable results.

When we fail to create space for employees with more introverted tendencies to contemplate ideas quietly, we miss out on countless creative solutions and tools that could raise the potential of the programs we're leading.

One super easy way to assist more introverted employees in collaborative brainstorming is to ensure you send out the agenda ahead of time. Sending it thirty minutes before the meeting is not practical. Try to make it a personal goal to send it out three to five business days before the meeting. Ask everyone to review and come prepared with three ideas to present. Given time to think ahead, you'll find your employees more engaged during meetings.

Another way to increase engagement is to create a chat room or TEAMS channel where attendees can also write out their thoughts. Some individuals process ideas better by messaging in an email or text format. I typically offer the chat room discussion as a tool between our live meetings.

"The intuitive mind is a sacred gift,
and the rational mind is a faithful servant."

~ Albert Einstein

I've been leading spiritual circles for many years, working with intuitive gifts and nighttime dreams to create solutions in community settings. I began incorporating intuitive practices into my business meetings as well and find it to be gratifying for my employees as well as the programs and systems in which we lead.

Our thoughts and memories are energy, and every existing problem has multiple solutions floating around in the multiverse. I mentioned before that the more connected your team members are, the more open, secure, and engaged they'll feel. When a team works well together, and the environment supports cooperation instead of competition, a beautiful synergy forms where employees are in flow and creativity and ingenuity are at peak resonance. The complex problems you may have been working to solve for months and even years will suddenly align with perfect solutions. It will feel as though solutions drop out of thin air.

Trusting and working to grow your intuitive gifts—your instincts—is how you and your entire program can shift performance to the next level.

"The individual is ephemeral; races and nations come and pass away, but man remains. But instinct is something that transcends knowledge. We have, undoubtedly, certain finer fibers that enable us to perceive truths when logical deduction, or any other willful effort of the brain, is futile."

~ Nikola Tesla

One of the easiest ways to help expand your intuitive gifts is to work with your dreams. The Dreamtime is the name given to the liminal space we enter when we sleep. Many believe this is the same place we can travel to, even when awake, to gather wisdom and knowledge from the collective unconscious. You can think of it as a giant library—the library of all libraries, where all questions can be answered. Again, this is all just energy, so we tune our radio receivers to pick up the station/channel broadcasting the specific message or solution we seek.

You can enter the Dreamtime through active dreaming, breathwork, guided meditations, sound baths, and plant medicines. Note: not all plant medicines are illegal. Many legal plant medicines can help open up your intuitive centers.

Cacao is the pure form of chocolate and can be a beautiful way to connect more deeply with your intuition through the heart space. Different herbal tea blends can also help to activate the pineal gland. Mugwort, butterfly pea, and blue lotus are a few herbs and florals that are easy to grow or purchase. Steep as a tea or create a tincture to add to your water or juice. Adaptogenic mushrooms can help focus, cognitive function, memory, and intuition. Lion's mane is my go-to favorite shroomy friend. Ensuring your diet is high in B Vitamins helps to also nurture and support your intuitive centers.

In the business setting, allowing the mind to be quiet and centered, you can travel into a question or problem to better understand and wait for the dream to reveal a solution, often in imagery and coded messages. Doing this as a group and then sharing what each individual experienced can bring huge "Ah-Ha" breakthroughs for problem-solving.

Even just starting each day or staff meeting with a mindful minute of silence is a great way to begin welcoming intuition back into your team's workflow. Adding a small basket of fidget toys, bouncy balls, and other items they can play with when thinking can aid in stimulating both sides of the brain so that creative ideas can flow through more easily. This is why we have what I like to call "creative pop-ups" when in the shower or driving our cars. Giving our hands something to do as our brains process data allows for better problem-solving.

THE TOOL

I lead circles that work with our dreams and the energy of the bees to help connect to and explore collective consciousness. Bees are known for their productivity, communication, and sensing skills. They're the ultimate model of teamwork. They are so interconnected that they're said to function within a single "hive mind."

Bees are able to pick up on the subtleties of the environment around them. Fine-tuning our own abilities to do the same, to learn to intuitively "read the room" before speaking can help foster communication that is better gauged to our audience.

An easy way to increase focused listening and speaking while also practicing time management is incorporating the ancient tradition of using a talking stick.

1. Choose a physical item to represent your talking stick. It can be a literal stick or really anything that is lightweight and easy to pass around. One program I worked with in the past used a silly rubber chicken. Adding a bit of fun helps foster team connection, which also encourages openness, security, and engagement.

2. Reserve time in meetings for your team to go around sharing any thoughts, questions, or feedback that needs to be shared with the group.

3. Incorporate voted-on rules around the talking stick rounds. For my group meetings, we honor the following simple rules:

    a. Only the person holding the talking stick may speak. There is zero cross-talk. This time is dedicated to focused listening and thinking in silence.

    b. The time limit for holding the talking stick and speaking is equally divided. At one minute before the time ends, we sound a little warning chime alerting the speaker to wrap up. This helps ensure one or two speakers don't monopolize all the meeting time.

I've outlined many tools you can use above to help connect more deeply with your intuition and lead your teams in mindful exploration to aid in process, program, and system improvements.

Please take a minute to visit my website (link below), where I share some additional tips and a beautiful guided meditation with the bees you can use with your teams to help welcome intuition back into your business meetings, expanding opportunities for sustained growth, employee engagement, and customer satisfaction.

I'm also available to lead group team building retreats where we work to engage our intuitive centers and explore activities that help to increase emotional intelligence, compassion, and active listening, which in turn helps to fortify relationships with our employees, peers and community as leaders. More importantly, we can reframe our relationship with ourselves and how we show up in service to the world and the greater needs of the collective heart.

https://www.dreamingwithbees.com

Click on the tab labeled - The Healing Hive - Book Medicine - Transformative Leadership Guided Meditation

Click to purchase and enter discount code: HiveMind8 (course will be free with code).

Dasha Allred Bond has been a healthcare leader for 20+ years. She is also a certified Dream Coach and Shamanic Healer who has studied with several world-renowned teachers. She and her family have pilgrimaged across Europe, Greece, and sacred parts of Mexico and North America, attuning to the energetic ley lines of our lands and the stories carried by the rocks, the rivers, the trees, and the bees. She feels a deep connection to the language of nature and how it is revealed to her through the dream archetypes found in classic myths and personal stories.

In 2021, she began dreaming with the bees and Our Lady of Guadalupe. Answering their calls, she visited Our Lady's Shrine in Mexico City and the Pyramids of Teotihuacan. This journey catalyzed the rebirth of her true story and more profound work into the mysteries of consciousness, the multiverse, and how trauma shows up in our minds and bodies.

Dasha is a certified End of Life Doula. Much of her focus is on helping dreamers move through their seasons of grief. In early 2023, Dasha created the nonprofit Aluna Bridge - Hospice Sanctuary for the Homeless. Dasha is also a bestselling author of three books, *Dreaming with Bees: Sacred Medicine from Beyond the Veil of Grief*, *Shaman Heart: Sacred Rebel* and *The Life-Changing Power of Self-Love*. Her current works include a memoir, a novel, and a young adult series. You can find details about her sacred circles and other intuitive offerings at the links below.

http://www.dreamingwithbees.com

http://www.penelopeponders.com

http://www.alunabridge.org

http://www.instagram.com/penelopeponders

http://www.instagram.com/dreamingwithbees

https://www.youtube.com/@dreamingwithbees/videos

http://www.facebook.com/dreamingwithbees

CHAPTER 16

SERVANT LEADERSHIP

TRANSFORM YOUR LIFE AND BUSINESS WITH A PEOPLE OVER PROFIT APPROACH

Gary Mueller

*"Leadership is not about being in charge.
Leadership is about taking care of those in your charge."*

~ Simon Sinek, author and inspirational speaker

MY STORY

"It's never going to happen," I grumbled under my breath.

"What?" asked my wife as we drove to church Sunday morning.

"The partnership I've been promised," I snapped back.

"I'm one of the best Creative Directors in the whole city. I helped build this agency. When people say BVK, they think of me. I should've been a partner in the agency by now. I'm done. I'm ready to quit."

That was the one-sided conversation I had with my wife right before we pulled into the parking lot for Sunday church—a church we'd never been to, but one we decided to go to on a whim that morning. Obviously, I had my mind on things other than God.

Little did I know as I walked through the doors that day that my career, business, and life would change forever.

I was 38 and one of the most highly acclaimed creative directors in the Midwest, racking up hundreds of national and international awards for my work. At the same time, the agency ballooned in size from a modest 18-person staff when I started in 1990 to just over 100. I grew to become the face of the agency and was one of the leaders to whom much of the credit for our growth was given.

Although I showed flashes of servant leadership, my focus was firmly planted on myself and my national notoriety. I thought that for BVK to succeed, I had to continue to be hyper-focused on doing the best work for the most high-profile accounts. And if you worked for me and were struggling or unhappy, it was best to go elsewhere.

Of course, the byproduct of that leadership style was a high turnover, especially in the 20-person creative department I managed. BVK became a stepping stone job for its creatives to move on to bigger and better opportunities. Instead of seeing leadership as a gift from those I served, I saw it as an entitlement. All that mattered to me were results—creating and producing award-winning work, making more money, and getting a partnership in the agency—a lot of me, me, me.

Even though I was at the peak of my career, I isolated myself as a leader. And now everything was unraveling. I wanted to quit BVK and go somewhere else.

At least, that's how I felt until two minutes into the pastor's sermon. As he spoke, I soaked in every word like manna from heaven.

"None of us were put on this Earth to live a comfortable life. Each one of us is meant to live for a bigger purpose. We need to use the unique gifts and talents that God gave us in the service of others. And he puts us in exactly the right place to live out that purpose…"

At this point, I stopped hearing the pastor's voice and instead heard another inside my head. This voice laid out my purpose, why I was given the gifts I had, why I was at BVK, and what I was to do next.

Your calling is to start a non-profit ad agency called Serve.

Its mission will be to shine a light on underserved causes.

Organizations with no money.

That will be the most challenging to work with.

Who other ad agencies would never even think to help.

These are the organizations Serve will help, and in doing so, will donate all the work for free.

The voice continued.

BVK will donate its employees' time and talents to do the work and fund two full-time employees. You will also inspire other people from the ad industry to join you and donate their skills to help.

In return, you must agree to give up your planned future partnership in BVK and any additional raises for the next ten years.

When the sermon ended, the voice inside my head stopped simultaneously. The joy I felt at that moment was indescribable. I felt as if a massive weight lifted off my shoulders. I walked into church angry and disillusioned about my job and life, and as I walked out, I felt like I just won the lottery. I had a bigger purpose, and it had nothing to do with me or money and everything to do with serving others.

As we walked out of church, I could not contain my giddiness. With a smile a mile wide, I grabbed my wife's arm and told her, "Honey, I know what I'm supposed to do with the rest of my life."

After strapping our daughter into her car seat, I turned to her and unloaded everything that had just happened, including the part about giving up some potentially significant future earnings. She didn't bat an eyelash. In fact, she seemed equally excited.

That night, I wrote a two-page document outlining the details of the deal to start Serve. The next morning, I walked into my boss's office, told him everything that had happened, and handed it to him.

Without hesitation, he smiled and asked, "So, do you need me to sign this, or can we just shake hands?

Stunned that he didn't ask questions or have even a single concern, I blurted out, "So, is that a yes?"

"Of course, it's yes," he said laughing, as he extended his hand to shake on it.

The next day, I started the long and challenging process of starting a 501(c)(3) without any non-profit experience. Three months later, Serve Marketing was born.

Not only did the epiphany change my life, but it also changed my leadership style at BVK.

I was called to learn what it meant to be a servant leader, which started with understanding the value of putting people first and empowering them to be great. Instead of worrying about my work success, I focused on giving others better opportunities to succeed, starting with who worked on the agency's best clients.

I no longer assigned myself the most coveted creative assignments. I did the opposite. I gave my team the tourism, sports, and high-profile public service jobs and took the most challenging clients in healthcare and higher education.

Not only did it uplift the department's morale, but it showed them I had the utmost faith in them and that I no longer thought the agency's success revolved around me. It was a pivotal moment in my leadership transformation. It also led to implementing a new rule I created as a servant leader—never giving anyone a job I wasn't first willing to do myself.

At the same time, I hired other talented creative directors and associate creative directors to run the creative department alongside me. Unlike traditional creative departments, where all the campaigns are run by a single executive creative director for approval (me), I gave my team full autonomy to make their own decisions. I cultivated an environment of trust, respect, and shared values. When issues arose, like disagreements between account people and the creatives over a campaign direction or a production, I unequivocally had their backs, and people knew it. I made it clear that my teammates were the agency's future, and we needed them to continue to grow and develop to be successful.

"Gary, I can't work with Mark and Kelly anymore. You gotta give me another creative team," pleaded Stacey, the account director on our most coveted travel account.

"They're two of the best writers and art directors in town, and their campaigns keep winning national awards for us, and you want to replace them?" I asked.

"Yes. They're both moody. They don't get along. I'm tired of being their babysitter," she snapped back.

The old Gary would've said, "Enough is enough. I have no patience for this either. We'll give you a new team tomorrow." However, the new Gary worried more about how removing them from their best account would affect them as people.

"I understand they both have baggage. We all do. I do," I tried to explain. "But they're both good people. Please find a way to bring them together and help them mend their fences. Can you do that for me?"

"Yes, I'll try."

Virtually overnight, I went from a me-first leader who looked out for my interests above everyone else's to one who ensured everyone else felt essential and valued. And it felt good. I finally learned the most important tenet of servant leadership, something my dad, a plumber, role modeled to me from an early age. When you put the best interests of your people ahead of everything, including clients or profits, success will follow.

As our non-profit work grew (by year three, BVK was donating over $1 million annually in time, salary, and creative production), so did the size of our agency and our profits. In the ten years following Serve's launch, BVK swelled to over 200 people and over $200 million in billings. Being headquartered in Milwaukee, once seen as an impediment to attracting top creative talent here, became a moot point. Suddenly, amazing people came from all over the country to work for us because of our culture of service and giving. But now, they wanted to stay because they shared our values and felt like they were a part of something bigger.

My leadership mantra shifted from command and control to trust and camaraderie. People felt empowered. They pitched in to help others who struggled, even on the eve of one of the most significant new business pitches BVK was ever invited to, and the person struggling was me.

"Kevin, my back is out," I grimaced. "I can't sit. I can't walk. I can only lie flat and kneel."

Kevin was one of my best and busiest creative directors and my right-hand man.

"How are you going to do the Orlando pitch?" he asked. "Isn't it the day after tomorrow?

"I'm not. I need you to."

Without missing a beat, he rearranged his entire schedule, got two other creatives to take three of his jobs, and booked his flight to Florida the following day. And he played a pivotal role in helping us win the business.

A few years earlier, I would've never considered subbing myself out of a presentation that important, even if I had to be carried onto the plane. But

I trusted my team and would accept the consequences if we didn't win. My team members' success was now more important to me than my own, so much so that I even changed the title on my business card from Executive Creative Director to "Cheerleader." Because that's what I became—and I loved it.

I finally understood what so many servant leaders before me understood: when people feel supported, empowered, and celebrated, they work harder and are more productive. Because your company is only as good as its people, as leaders, it's our job to nurture and invest in them. When you do that, great things happen.

And as Eleanor Roosevelt once said, "Good leaders inspire people to have confidence in their leader. Great leaders inspire people to have confidence in themselves."

I couldn't agree more.

THE TOOL

HOW TO MAXIMIZE YOUR INNER SERVANT HEART.

Ask anyone who has ever had a great boss to describe what they admired about them, and they're likely to represent the qualities of a servant leader. Humble. Ethical. Empathetic. Positive.

But authentic servant leadership goes deeper than that. It's a calling to lead with your heart. When you lead with a servant's heart and your focus is firmly planted on your team members' personal and professional growth, morale skyrockets, productivity increases, employee retention improves, and, not surprisingly, earnings grow.

Look no further than the remarkable success of servant-led companies like Southwest Airlines, Patagonia, Marriott, Starbucks, Nordstrom, and Chick-fil-A.

But what steps must you take to be that kind of transformative leader? To make the most of your servant's heart.

1. Value the person, not just the employee.

I was once told by another leader in our organization that there is no way to make everyone happy. There's no way to give everyone the raises they deserve, promotions, or the more prominent offices. I'd argue that focusing on smaller but equally valuable gestures of human kindness is a better way to make your employees feel appreciated than simply rewarding them with more money. Calling a team member immediately after a pitch from the car to tell them how it went. Or stopping by someone's cube to ask about their sick kid and going out to pick up dinner for a team working late on a campaign and leaving a simple handwritten note of thanks instead of sending an email. Or even going to the funeral of an employee's parents.

The simple act of going out of one's way to help an employee, acknowledge them, or listen shows you value their humanity and not just their talent. When you show kindness to someone on a human level, it creates an emotional bond with you as a leader that inspires them to want to contribute even more to the company's success.

2. Serve humbly.

After starting Serve, one of the first things we did was make a sign for the front lobby with a giant word, EGO, on it. Underneath it, in small type, were the words "This is the only one you'll find here." Because we wanted to establish a culture of servant leadership, the sign served as a visible daily reminder that it's not about me as a leader. It's about asking, "How can I help make the people around me better?"

When you serve each day with a humble heart, you become more approachable, relatable, and human to your team. It allows you to demonstrate more purposeful care and appreciation for the people around you. Whether you're deflecting praise from a client to your team for a job well done, taking a turn washing dishes in the company cafeteria, or publicly acknowledging your own mistakes, serving humbly shows you care.

3. Have an inspiring vision.

Another essential tool of servant leadership is having an inspiring vision. Great leaders possess the ability to envision a future that ignites passion and purpose within their followers. When I led the effort to start Serve, it was the country's only all-volunteer, non-profit ad agency. No other ad agency had ever committed to such a significant and impactful corporate social responsibility program as Serve. Our vision for it was to show that bold and provocative public service campaigns can help underserved causes accomplish their missions. And, when we began to see the impact of our groundbreaking PSA work—like a 65% drop in teen pregnancy in Milwaukee or twice stopping city-wide shaken baby epidemics, our vision inspired even more people from all across the country to volunteer and join BVK.

4. Wear your heart on your sleeve.

One of the things that sets servant leaders apart from traditional business leaders is their unbridled passion for doing good and helping others. They speak unapologetically about prioritizing their ethics and values before profits.

They also aren't afraid to show you their authentic self or share what they stand for.

When I started Serve, I made it my mission to tell the story of how it began and what BVK was doing to support it. We told the world we were looking for like-minded people with a passion for giving back, which I still do today. I know that when you wear your heart on your sleeve and show the world what you believe in, you inspire others to join you.

5. Lead from the back.

Great leaders inspire the next generation of leaders. Instead of exercising power and control, they share their leadership mantle with others, acting more as stewards of the organization. One of the first things I changed in the management structure of our creative department after adopting a servant leadership model was to empower creatives at all levels of leadership to manage their teams and their own client accounts. That meant if you were an associate creative director on an account where you managed the entire team, the creative presentations, and had a great relationship with the client, you were now in charge of that account. And you no longer were required to run your work past me for approval.

When you share the leadership platform and empower others to become better leaders, you create an environment of trust. Team members feel free to take more risks, which, more often than not, leads to bigger and better results.

6. Listen, then do.

Servant leaders know that leadership starts with listening. They value input from their team members. They build an inclusive environment where people feel comfortable enough to share their opinions, suggestions, and concerns in the first place. And they always make time to listen, even when it's inconvenient. In other words, they don't just wait for the annual review to hear what's on people's minds.

But where most leaders fail is in the follow-up to listening—the doing. As a servant leader, always prioritize follow-up actions resulting from listening to your employees. As important as it is for your team members to be heard and have their ideas and opinions acknowledged, it's equally important that there's a resulting action.

The journey of servant leadership is paved with humility, empathy, and trust. It's about being selfless and always putting other people first—the people you manage, the vendors you work for, the UPS guy who delivers your packages, and even the night janitor who cleans your office. But it's not a sometime thing. It's a daily action that brings a responsibility to help others thrive and reach their full potential. And the results of this transformative style of leadership are remarkable.

By embracing these seven tools, you, too, can inspire positive change and create a lasting and profitable impact on your organization and beyond.

So what are you waiting for? Get started.

Gary Mueller is an Executive Creative Director at BVK in Milwaukee. His bold and provocative campaigns in healthcare, higher education, and public service marketing spaces have won every award imaginable, from Cannes Lions and One Show Pencils to Clios, Obies, and Emmys. His creative works have been lauded by everyone from *Adweek, Ad Age*, and the *New York Times* to *Newsweek, CNN, BBC*, and *The View*. He is also a recent inductee into the Wisconsin Advertising Hall of Fame.

Gary is most proud of his public service work, however. As the founder of Serve, the country's first and only all-volunteer, non-profit ad agency, he and his staff at BVK have donated over $20 million in cause marketing campaigns to help shine a light on more than 75 underserved crisis causes, including domestic violence, teen homelessness, and sex trafficking, as well as infant mortality, drug addiction, and teen pregnancy.

When he's not out trying to save the world through his non-profit work or receiving awards for his good deeds, Gary can be found emceeing local charity galas, barefoot water skiing, traveling with his wife, or sampling expensive tequilas at his backyard tequila bar.

Connect with Gary:

Website: https://servemarketing.org

E-mail: Garym@bvk.com

LinkedIn: https://www.linkedin.com/in/gary-mueller-a8772a16/

Facebook: https://www.facebook.com/garymuellerII

Instagram: https://www.instagram.com/garyrmueller/

CHAPTER 17

WHY LEAD ALONE?

SHARING THE POWER FOR GREATER IMPACT

James M. Blazar, MBA, HA

"I start with the premise that the function of leadership is to produce more leaders, not more followers."

~ Ralph Nader

MY STORY

With more than three decades of experience as an executive, I'm often asked to present on leadership. It's always been an honor to share my experiences and advice. The funny thing is, **I had it all wrong until eight years ago.**

Early in my career, the formula for success was simple.

I burned the midnight oil, surpassed goals, and knocked down barriers along the way. I was "the person to see if there was a problem to solve" and the guy people wanted on their team.

I quickly grew in my career, and the organizations where I worked were successful. I was rewarded with new professional responsibilities, titles, and opportunities. By all accounts, this approach worked. Sound familiar?

I'll never forget the day that changed my entire mindset. I woke up early to prepare for another Monday as the chief strategy and transformation officer at Hartford Healthcare in Connecticut. I put on my suit, tightened my tie, hopped in the car, and headed to the office for a typical day full of meetings.

Noon rolled around, and my calendar directed me to a mid-sized conference room with many peers. A gentleman stood at the front of the room, and the words "Leadership Coaching" were front and center in bold blue font on the screen next to him.

With more than three decades of leadership under my belt, I walked in with my chest proud, grabbing a seat near a friend and opening my laptop so I could multitask through another meeting.

There's nothing new for me here...I could probably teach this course.

I was wrong.

As the presentation continued, my ears perked up, I closed my computer, and my gaze was drawn to the screen as the leadership coach spoke. "You should spend at least half of your time developing others," he explained. "You'll achieve better results by giving others the power to lead."

Curiosity sank in.

Maybe I'm not as great as I think I am.

He proceeded to walk us through the "10 Principles of Personal Leadership." As I leaned in to listen, my mind was spinning with different leadership scenarios from my past.

Could I have handled them better?

I thought back to the mishap I had early in my career with a hospital receptionist. She walked into work with torn-up jeans and sneakers. I pulled her aside and told her, "You need to dress your best at work."

The next day, she walked in with a low-cut, skintight dress meant for the disco – the best outfit she had in her closet. Oops.

As the presentation went on, I felt that terrible feeling in my gut, realizing the world changed, and to be successful, I had to change too. I had to unlearn most of what helped me excel in my career for more than 30 years.

He continued to walk through the 10 Principles, giving detailed examples of each in action, such as:

- Respect and leverage separate realities.
- Be curious versus judgmental.
- Look in the mirror first and be accountable.
- Have courageous conversations.

It wasn't the principles alone that rattled my thinking; it was how he described the difference they make when applied daily: "By disrupting and changing your unproductive habits, you can achieve outstanding performance results from your team."

Who doesn't want that?

After that initial meeting, we engaged in one-on-one coaching sessions, and a leadership development plan landed on my desk. Over the next few months, my comfortable and go-to leadership behaviors were challenged left, right, and center.

Have I done a disservice to my team and this organization?

Is it too late to make an impactful change?

LEADERSHIP OF THE PAST

The style I, and many other leaders, practiced for years was to take charge. I was the leader, surrounded by a team of contributors. If a peer or someone on my team had a problem, I jumped right in and solved it.

We forged ahead and focused our time on raising the bar, working harder, and rewarding those who outperformed others. At the end of the day, I made the decisions.

FLIPPING THE SWITCH

In deep learning and practice, I realized we would achieve better results if I were no longer the primary source of problem-solving and innovation. I had to focus on building a team of leaders who'd make their own decisions and solve problems themselves.

I had to teach and mentor rather than fix all the issues and provide all the answers. Initially, I really struggled to switch my mindset and had some unsettling thoughts.

What will my team or colleagues think?

Will I lose their respect?

Will I lose their trust?

Will I bring less value to the organization?

If my team learns to solve more problems and create better processes and outcomes, will they still need a leader like me?

I didn't remember feeling that insecure since I took my microeconomics final in graduate school. I felt like I was sliding from the top of my game to unknown territory in real-time. I was less confident as a leader and completely vulnerable, but I kept at it, and the results were life-changing.

FROM CONCEPT TO REALITY

How did I put these behaviors into practice? Below are some real-life examples demonstrating how my approach changed and the positive outcomes that occurred as a result.

New Brand Launch

Problem:

I was the chief strategy and transformation officer at a health system. Our marketing team wanted to launch our new brand by writing and recording an "anthem" that would appear in our commercials and across other brand channels. When I heard the idea, I looked down and shook my head.

There's no way that'll work.

My Approach:

Instead of being judgmental and dismissive about the idea because I thought I knew best, I asked questions and learned more about their vision. It was clear there was passion behind the idea. Although I disagreed with the campaign approach, I stood behind their decision and empowered them to move forward.

Leadership of the Past:

Former me would've brushed off the idea completely and said, "Nice idea, we'll try another time," ultimately moving forward with launching the campaign the way I envisioned. The campaign would've never happened if I hadn't applied the principles, moved out of my comfort zone, and played it out.

Results:

To date, this was one of the most successful campaigns of my career. Team culture and excitement were at an all-time high because new ideas were heard, and the team contributed in a big way. I learned that unless I know from prior experience that taking a risk will hurt us, I'm going to support the team in trying.

Principles to Use When You Disagree:

- Leverage separate realities.

- Be curious vs. judgmental.

Policy Harmonization

Problem:

I watched multiple HR departments from recently merged hospitals work on harmonizing their policies. We spent hours in a room but barely made any progress. At the end of the meeting, the team looked at our internal communications lead, who reported to me and said, "Put the communications plan together." She rushed into my office shaking and near tears while vocalizing the challenge of delivering a plan when the direction was unclear. One of my most valuable team members was ready to quit.

My Approach:

I encouraged her to have a courageous conversation with our HR lead. I taught her how to resolve the problem herself rather than stepping in to improve things. We even role-played, where I shared tips on how to communicate honestly and effectively and gave guidance on how to respond to different scenarios with professionalism and respect.

Leadership of the Past:

I would've marched right into the HR lead's office, strongly defending my team and demanding they provide clarity. I would've made it my personal mission to fix things.

Results:

The internal communications lead had a courageous conversation. A significant bond developed between the two, especially when the head of HR opened up about having similar feelings of frustration. They resolved the issue, got clarity together, and built a lasting friendship in the process.

Principles to Use When You or a Team Member is Emotional and Upset:

- Teach, coach, and mentor—spend at least half of your time developing others.

- Have courageous conversations.
- Be curious vs. judgmental.

Logo Development

Problem:

I'm the chief strategy officer at a newly formed organization. On one of my first days, I sat down with two of my bosses, who slapped a sheet of paper in front of me with a home-grown logo at the top. "Look," they said excitedly, "we saved you a lot of money because we already came up with a logo."

Oh no, this will never work; it won't differentiate us in the market.

My Approach:

I thanked them for the contribution and suggested we run it through market research, along with some other logo options, just to make sure it's what's best for our brand. We included their design in all of our testing and gave it a fair shot at success.

Leadership of the Past:

I never would've pushed the logo through testing. I would've dismissed their request immediately and taken charge by leading with the creative concepts I believed would work best.

Results:

It was a wonderful teaching moment for all of us. We ran the test with their logo in place, and it failed. But we gave it a fair opportunity, and they were incredibly receptive to the feedback from the market. And I learned how well these leadership principles work with your peers and leadership. It's not only about how you treat your direct team but all levels of the organization.

Principles to Use When Your Expertise is Undermined:

- Be curious versus judgmental.
- Respect and leverage separate realities.
- Teach, coach, and mentor.

Request for Proposal

Problem:

We were spending a boatload of money on a newsletter program. The newsletter was in distribution for over 19 years, and the team adored our agency partners. I, on the other hand, grew increasingly less impressed with the product and felt strongly that we needed to evaluate the program.

My Approach:

I suggested (not demanded, there's a difference) that we put out a request for proposal (RFP) for a new partner. I stayed out of the process. The team was apprehensive but took ownership and gave it a shot. They wrote and distributed the RFP and brought in three vendors, including the current partner, to pitch the business. Although I felt strongly about the need for change, I empowered the team to lead the process and make their own decisions.

Leadership of the Past:

I would've been much more vocal about my opinion and very involved in the RFP process. I would've strongly encouraged the team to find a new partner versus positioning it as a purely exploratory exercise.

Results:

The team later admitted that they had every intention of going through the motions but remaining with the partner we had for more than 19 years. They were comfortable, happy, and trusted the group. However, during the pitch process, another agency surprised them with innovative ideas and fresh perspectives. They ended up switching partners, completely revamping the program with greater success and saving money along the way.

Principles to Use When You Want to Inspire Change:

• Teach, coach, and mentor.

• Be curious versus judgmental.

• Respect and leverage different realities.

• Remember, it's about progress, not perfection.

In sharing these examples, I hope you realize how impactful it was to "share the power" with others on the team. In these cases and many others in my career, the outcome was significantly better than if I handled it independently.

The lesson: Even though it's scary, you have to let go and trust that applying these behaviors will always yield better results.

When you spend time creating a team of leaders, you bring out the best in others and generate a lasting impact.

In the tool below, I challenge you to evaluate your leadership style and look in the mirror first. Being accountable and committing to continuous improvement through proven leadership principles will make a difference in your life, both professionally and personally.

THE TOOL

One of the "10 Principles of Personal Leadership" is to look in the mirror first and be accountable.

To get started, ask yourself these key questions every day to build a culture of accountability:

1. What more can I do right now to be a role model for those around me?

2. What more can I do right now to achieve the outcome I/we desire?

3. What more can I do right now to prevent something undesired from occurring?

4. What expectations or feedback can I deliver right now to make a positive difference in individual or team performance?

5. What more can I do right now to seek or provide the clarity I think doesn't exist?

6. What more can I do right now to make this meeting more productive?

7. What more can I do right now to say what needs to be said that no one else is saying?

8. When someone or some outcome has not met my expectations, ask, "How did I contribute to that?" and "What more will I do next time to make it successful?"

Another principle is "Teach, coach, and mentor—spend at least half of your time developing others." Coaching and mentoring are so valuable because today's workforce wants to connect to a purpose, feel valued, and contribute.

When you put this into practice, consider these tips:

1. Don't tell your team what to do; ask them how they'd solve a problem or approach a situation. Then, review their thoughts together and build a plan.

2. Try role-playing and providing constructive feedback in real time.

3. Assign new and out-of-scope projects to expand someone's experience and exposure.

4. Keep in mind: Building a team of leaders builds a legacy of continued success long after an individual leader is gone.

Mark Sasscer, Founder at LeadQuest Consulting, Inc. is responsible for developing "The 10 Principles of Personal Leadership." To see the full list of leadership principles, visit LeadQuestConsulting.com.

James M. Blazar, a titan in the healthcare industry, serves as the strategic advisor to the CEO at Hackensack Meridian Health, the largest integrated healthcare network in New Jersey. His strategic prowess has propelled the network's growth through mergers, acquisitions, and innovative partnerships, solidifying its position as a national leader in patient care and medical advancements.

James's impact extends far beyond Hackensack Meridian Health, and his career is a testament to his visionary leadership and strategic acumen. While in New Jersey, his contributions to Governor Murphy's Healthcare Committee left an indelible mark on the healthcare landscape.

Prior to Hackensack Meridian Health, James served as senior vice president and chief strategy and transformation officer at Hartford Healthcare in Connecticut, president and CEO of Cleveland Clinic Canada, and chief marketing officer at Cleveland Clinic in Ohio.

James's accomplishments have garnered him numerous accolades, including a place among Becker's 52 Great Health System Chief Strategy Officers. With his unwavering dedication to improving healthcare, he continues to shape the future of medicine, leaving a legacy of innovation and excellence.

When James is not working, he's spending time with his wife, Nancy, two kids and four grandchildren either going for a hike, enjoying a delicious meal, or enjoying the ocean breeze at their home in Cape Cod.

Connect with James:

Email: Jmblazar@gmail.com

LinkedIn: linkedin.com/in/jim-blazar

CHAPTER 18

PAYING IT FORWARD

MENTORING TO LEVEL-UP YOUR LEADERSHIP

Daniel Fell

*"A mentor is someone who allows you
to see the hope inside yourself."*

~ Oprah Winfrey

MY STORY

"Are you sure you want to be an engineer?"

The words rang in my head as I exited my professor's office in McBryde Hall and shuffled back to my dorm room across the snowy quad. I couldn't do calculus, but I could do this math. I had to ace the final exam to pass the class. And the odds of that were, let's say, not heavily in my favor.

I entered Virginia Tech thinking I wanted to be an engineer. My father was a chemical engineer, and I liked science, and it seemed like a respectable career. He succeeded with it and even traveled the world as a chemical researcher, practicing engineer, and eventually senior manager with one of the world's largest energy companies.

I was born while my family was living in Yokohama, Japan, and my father was managing an international joint venture. I still have the original paper telegram (this was way before email) a stateside co-worker sent to Dad congratulating him on my birth. Tongue-in-cheek, it reads, "Congratulations on a successful launch. Stop. Trust product stamped 'Made in Japan.' Stop."

If I ever get a tattoo, it will say 'Made in Japan.'

Nineteen years later, I was failing in his eyes and mine and failing five-hour calculus for sure. It was also the first time anyone even asked me that question: *Did I want to be an engineer?*

The more I thought about it, the more I realized I didn't. While I enjoyed some of the courses—chemistry and even engineering economics—my passions aligned more with biology than engineering. So, two years into college, I switched majors and took up microbiology. I also added some elective courses in psychology, business, and consumerism out of curiosity and exploration.

It wasn't until my senior year that I realized I needed to translate my newfound interests and studies into a real job. Engineering majors graduated and became engineers. But what did biology majors do? I had no idea.

Although I volunteered as an emergency medical technician during the summers, I long ruled out medicine as a career. And while research was an option, I preferred being around people more than Petri dishes.

Eventually—and practically in the last hours of my last semester in college—my curiosity about business and marketing led me to apply for an unpaid internship in the marketing department of a small community hospital in Southwest Virginia.

That decision, and the chance opportunity to work for an incredibly dynamic marketing leader who herself was going back to school to get her master's degree (and would eventually earn her PhD and start her own market research company), was the defining moment of my education and ultimately, my entire career.

Christine Meade's enthusiasm and willingness to take me on as a college intern and introduce me to a career in marketing opened my eyes to a world I didn't even know existed. It also led me to a national association that became my professional network and a collection of industry contacts who, over many decades, I'd work for, collaborate with, compete against, and come to count on as dear friends and colleagues to this day.

Her passion for the evolving marketing world, specifically healthcare marketing, was contagious (to use a medical term), and I caught the bug. It also became my passion, and I built my career around that passion and work.

One of my first steps was convincing my parents to pay for me to fly to San Antonio, Texas that fall to attend the American Society for Healthcare

Marketing and Public Relations Annual Conference. Once there, I registered as a student (fortunately cheaper than the total fee) and walked around the exhibit hall, introducing myself to people Chris arranged for me to meet.

Two companies, one in Tennessee, where I eventually landed my first job, and another in Virginia, where I joined forces almost two decades later and well into my career and running my own company, were the first healthcare marketing professionals I met outside of Chris. The decision to attend that one conference led me to all kinds of opportunities and connections, including accepting a seat on the society's board of directors.

I credit Chris for introducing me to my career path and, more importantly, for taking me by the hand and helping me start the journey. I failed out of engineering school, graduated with a degree in biology, and decided at the last minute I wanted to be in marketing.

How much more circuitous of a career path could I take? And yet, she was one hundred percent confident in my ability to be a success. She didn't advise me so much as cheer me on like a coach.

FINDING MY OWN MENTORING PATH

Chris' enthusiasm, passion, and commitment to helping me get started in my career are something I greatly value to this day. But it wasn't until later that I understood and appreciated the real power of mentoring and how much it'd help me be a better leader. Having been mentored by someone else is a tremendous gift, although it's certainly not a requirement for being a good mentor.

I've always tried to help others and be a resource when I could, but developing more formal mentoring relationships—both at work and outside of work—helped me improve my communication skills and hone my ability to prioritize and focus on the essential things in life.

One of the things you must do as a teacher, mentor, or coach is zero in on the essential activities and tasks and understand the sequence of learning those skills. For instance, if you're learning to play basketball, you don't go from picking up a ball to dunking it. This is where a mentor can help someone understand the right steps to achieving a goal or see the best path more clearly.

I believe good mentoring is almost indistinguishable from good leadership. While leadership encompasses many roles and tasks that probably don't apply to mentoring (at least not informal mentoring encounters outside of work), the core dynamic of helping someone better themselves—or be their best selves—is core to both skills.

I enjoy working with entrepreneurs and founders because I started my own business. Not only do I have many lessons and failures others can learn from, but I also have a passion for anyone wanting to go into business. It's not for everyone, but I see it as one of the most creative and thrilling things you can do. Starting a business is high risk at times, but it also comes with high rewards.

We sometimes use the term "makers" in the startup space, and I love asking people, "What would you make if time and money weren't an issue?" It opens people to their creativity and imagination and often leads them in new directions they hadn't thought were possible or even contemplated.

Seeing others grow and succeed is rewarding. Whatever your interests or passions, consider finding others you believe in and sharing those passions with them through mentoring. I guarantee you will benefit in ways you've never experienced. Developing the next generation of leaders is a big part of being a good leader. And I believe mentoring is one of the most powerful ways to do that.

THREE WAYS TO APPLY MENTORING

While there are lots of structured mentoring programs out there (and I encourage everyone to learn more about the different types of programs and opportunities that may appeal to them and even consider volunteering for some), you don't have to be part of a formal mentoring program to help others. In fact, like my mentor and friend Chris, the most prevalent form of mentoring happens every day inside and outside of work, around the community, and between individuals who simply share a standard connection or interest. You can be a valuable mentor to others in three ways.

Industry Mentoring: Perhaps you work in an industry like banking, higher education, or renewable energy, that gives you particular knowledge or expertise than others in that industry, especially those new to it or looking to advance within the same industry. And the more specialized your knowledge and experience within an industry, the more unique and valuable that experience becomes. I spent my career in healthcare and have met many industry experts and people who understand niche areas of healthcare like health insurance, long-term care, and rehabilitation. Even though I know a lot about the healthcare industry in general, it's always valuable to have go-to experts in specialized areas of your industry.

Career Mentoring: Career mentoring is less about a particular industry and more about careers or jobs. Understanding and being good at sales is a real talent and applies to many different industries. Even if you work in one type of manufacturing, your talents as a sales executive can be valuable to someone coming up in the field of sales in any industry. Maybe you have spent your career in human resources and want to mentor others to join the field. You likely have a lot to share with others about how human resources has evolved, the latest trends and skills needed, and where to go for education and training, regardless of a particular industry. Career mentoring is one of the most practical and valuable types of mentoring you can be involved in today.

Skills Mentoring: Skills mentoring centers on skills or talents you can develop in others. They could be related to or associated with a particular industry or career role, but more often, they are cross-industry and job function or simply life skills and passions. There are lots of different types of skills, such as practical skills (think automobile or machine repair, personal finance, and cooking), artistic skills (like painting, throwing pottery, or sewing), and athletic skills (such as tennis, golf, yoga, or martial arts). Hobbies and interests are in the skills category. Maybe you have a passion for gardening or growing roses specifically. Perhaps you collect stamps and want to encourage the next generation of philatelists. Sometimes, your professional and personal interests are intertwined. My sister works in animal rescue professionally but is also passionate about helping feral cats, which she does on her own time. She often helps others to do the same.

THE TOOL

MENTORING SUCCESS FRAMEWORK

While many mentoring relationships evolve informally and have little structure, it can be ideal when some parameters guide the mentee and mentor and help establish some structure. Here are a few things to consider:

Find the right match.

While mentees and mentors don't have everything in common (in fact, it's probably better they don't), they do need to get along and share at least one common interest—the subject matter for the mentoring. Beyond that, having compatible personalities, communication styles, and other shared interests can be helpful to the relationship.

Align expectations and goals.

Spell out the objectives of the mentoring relationship in the beginning. They don't necessarily need to be written down and signed but should be articulated and agreed to. Depending on the goals, you may want to be descriptive and specific. For instance, teaching someone a task, like woodworking, will be more specific than helping them with their career path.

Agree on a cadence and timeline.

Similarly, it's essential to understand the time commitment involved, the time you might be working together, and the cadence of meetings or encounters. Here, it may vary greatly depending on the relationship and goals for the mentoring. Some mentoring happens rather briefly over a short time. Other relationships can go on for years. There is no right or wrong way to do it, and it's heavily dependent on the parties involved and the subject of the mentoring. Mentoring can happen intermittently as well. There may be specific times or cycles in the relationship that drive more engagement, and that's perfectly fine, too. However, having a shared understanding of the timing is essential, especially when it may be in intervals.

Schedule regular progress checks.

Mentoring relationships can be a lot of fun and evolve from or even turn into general friendships. However, it's essential to have regular check-ins about the relationship to ensure that the mentor and the mentee benefit from the relationship. Seeing progress and productivity is an integral part of mentoring relationships, and exploring the relationship and how it's evolving and progressing is an excellent way to ensure success. These can be formal or informal, regular or periodic, but assessing the relationship and progress related to the original expectations and goals allows for updates and adjustments.

Show you're thinking about them.

An easy way to stay in touch and show your mentee you're thinking of them is to drop them a note or email anytime you encounter something that might interest them. Maybe share a news story or article related to their job or interests. Or something encouraging like a tip or feature about someone else's success. Little moments like this don't take much time or require meeting up, but they show you care, and you're always thinking about them.

Allow for two-way feedback.

At the same time, feedback must be bi-directional, meaning the mentor should give feedback to the mentee, and the mentee should also give feedback to the mentor. A mentor providing feedback seems obvious and natural—after all, the point of the mentoring is that one individual (the mentor) can help coach or encourage another (the mentee). But it's also important that the mentee has the opportunity and takes the initiative to provide feedback to the mentor. And you, as the mentor, should encourage this. It provides valuable insight into if (and how) you're helping the other person, and it also helps you adjust and tailor your efforts and, most importantly, improve as a mentor overall. After all, if you enjoy mentoring, you should want to enhance and share your mentoring skills with even more people!

Explore growth and development.

Finally, mentoring relationships often start in one specific area or focus on one defined objective but evolve. Perhaps the mentor has more to offer, or the mentee realizes how valuable the opportunity is to them and wants to expand the relationship. Other times, the mentoring process opens up conversations and grows organically into different topics, and a longer-term relationship forms. This can be a positive if both parties agree and seek more time together. You can always use your progress checks and two-way feedback sessions to explore this further and see where it takes you.

Danny Fell has over thirty years of healthcare marketing and advertising experience working with some of the country's largest healthcare brands, including Geisinger, Massachusetts General Hospital, HP Medical, Siemens Healthcare Diagnostics, and UnitedHealth Group. In addition to working with a wide range of businesses, from Fortune 500 firms to non-profits, Danny co-founded and ran a successful national marketing agency, established a professional networking group to help connect healthcare startup founders, and has invested in dozens of companies as an angel investor and marketing mentor. He is currently a senior vice president at BVK in Milwaukee, WI, where he helps lead the healthcare practice. Nationally recognized for his writing and speaking on topics ranging from healthcare ratings and rankings to digital health strategies to AI, Danny's articles have appeared in *HealthLeaders, Modern Healthcare, Strategic Health Care Marketing*, and the *Journal of Healthcare Management*, among others. He is the co-author of *A Marketer's Guide to Market Research* and a member of the eHealthcare Strategy and Trends editorial advisory board. In 2012, Danny was honored as the first recipient of the John A. Eudes Vision & Excellence Award for his contributions to digital marketing and thought leadership in healthcare.

If you are interested in learning more about the power of mentoring or want to share some of your experiences and best practices, reach out to me on LinkedIn at https://www.linkedin.com/in/dannyfell/ or through my work at www.bvk.com. I'd love to hear from you, exchange ideas, and talk about mentoring in both professional and personal settings.

CHAPTER 19

THE COLOR OF LEADERSHIP

HOW A BOLD CHOICE HELPED A NEW BRAND SUCCEED

David A. Feinberg

"It's only by being bold that you get anywhere."

~ Richard Branson

MY STORY

THE SITUATION

"You've got to be kidding."

"You're not serious."

"That's the school's color. We can't use it."

"Do you know what that represents?"

"We're a healthcare company. You can't use that color to represent healthcare."

These are just some of the comments I heard as I prepared my recommendation to use a bold red as the color for the new NewYork-Presbyterian brand. Folks could barely accept the brand name, and now, to add insult to injury, I proposed a radical color choice.

"Red means blood. That's the wrong image for a hospital."

"This is not consumer products; it's healthcare. You need to learn this new field."

But I knew it was the right choice. I also knew it would be a tough sell. And being new myself—I had just joined the organization—I took a big risk recommending something neither obvious nor safe. As I look back on it over two decades later, I almost can't believe I did it.

This is the story of how and why Pantone 485 became the brand color for one of the most successful new brands in the history of hospital healthcare marketing and what this story teaches us about the power of leadership.

THE CHALLENGE

The year was 1998, and two of the most storied names in hospital history decided to merge to address market conditions that challenged their ability to thrive.

One was The New York Hospital, the second-oldest hospital in America, chartered in 1771 by King George III, the same King George who tried quite unsuccessfully to stop the United States from ever being born. Located on the very tony Upper East Side of Manhattan, an area once known as the Silk-Stocking District, it was the anchor hospital of The New York Hospital-Cornell University Medical Center, highly regarded for its brilliant physicians and high-quality care. You get the picture—a proud heritage of excellence and elegance befitting its history and location.

The other was The Presbyterian Hospital in the City of New York, founded in 1868 by James Lennox and, by the early 1900s, located in Washington Heights, a decidedly working-class, diverse, and vibrant neighborhood famously depicted on Broadway and in the movie *In The Heights*. It leaned proudly into its role as a leader in medical research and teaching as the anchor hospital of the world-famous Columbia-Presbyterian Medical Center. Presby, as it was commonly referred to, was proudly gritty and feisty; an urban hospital that cared for all comers, regardless of class, as befitting its founding as a place where all who needed care could find it.

On the surface, in many ways, there weren't two more different institutions. But beneath the surface was a common thread: both considered themselves "The Best." Each was a proud organization with a long, deep history of service and accomplishment. Along with that, unsurprisingly, came this: each thought it was better than the other.

The challenge was clear. How do you bring these two staunchly separate institutions together under one common theme?

The answer was found in the strategy of the merger. This new organization had to be as fully integrated as possible, a true full-asset merger. It wouldn't be two equal entities working separately under a holding company. Leadership would be singular, with one board, one CEO, one executive team, and one set of books. This approach was key to success. To take full advantage of the combined resources and expertise of each hospital required a complete coming together.

The ultimate goal was equally clear, derived from the common aim of both institutions: to be the best. NewYork-Presbyterian wasn't formed to be just another large academic health system. It aspired to be among the top tier of peer institutions, and full integration was key to achieving that goal.

For me, personally, the stakes could not have been higher. It was less than a year since I had started, so I was still establishing myself. This was my first major proposal. I knew that if this didn't go well, it might be my last. It felt as if my entire future was on the line.

THE CHOICE

From a marketing standpoint, the goal and strategy drove the solution. Several choices were clear.

First, this would be a branded house, not a house of brands. No other approach could support the strategy of full integration. Further, one of the key drivers was efficiency through synergy. Marketing each brand separately would be more costly, complicated, and ultimately less effective. Thus, a single brand name with a single color or set of colors.

Next, the color choice had to be new. It would be wrong to pick one of the legacy colors, implying one side won and the other lost—not a good basis for bringing folks together. And the legacy colors were both variations of blue, the most common, least distinctive color palette in the category. The new color had to be bold, distinctive and supportive of the leadership goal.

As we went through the rainbow, the choice became clear. Blue was out. Green isn't bad but not bold or distinctive; it's the second most common color in the category. And it began taking on a secondary meaning of environmental advocacy, not a bad message but not the core message of the brand. Purple could've been interesting, but it was already taken in the market. That leaves orange, yellow, and red, and of those, red was the clear winner.

Red represented everything we wanted the brand to be:

- It's distinctive. Many staff and colleagues expressed a natural reluctance to use red because of some negative associations and its uniqueness in the category. The only other systems that used red were those associated with a university whose color was red, and those were relatively rare. Thus, the choice of red automatically distinguished the brand.

- It's bold. From a marketing standpoint, no color makes a greater impact than red.

- It's the color of leadership. Coke vs. Pepsi. McDonald's vs. Burger King. Colgate vs. Crest. The list goes on.

- And it's a great healthcare color. Many leading healthcare brands use red, including Tylenol, Red Cross, Band-Aid, and Theracare, to name just a few.

The final hurdle was reconciling this choice with the color of Cornell, the academic partner of The New York Hospital, whose sports teams are known as "Big Red." The choice of red might seem to favor one academic partner, Cornell, over the other, Columbia. Fortunately, Cornell-red was never part of the marketing of The New York Hospital-Cornell Medical Center. There was no association between red and the medical center. In addition, red represents a wide palette of colors. Working with a very talented design and creative team, we picked a shade very different from that of Cornell. Once folks saw how different the colors were, the objections diminished, and we moved forward aggressively using the new color for the new brand.

THE SELL

My heart pounded, my palms sweated, my legs shook. This was about as intimidating a room as you can imagine. Picture deep mahogany all around, adorned by painted portraits of past hospital presidents and trustees looking down on us in apparent judgment. Just outside was a reproduction on parchment of the original charter signed by George III. The huge dark wood table was alleged to have come from J.P. Morgan's board room.

The chairs were university chairs with the seal of The New York Hospital emblazoned in gold on the back panel.

And if the surroundings weren't intimidating enough, the attendees were even more so. Many of the nation's most powerful, bold-faced industry leaders were collected in one room at one time on the institution's board, representing some of the largest, most powerful corporations in the world: Morgan Stanley, American Express, Citigroup, Hearst, Ogilvy, McKinsey, Verizon, and more. Add to that the deans of both the Columbia and Cornell medical schools, as well as the management and clinical leaders of both hospitals.

I wondered and worried. What was I doing here in the presence of these titans of industry and brilliant minds? Why would they listen to me? What made me think I was worthy of their attention and respect? I felt a level of pressure I had never experienced before.

Fortunately, I had the backing of my leadership. They had the vision to support our bold recommendation. The logic was sound, and they wanted to shake things up. The brand was a big part of that. And several influential trustees also backed our choices, including a few highly respected marketing experts who served as valuable advisors during the process.

Importantly, this was far from a one-man show. I worked with a very talented team of creative strategists, marketers, designers, and researchers who helped put the plan together. While I was the only presenter, I represented a large group of professionals who did the very hard work of bringing our strategy to life.

The specific board action was the approval of the name, NewYork-Presbyterian Hospital, but we chose to show it in context, including the logo, how it would be used, some signage, and the tagline—The University Hospital of Columbia and Cornell—which we incorporated into the logo.

The final chapter of the presentation was the color. Rather than just show the color in our materials, I chose to describe it as a strategic choice. I knew it would be met viscerally with some resistance. So when I said, "Red is the color of leadership," and I backed it up with examples, I sensed a positive reaction in the room. They wanted the new organization to achieve even greater heights of excellence. This explained how the choice of red advanced that goal. While these are some of the most brilliant and accomplished people in the world, few of them are marketers. Making the connection in a way they could understand helped gain support and overcome concerns.

Another key choice was the avoidance of marketing jargon. We all revert to terms only understood by those who work in the field, like *positioning, share of voice, reason-why, brand voice,* and *leverage.* I did my best to expunge them from my narrative and speak in plain, understandable English. This respects the audience and invites them into the story rather than trying to impress them with meaningless sophistication.

The immediate response to the presentation was almost universally positive. People related to the explanation of why we made our choices and how they all fit together to support the vision. We helped our audience appreciate the rigor that goes into professional marketing—that it's not a bunch of folks sitting around a table spitballing ideas, "Mad Men" style. There is a science to the art of marketing, and working to help your constituents understand that yields great dividends.

MAKING IT WORK

Now that the choice was made and approved, the hard work of implementation began. No matter how sound the strategy, without excellent execution the effort will not fully succeed. Our team began rolling out all the brand elements using bold red as our color. These included logo and graphic standards, signage and wayfinding, promotional materials, marketing collateral, business cards, stationery, brochures, and print and TV advertising, among others.

While getting approval for the bold choice of color was gratifying, seeing it come to life was even more rewarding. The presence of red had the desired effect of distinguishing NewYork-Presbyterian from the competition and of communicating a strong image of excellence and leadership. As the various elements rolled out, the impact strengthened, and the many concerns expressed prior to the selection largely faded away. It became apparent that their concerns were unfounded. It was wonderful to receive positive feedback from across our various constituencies, including employees, nurses, physicians, other medical staff, patients, the public, and our trustees.

LONGER TERM

Bold choices can yield bold benefits for many years into the future. About ten years after the red brand color was chosen, the highly successful "Amazing Things are Happening Here" advertising campaign was launched.

The brand color was a major contributor to this success. The creative agency designed a bold graphic symbol with the tagline in white type against a red rectangle, thus making strong use of the brand color in presenting the selling idea. This graphic became a ubiquitous and powerful symbol of the brand and its unique selling proposition. The "Amazing Things" campaign continued for over a decade, built upon the power of that simple but distinctive red graphic.

It's almost impossible to believe it has been over twenty years since that approval presentation. But the branding and color choices have held up very well. The merger has been a huge success, to the benefit of so many patients who received better care and for all the people whose hard work and dedication made it possible. While that success is attributable to many things more important than the marketing, or specifically the choice of red, hopefully the marketing decisions contributed in some meaningful way to make that positive outcome easier and more likely.

THE TOOL

LESSONS OF LEADERSHIP

To drive transformational leadership, here are some key steps as derived from the example described in this chapter:

1. Choose When to Be Transformational

   Carefully assess the situation. What is the need for transformational leadership? What's being transformed? And why? Is the organization ready for it? Not all situations require transformation, which is the most difficult kind of leadership to achieve. The need and motivation must be great to be successful. And the conditions for change must be in place. If not, perhaps pivot to a less dramatic, more gradual change plan.

2. Understand the Why and Use That to Drive Change

   Transformation can only occur when there is a clear reason and commitment. Sometimes, it's an opportunity, a threat, a crisis, or perhaps a change in leadership. The nature of the why will drive the plan for transformation. Alignment among your key constituents and participants will help foster support for and participation in your plan.

3. Be Bold

Transformational leadership requires bold thinking and initiative. It's not the time to hold back. A clear need and alignment can provide the opportunity to be bold. Actions that would normally be off-limits could now be considered. It's a good time to stretch the possible and suggest the radical. And even if some of your ideas are rejected, as long as they're rooted in the situation and have a good rationale, they'll be appreciated if not accepted. In these circumstances, being bold isn't as risky as might otherwise be the case. In fact, the greater risk might be to lie back and not lean into the situation.

4. Speak to the People's Concerns and Interests

Real transformation is ultimately about the folks who need to transform. The why works best when put in terms that make the benefits clear to those involved—the classic "What's in it for me?" rather than why it's good for the department or organization. Self-interest is always the greatest motivator. Try to tell the transformation story in terms that make the self-interest obvious; this is good for you as well as the organization.

David A. Feinberg is Senior Vice President, Chief Marketing and Communications Officer for the Mount Sinai Health System and Dean for Marketing and Communications for the Icahn School of Medicine at Mount Sinai, providing leadership and strategic guidance for all marketing, communications, public relations, digital and branding efforts.

Mr. Feinberg joined Mount Sinai in November 2018 from the Dana-Farber Cancer Institute in Boston, where he was Vice President and Chief Marketing Officer. Before that, Mr. Feinberg held marketing leadership roles for nearly 20 years at NewYork-Presbyterian Hospital, where he was Vice President of Marketing from 1997 to 2011 and Chief Marketing Officer from 2012 to 2016.

Prior to joining NewYork-Presbyterian Hospital, Mr. Feinberg led the healthcare practice of The Seiden Group, an advertising and marketing firm, helping to develop strategies and programs for clients such as Novartis and Bayer. His other previous experience includes Ciba-Geigy, where he helped establish their consumer division; Biocyte, an early-stage pioneer in the field of cord blood stem cells; Procter & Gamble and Clairol.

Mr. Feinberg holds a Master's in Management, Marketing, degree from Northwestern University's Kellogg School of Management and a BS in Economics from The Wharton School of the University of Pennsylvania.

CHAPTER 20

SELF-LEADERSHIP VS. SELF-MASTERY

THE KEY TO LEADING WITH CLARITY, COURAGE, AND HEART

Jenny Gladding

"I'm out with lanterns looking for myself"

~ Emily Dickinson

"It is only with the heart that one can see rightly; what is essential is invisible to the eye."

~ Antoine de Saint-Exupéry

MY STORY

"Flashes of Brilliance" was the phrase that caught my attention. I was allowed access to my college admission files the first year I'd left home to attend college. I was seventeen, and I'd left behind a family broken by divorce and emotional dysfunction. Part of me felt exhilarated, even liberated, with my new adventure far from home. However, the fog of my high school years, which impeded my effort to think clearly and access my creativity, seemed to hover nearby. I didn't feel brilliant and wondered about the "flashes."

This phrase came to define my identity over time. I didn't trust myself as the source of my knowing but imagined instead that any brilliance was bestowed upon me at random, leaving me uncertain how to access this gift when needed. I lived in a state of anxiety about making myself fully visible. The larger question that occupied my concerns was what caused me to be either favored and lit up or forgotten and left behind to fend for myself like an orphaned boxcar child.

The issue of visibility afflicted me in more than one way. Throughout my twenties, I worked as a photographic fashion model. This, too, felt like a perilous charade in which I might, at any moment, be discovered to be inadequate for the role. I recall standing against the white-papered backdrop in a photographer's studio while an assistant peered at me through the camera's lens, making lighting adjustments in preparation for the photographer. During the preceding hour, I'd been visibly transformed as the makeup artist painted my face and the hairstylist worked on my hair. I'd been dressed by the clothing stylist and deemed ready for the photo shoot. When the photographer arrived and peered into the camera's lens, I held my breath and froze, imagining his annoyance as he'd look up and shout, "Who is this? Where is the model?" *Even beauty was intermittently bestowed upon me.*

I've been a seeker for as long as I can remember. I've read, studied, and pondered the mysteries of life. I've explored various spiritual and personal development practices, pursued degrees in higher education, and received honors and a prestigious fellowship. Yet, after all these accomplishments, I felt uncertain about my capacity to rise to a more powerful version of myself. I sensed I had important gifts to offer but kept my light dim, believing I wasn't yet deserving to make myself visible enough to lead and inspire others. The parts of me in the lead were operating from a limited and fear-based perspective. *Better not to shine too brightly if you can't be sure that light will endure.*

Along the way, a mentor suggested the power of doing Jungian shadow work to generate awareness in the areas of my life where I felt most stuck. By the age of twelve, I'd become interested in my mother's quest for deeper meaning, exploring her books on philosophy, psychology, and spirituality. She was fond of quoting a Jungian phrase, "The gold is in the dark." This idea fascinated me for many years, reverberating inside me like the koan the Zen masters use to reveal the limits of rational inquiry. I was sure it held the key to something I did not yet understand. When my mentor suggested the shadow practice, I felt ready to find the gold.

"Begin," she said, "with your most challenging relationship–the one where you have the most aversion. List all the qualities you dislike or judge in this person and then search to see where these same qualities live inside of you, even if only a small percent."

The task was difficult at first. I spent so many years seeing my father as wrong because he was critical and emotionally distant, and I'd felt abandoned when he remarried more than once. Slowly, a window of awareness began to open. As I noticed how I often disconnected from relationships and moved on in life, and more importantly, why I behaved this way, I found the bridge to understanding my father. I had been running from losses for so long. I understood then that perhaps he cut off from our family as the only way he knew to protect his vulnerable feelings. This new perspective, imbued with understanding, seemed to shift the dynamic between us. In time, I witnessed how, when I softened towards him, he began to soften towards me.

I have butterflies in my stomach. I've come to make an offering of peace, to own my part in the decades-long cold war of my relationship with my father. I'm so nervous; I'm unsure I'll say anything of real meaning and have the usual polite conversation instead. It's the week after Christmas; the sky is grey, and the air is heavy with the promise of snow. I park the car and hug the soft wool of my jacket close as I approach the hip restaurant he's chosen for our meeting. I note his gracious nod to my food preferences.

Inside, I find my father waiting at a table against the banquette. I take the chair facing him. We order lunch and begin to chat. I take comfort in the warm glow of the lights above and the steaming cup of golden latte pressed against my fingers, struggling, as always, with the sense that I'm invisible to him. Lunch arrives, and the words I'd intended to speak remain just below the surface of our conversation. The part of me that feels invisible and powerless seems unaware of a deeper presence in me, the one holding the vision for this brave conversation to take place. And then, at last, I begin.

"The reason I asked to have lunch with you is because I have some things I want to share. " I say. My heart is racing, and I feel that familiar emptiness at my center. *Is it because he feels empty, too?* I admire my father's courtly manners–he's good at the outward gestures of hospitality, but I've always longed for a deeper sense of welcome.

"Okay," he responds. *His eyes look curious.* As I think about it, he has kind eyes, but I've generally been too alienated and shut down to take that in fully.

"I've been reflecting," I say, "and I have some things to share about my part in our relationship." I feel trembly and untethered, but the brave part of me is determined.

"I see now how I've contributed to the distance between us," I continue. "I've blamed you for years, but now I see how I helped to perpetuate this dynamic, and I want to apologize."

My father reaches over, places his hand on top of mine, and says, "Well, that's quite a confession."

I could feel my rebellious parts rising up, unfurling like a coiled serpent. *How can he not take some responsibility?* I heard. *It's not fair! He always blames me!*

But my higher Self was more present, calming the excited parts and staying grounded, allowing the heart's alchemy to hold my father and me in this new moment. It was no longer about me or what I was lacking, nor was it about my father and what he lacked. The mind always searches for what's missing and what can be fixed. Yet there, centered in the compassionate energy of the heart, shining the light of awareness on myself, I found my capacity to effect transformation in a relationship long marked by resentment and disconnection.

Einstein tells us, "No problem can be solved from the same level of consciousness that created it." The exercise in shadow work with my father provided a flash of insight, shifting my identity as an abandoned daughter who struggled to be worthy of shining my light to aligning with a higher version of myself. The impact of this revelation was limited as the framework for shadow practice is a cognitive one. I found the flash of gold in the process, yet I longed to experience how I could more confidently connect with the source of my light. I had more to learn before arriving at the heart's core.

WAKING UP IN YOGA CLASS

For a long while, I'd faithfully come to the yoga studio five days a week. I'd laid my yoga mat in the front row and surrendered to the next hour of being led to breathe and move through the asana practice. Yoga teachers seemed to possess a confidence, presence, and knowledge, which I aspired to embody one day; however, the chasm between who I was and that future version of myself seemed quite wide. Though I completed the 200-hour yoga teacher training just before the pandemic, I still imagined it would take years of training and practice to become that version of myself.

In the years following my yoga teacher training, I was also studying to be a life coach and eventually focused my interest on IFS (Internal Family Systems) for coaches. Slowly, I was learning to access more confidence and clarity as I practiced this model.

"I told my boss that you're a yoga teacher, and she wants you to come in and audition to teach," my daughter announced one afternoon a few years ago. She was living at home while attending college and worked at a local fitness center.

I felt both horrified and excited. *The deeper part of me is telling me this is the moment—the invitation has arrived for me to step into a larger vision of myself, the one I've held for so many years.*

I was going to say yes, or I was going to hold back and believe I wasn't ready. I accepted the invitation to audition and watched in amazement as the golden thread of my future self began to pull me forward.

Gradually, a kind of alchemy began to take place. My intellectual seeking shifted to a knowing in the body (first revealed to me in the practice of yoga). Yogic philosophy tells us the heart center is the seat of intelligence and intuition, in contrast with the mind center, where reason and intellect reside. The mind constantly makes meaning of our present experience through the lens of our previous experiences and beliefs. Heart-centered knowing brings us into the present moment, deepening our awareness and ability to access intuition and creativity and revealing our connection with the infinite. I'd been on a lifelong quest to discover my calling and feel worthy to share my gifts of keen intuition, wisdom, and compassion to benefit others. The more I experienced the intelligence at my heart center, the clearer and more aligned I became with my purpose. In the language of IFS, we'd say I was becoming more and more Self-led.

SELF-LEADERSHIP VS. SELF-MASTERY

In my story above, I experienced a part of me that doubted it could trust my knowing enough to fulfill a greater, more visible role in my life. This part formed its identity around the idea that any brilliance I possessed was unreliable and random. I also had a very active thinking/learning part who pushed back against any experience of uncertainty, preoccupied with helping me to keep acquiring knowledge so that I might one day be ready to shine in all my radiance. Often, these internal parts oppose one another, and we wonder why we do and say things that conflict with our stated intentions. I believed that I had an important and powerful purpose, but the uncertain and intellectual parts kept me locked in a pattern of never quite fulfilling the larger vision I had for my life.

How, then, does one acquire mastery with these conflicting internal points of view? I would suggest that the common self-mastery model rests on a notion of self-discipline which conceives of a central self that "rules" with reason or will, bringing all the disparate parts of our personality into alignment. Similarly, certain mindfulness practices encourage us to transcend or let go of our thoughts and feelings and disarm the offending ego. These models of self-mastery reflect our dominant culture, judging the feelings and wounds of our triggered parts as illusory, weak, self-indulgent, and shameful. Our difficult feelings don't really go away and often exert a profound influence over our lives when we ignore them. Jung writes, "Until you make the unconscious conscious, it will direct your life, and you will call it fate." Let us consider an alternative practice to the common notion of self-mastery. If our sometimes overwhelming emotions can't be controlled or eliminated, what else is possible?

Various belief systems refer to a part of us that is eternal, true, awake, and aware using different terms. In spiritual traditions, the higher self is that part of us that connects with the sacred source of all life. The idea of Self with a capital "S" from Internal Family Systems (IFS) is an embodied experience of wholeness, wisdom and well-being that has the power to bring about our healing. Internal Family Systems (IFS) is a model created by Dr. Richard C. Schwartz, PhD, which enables us to bring compassion and understanding to all the parts of our inner experience towards becoming more conscious; more Self-led. In IFS, we learn to center our awareness in this Self energy and then begin to connect with the parts or aspects of our personality that suffer from disconnection, develop defensive strategies, and believe they are in the driver's seat of our lives. It's as if we have an internal family of child-like sub-personalities who believe they must rely on their limited perspectives and resources to guide our actions and protect us.

When we tap into a deeper well of wisdom and compassion and extend that energy toward the "unruly" parts that derail us from our intentions, we experience Self-leadership. Self, from the perspective of IFS, includes certain qualities of experience: a sense of calm, connectedness, clarity, curiosity, courage, compassion, and creativity. These qualities let us know when the energy of Self is at the helm. We can begin to see the good intentions behind destructive or self-sabotaging behavior as a sincere effort to cope with overwhelming experiences and emotions that continue to live inside us. In time, using the tools of IFS, the parts who've kept me stuck have begun to heal and blossom. I experience more spaciousness, less reactivity, and my capacity for understanding others has grown as well. I now show up in my life and relationships in ways I never imagined possible. With the powerful qualities of Self-leadership, we can begin to express our unique gifts and shine in all our brilliance; the world needs our light. Using IFS in the coaching relationship allows this transformation to unfold. I offer a glimpse into this process using a self-practice below.

THE TOOL

SOMATIC HEART CENTERING

Begin by focusing on your breath.

Deepen on the inhale, through your nose, as if you could breathe all the way down into the bowl of your pelvis. Pause for a moment and notice the space between the breaths.

As you exhale, notice the breath as it releases slowly from your belly and up through your chest. When you are empty, pause again before the next breath in. Continue for several rounds of breath. Sigh the breath out through your open mouth a few times to release any tension. Breathing in this way shifts us into the parasympathetic nervous system, bringing about a greater sense of calm.

If thoughts are present, envision the breath carrying those thoughts down into your heart center. Experiment with placing your hand over your heart to sense into this center of awareness somatically.

Now, bring your awareness to your inner experience as if you're shining a light into the dark interior. See if you can notice any sensations in or around your body. As you bring your focus to the inside, thoughts, feelings, or images may also appear. For instance, you might notice a swirling feeling in your belly, some tightness in the throat, or perhaps a concerning thought or emotion that feels omnipresent. Continue with the exercise below.

SELF-LEADERSHIP THROUGH PARTS AWARENESS

Begin to get curious about the sensation/feeling/thought/image that shows up in or around your body. Think of this as a part or aspect of your personality which is asking for your deeper attention.

Visualize the part you've identified separating from you and taking a seat in front of you. Check to see how you feel toward this part, noticing if you're able to approach it with curiosity and an open heart. If so, extend your kindness and compassion, sharing your intention to understand and witness its experience.

If you feel overwhelmed with any particular emotions or beliefs, take the un-blending steps below to return to the heart-centered awareness of Self-leadership. Imagine this perspective as the seat of awareness, the Self through which we're connected with a greater, more transcendent presence and the source of all healing.

UNBLENDING

Focus again on the breath, deepening on the inhale. Shift awareness again to the heart center. Notice any feelings, thoughts, or sensations. Invite these aspects or parts of your personality to take a seat in front of you. See if you can describe how they appear. Notice who is observing and describing the part and how doing so enables you to create a bit of separation between the part and your wise Self. You can also do this step as a journaling exercise.

Continue to check to see if you're feeling open-hearted and curious towards these parts of your personality. You're looking for an experience of calm, compassion, and curiosity, to name a few of the qualities of Self energy. Unblending from a part enables this energy to become available.

Jenny Gladding is an RYT 200 Yoga Teacher and Transformative Life Coach with Level 1 training in IFS (Internal Family Systems). For the past 40 years, she has studied spiritual and psychological development both in and outside academia. She has completed multiple coach training programs focusing on interpersonal relationships, presence-based leadership, and coaching with the IFS model.

Jenny helps clients release the emotional patterns and limiting beliefs that keep them from rising into the highest expression of their authentic gifts. The wholeness, healing, clarity, and power we seek is in the heart of our most painful and confusing experiences. With her warm presence, wisdom, and keen intuition, she guides her clients to align with their higher Self, making healing and transformation possible.

Jenny is the adoring mother of two adult daughters, a daily seeker of enchantment, a passionate yogi, lover of beauty, afternoon tea, and the culinary arts, with a relentless passion to awaken you to the heart centered wisdom of your authentic self.

Do you sense a potential you've not yet realized, struggling to shine your unique brilliance in the world? Do you long to create a life of meaning and joy? Follow the link below to learn more about coaching with IFS.

Connect with Jenny Gladding

Website: https://JennyGladding.com

Email: jennygladdingcoaching@gmail.com

CHAPTER 21

CAREER–BUILDING LEADERSHIP COMPETENCIES

LESSONS FROM THE SOFT COOKIE WARS FOR ASPIRING LEADERS

Mark J. Bohen, MBA

"I learned to always take on things I'd never done before. Growth and comfort do not coexist."

~ Ginni Rometty,
former Chairman, president and CEO of IBM

MY STORY

I LEARNED THAT IT TAKES A LOT MORE THAN SKILLS TO BE SUCCESSFUL.

When I entered the Nabisco offices on my first day of work, my heart was beating fast. I was nervous. I felt overmatched. Most MBA graduates worked before business school. I went to business school right from college and started at Nabisco when I was 24. I wasn't sure I had enough skills or any skills to be successful in the business world.

That day as I started my first job at Nabisco as an assistant brand manager, I had no idea this experience would not only develop my skills but also profoundly shape my thoughts on leadership. Now I'd like to pass on what I discovered to you-emerging leaders in marketing.

My first assignment was to work on Almost Home, Nabisco's soft cookie entrant, designed to blunt Proctor and Gamble's expansion in the cookie category behind their new fat substitute, Olestra. This battle became known as the Soft Cookie Wars of the 1980s. Millions in marketing were spent by Nabisco, Proctor and Gamble, and Keebler. The war ended when it was discovered that Olestra caused diarrhea, and soft cookies couldn't come close to homemade cookies.

My job was to clean up after the soft cookie wars. I discontinued flavors and sizes, took price increases, cut marketing programs, and restored profitability.

Some people consider this an undesirable assignment, but to me, I learned and gained experience in marketing skills, but more importantly, in the leadership competencies that allow people to be successful, especially in times of change and upheaval. I learned critical skills such as understanding an income statement, forecasting, budgeting, mining for consumer insights that could be leveraged for growth, and, most importantly, positioning a product and brand.

Although I didn't appreciate it then, I was also developing important leadership competencies such as impact and influence, strategic thinking, critical thinking, resiliency, persistency, agility, collaboration, and a growth and experimental mindset.

I needed both marketing skills and leadership competencies to be successful in my jobs, but it was the leadership competencies that advanced my career.

After my Almost Home assignment, I worked on Barnum's, Newtons, Cookies n Fudge, new products, and eventually iconic brands like Oreo and Ritz. Nabisco moved brand people around to different businesses frequently. Getting comfortable with change and ambiguity has served me well throughout my career and is a prerequisite for success today. When I worked on Barnum's, a small business in the Cookie and Cracker portfolio, I didn't have big budgets. Understandably, most marketing dollars, research and development (R&D) resources, and manufacturing time went to Oreos, Ritz and other larger brands that drove most of the growth for the company. Still, I was accountable for the volume and profit growth of Barnum's. I had to be innovative.

DEVELOPING COMPETENCIES IS AN ART.

The practice of marketing is both a science and an art. Segmentation and targeting, data analysis, and tracking return on investment are all examples of the science of marketing. When some people think of the art of marketing, they think of the creative process. It's true—that is an art.

In brand management, one has no direct authority over R&D, manufacturing, or sales. A brand manager needs to think like an orchestra conductor and use impact and influence to bring everyone together. That and a lot of collaboration, resilience, and persistence go a long way, particularly when working on a small business such as Barnum's or when an industry or business is rapidly changing.

Back in the late 1980s, before the internet and email, when inter-office mail was delivered by people pushing carts and dropping the mail at your desk, business moved at a slower pace. There were many more in-person meetings and drop-by conversations, with agreements written in memos, delivered through inter-office mail, or dropped on your desk.

The Romans used the expression 'Barbarians at the Gate' to describe foreign attacks against their empire. For some in the business world, 'Barbarians at the Gate' evokes memories of the events surrounding the 1988 leveraged buyout (LBO) of RJR Nabisco, the largest in corporate history at the time.

During the LBO, just two years into my career, change happened at a furious pace. The only way to keep up was to read the Wall Street Journal in the morning to get the latest Nabisco news, as inter-office mail wasn't delivered until the afternoon.

So, who thrived in an environment of ambiguity, fast change, and stress?

It wasn't those better at forecasting or budgeting. It wasn't those with the most experience or expertise. Leaders who were agile, resilient, and comfortable with constant pivots and ambiguity outperformed others. Still, early in my career, I learned to function and excel in an environment of ambiguity.

After many years in consumer-packaged goods, I was recruited by a large, European-owned specialty insurance company. In 1998, I interviewed to become the Chief Marketing Officer for one of its business units, specializing in employee benefits like disability, dental, and life insurance, based in Kansas City, Missouri.

I recall walking into the CEO's office for my interview.

I was nervous. *Maybe I'll just walk out and get back on the plane. I can't do this job.*

All my experience was in consumer-packaged goods. I didn't know the first thing about the insurance industry, how insurance policies worked, how an insurance company made money, or how they were sold to an employee through their employer.

Even though I had all these employee benefits at Nabisco plus health insurance, I never paid any attention to them. I went for my annual physical and dental cleanings, and that was it.

I can't bluff my way through this interview; I must tell the CEO that I'm the wrong person for the job!

The interview began. I said to the CEO, "I have strong classical marketing skills, acquired in the consumer-packaged goods industry, and I believe those skills translate to insurance, and are needed in insurance, but I don't have any insurance experience or knowledge; I'm not your guy."

Not wanting to waste his time, I offered to help find other candidates with strong marketing skills and insurance expertise.

Looking directly at my resume and then at me, with a straight face, he asked, "You don't have any insurance experience? That's perfect and just what we're looking for."

After a few more rounds of interviews, I accepted an offer to become the Chief Marketing Officer. Turns out he wanted someone with fresh eyes and who could lead through change. A few years after I started, the company was spun off by its European parent. I was involved in the initial public offering (IPO) of stock, moved around to other parts of the company, learned the insurance industry, and stayed for 15 years.

What was the lesson?

The insurance industry was slow to change. The business model, which was focused on the intermediary, needed to transform and become more oriented towards the customer, the one who put money into the system, not the one who was paid to sell policies. Other industries at the time, such as investments, were also becoming consumer-oriented.

My classical marketing skills, while important and valued for this position, weren't what separated me from other candidates. It was my leadership competencies-specifically bringing an experimental, growth mindset, being comfortable with change and ambiguity, and being resilient and agile. Back at Nabisco, these competencies separated the top performers from the pack, and it was true here as well.

Next stop: Healthcare. I can't say I had a strategic plan for my career when I started at Nabisco, and you may not, either. Careers evolve. What became clear over time was that businesses and many industries were changing rapidly and reinventing themselves, all in search of more growth. As I thought about what industries were evolving to become more consumer-focused and needed my combination of classical marketing skills and competencies, I received a call from a recruiting firm about a Chief Marketing and Communications position with Michigan's largest health system.

As I approached my first interview with the CEO, I again felt woefully unprepared as I knew little about healthcare delivery. Unlike my last interview in which I tried to talk myself out of a job, now I wanted to convince the CEO I had the marketing skills and competencies to be successful in healthcare.

As it turned out, the CEO's brother was an executive at Proctor and Gamble, a top-tier packaged goods company—one I was very familiar with—and my competitor when I was in the cookie wars. He was looking for a candidate with consumer-packaged goods experience.

I accepted the offer and became an executive in the fast-changing, complicated world of healthcare.

I joined the organization as three large health systems merged and integrated into one. Once again, I found myself in a leadership position during a time of major change with lots of ambiguity. To compound our challenges, we entered the pandemic.

The pandemic was difficult for everybody in healthcare—patients, nurses, doctors, and all other employees. With no playbook, we needed to lead to keep our health systems open to save lives, keep them safe for employees, and keep them financially viable. Talk about dealing with change, ambiguity, and complexity!

During the pandemic, I was recruited to join another health system, Mass General Brigham, located in Boston, Massachusetts. In September 2020, I started as Chief Marketing and Communications Officer.

Now, for the third time since I left Nabisco, my competencies in leading during change and ambiguity—agility, resiliency, impact, and influence, having an experimental and growth mindset—seemed to be more valued than my marketing skills.

Mass General Brigham is a large, integrated academic health system. It has two world-renowned academic medical centers (Massachusetts General Hospital and Brigham and Women's Hospital) and three specialty hospitals (all of which are Harvard Medical School teaching hospitals), as well as community hospitals, home care, a health plan, and community health centers. Its research organization is the largest health system-based research operation in the country. All told, there are over 80,000 employees. Mass General Brigham is large, complex, and undergoing tremendous change.

Healthcare across the country is under severe pressure and undergoing change as the mission-based, not-for-profit healthcare business model fights for survival in a post-pandemic, high-inflation environment. At Mass General Brigham, we're transforming from a holding company to an integrated academic health system. With this transformation comes plenty of ambiguity and a need for resiliency.

In Marketing and Communications, we've transformed from a generalist, hospital-based model to a specialist enterprise model. We were much more art than science, which is a nice way of saying we made marketing decisions based on others' opinions or gut feelings. Now, we're more analytical, research, and ROI-focused. I believe we have the right balance between art and science.

We have many marketing and communications employees new to Mass General Brigham. I've recruited many with specialized skills that we didn't have in abundance before and which I believe are required to compete on a national and global basis. We have specialized teams focused on consumer insights and research, data and analytics, brand management, clinical services and growth, digital marketing, and communications. On the communications team, we have leaders who specialize in government affairs communication, change management communication, and crisis communication, to name but a few specialized areas.

I mentioned that skills took a back seat to competencies earlier in my career. That doesn't mean I didn't keep my skills sharp. No matter your title or role, we all need to be life-long learners and keep our skills up to date. The practice of marketing and communications is constantly evolving, and we all need to be at the top of our game in our own specialized focus area and know enough about all areas as we grow in our careers. I've needed to learn about the specialized area of search engine optimization and search engine marketing. These skills became important to the practice of marketing after I became a Chief Marketing Officer. I've tried to learn from others and on my own, so I know enough to assess our performance.

While we recruit for specialized skills, that's not enough to land you a leadership role in Marketing and Communications at Mass General Brigham. As we transform from a holding company to an integrated system, we need employees with specialized skills **plus** the leadership competencies I found so important in my own career journey.

During times of high stress, ambiguity, and change, I always come back to the competencies I observed in others who were successful at Nabisco and that I worked to develop in myself during my career. These competencies helped me through challenging times in other industries and companies. Resiliency, persistence, collaboration, agility, impact and influence, and having an experimental and growth mindset are all important and keys to a successful career in businesses or industries undergoing major transformation.

Remember, as Ginny Rometty said, "Growth and comfort do not coexist."

Try these suggestions in the tool below.

THE TOOL

How do you develop leadership competencies like dealing with ambiguity, collaboration, becoming more resilient, being more persistent, and having a growth and experimental mindset?

- Seek new opportunities and experiences in your company. Even if you think the job is unappealing, there's always something to learn and always opportunities to build competencies.

- Seek mentors. Ask for their input and advice. Choose people who will be completely honest with you.

- If you have an opportunity to work with a coach, take it. Work on building competencies.

- Observe others you work with you feel consistently demonstrate these competencies.

- Intentionally demonstrate the competency and ask for feedback in specific areas with examples.

Take a new assignment, even if it means learning from a new experience or doing something when you don't feel quite comfortable or sure of your abilities. Take a risk!

Mark Bohen, MBA, is the Chief Marketing and Communications Officer at Mass General Brigham, a world-renowned integrated academic healthcare system with two leading academic medical centers in Massachusetts General Hospital and Brigham and Women's Hospital. Mass General Brigham generates over $20 billion in revenue and has over 80 thousand employees. He is responsible for building and leading a world-class marketing and communications organization and ensuring people around the globe know about the leading research, clinical care, innovations, and education taking place throughout the Mass General Brigham system. Mark leads all marketing and communications functions, including brand management, data analytics, consumer research and insights, digital marketing, clinical service and hospital marketing, marketing strategy, and internal and external communications.

Prior to joining Mass General Brigham in September 2020, Mark spent four years at Beaumont Health, the largest health system in Michigan at the time, as Chief Marketing and Communications Officer.

Previously, Mark was Senior Vice President of Marketing and Innovation at Assurant, a Fortune 500, publicly traded insurance company, and more than ten years in consumer-packaged goods, mostly at Nabisco in brand management roles on iconic brands such as Oreos and Ritz Crackers.

Mark earned his BA in marketing from Syracuse University and his MBA from Duke University's Fuqua School of Business.

CHAPTER 22

CATALYST

APPLYING AUTHENTICITY, VULNERABILITY, AND HOW TO LEAD BY EXAMPLE

Amy Moudy Comeau, MBA

"Growth and comfort do not co-exist."

~ Ginni Rometty, former IBM CEO

MY STORY

I got fired.

My infant son almost died.

I miscarried.

My husband had brain surgery.

These very personal events shaped my leadership style.

ACT 1: I GOT FIRED. AND IT WAS A GIFT.

I moved to Atlanta during the fall of 1997. I didn't know it then, but nearly 30 years later, I'm here to stay.

I was fortunate to be offered jobs in Seattle and Atlanta after being one of four individuals in North America to receive the prestigious OPERA America Fellowship, geared to groom the next generation of opera leaders—general managers, or, in biz speak, CEOs.

I studied for a year with the brightest marketing and communications minds in Seattle, Los Angeles, Atlanta, and Lake George, New York. It was so transformative to my career that I still include it as a footnote on my resume.

I nearly literally drove the entire circumference of the United States that year—my first solo road trip. GPS and iPhones didn't exist back then. I used old-school paper maps and had my mom's cell-phone-in-a-bag in the glove compartment to use only in case of emergency. Fortunately, it was never needed.

Triple A TripTiks, my favorite music cassettes (thank you, Columbia House), mixtapes, and library books-on-tape carried me from Buffalo to Seattle. Even shipped those library tapes back to my mom to return so I wouldn't incur a late fee.

I **loved** working in the arts. Planned to dedicate my career to it. And I did. Little did I know how short that arts career would be.

My OPERA America fellowship followed my first job as an administrative assistant at Lyric Opera of Chicago, where I learned so much about marketing without realizing it at the time: The art of monthly annual appeal direct mail, how to sort and bind newsletters for bulk mail, the concept of being sold out on subscription, how to write an expert run-of-show for complex events and more.

I found my job at Lyric working part-time as a student at Northwestern. Fun fact: I did telemarketing, securing season ticket renewals from subscribers. I hate cold-calling, but I did it to access internal job boards— literal bulletin boards where internal jobs were posted before paying for newspaper placements. It worked. I applied for two assistant jobs, landing one. This was the first time I remember stepping out of my comfort zone to develop my career. Decades later, I came across Northwestern alum and IBM CEO Ginni Rometty's quote: "Growth and comfort do not co-exist." She's absolutely correct.

Then I earned the OPERA America Fellowship, which led me to The Atlanta Opera.

Young, single, and without a friend there, I immersed myself in my work. I attended nearly all the evening and weekend rehearsals and every event. Bought my opening night dresses at the Junior League Nearly New shop, worried I'd show up in a board member's daughter's castaway. But you did what you needed to on a meager arts salary. I didn't care about the money. I cared about the craft and the work family.

Yes, the work family.

I need to belong. I need to be me. I had both at The Atlanta Opera. A small 25-ish-member team of year-round employees, we ate lunch together every day. The Artistic Director regaled us with endless stories. It was home, I loved it, and I learned a ton.

As PR/Promotions Manager, I quickly learned crisis communications. Within three months, we fired two lead singers, followed by a controversial production of Don Giovanni. Yep—growth and comfort do not co-exist.

Those pain points led us to hire a PR firm to train us in crisis communications, which opened the door to learning customer service straight from the Ritz-Carlton. I got to audit their new employee orientation, learning firsthand their service promise and CRM—theirs started old school on index cards!

Yep, dealing with the crises was tough, but they helped me learn how to build resilience and gave me literal on-the-job opportunities to learn and grow.

Then, my boss announced she was leaving for a great opportunity at a local PR firm. I stepped out of my comfort zone again. Not waiting to see how they'd fill her role, I walked into our managing director's office, a ball of nerves, voice shaking a bit, and told him I wanted her job.

"Can I speak with you for a moment? I'm very interested in and want to be considered for C's job."

He named me interim Director of Marketing and PR, which became permanent. I achieved my five-year career goal a year ahead of schedule.

More challenges and learning came: becoming my work BFF's boss, hiring new employees, firing others, managing a telemarketing team, setting ticket prices, predicting sales, managing front-of-house, and working with our artistic director setting the schedule to balance sell-outs with newer works to expand the genre.

We grew ticket sales exponentially to the point they became more than 60% of earned revenue. While a great resume boost, it was a red flag. I knew from my time at Lyric Opera the balance of earned to contributed revenue for an arts organization should be at least 60/40 contributed income to earned. Ours was flipped.

Cue the dotcom bust, September 11th, and move to a new venue.

Ticket sales flopped. They fired me.

A bitter pill to swallow. *Really* bitter.

A type-A overachiever, I never truly failed at anything. Embarrassed to call my parents with the news.

I didn't fail. The company failed.

Sure, I made mistakes. I didn't recognize the signs. A board member mentored me, "You should do market research." Me: "I already did some, don't have the budget or time for more." I was too naïve and proud to understand.

I learned from that loss—a lot.

I recoiled at the general manager's suggestion to say I was "moving on for other opportunities." I couldn't do it. I couldn't look my team in the face and tell them I was walking away from them. I think I tried, but a team member saw right through it, saying, "Wait, they fired you?" I nodded yes. A relief they finally knew.

Maybe it was not my first, but it was an early moment of leaning into vulnerability and authenticity.

The next month was tough. The official announcement to the company said I was moving on to other opportunities. But nearly everyone knew the real reason why—my team made sure of that. My boss threw me a fancy party, including gifting me a pair of lovely candlesticks. I held onto those a lot longer than I should've—a reminder that loyalty to a company isn't rewarded. In the decades since, I've seen this play out time after time with leaders, colleagues, and management changes. Now those candlesticks are sitting on someone else's table—a Goodwill treasure hunt find.

Getting fired hurt. I thought my career was over.

*How did this happen? I **moved** here for them. They wanted me, and now rejected me.*

How naïve I was.

This loss became a gift.

But a stark reminder that *loyalty* can have its scars.

I gave my all to the Opera. I was all in. And loyalty bit me in the butt.

I'd like to think I realized the loyalty game in that experience. I certainly did.

But it wasn't until the shocking experience I had two jobs later when my child almost died that it resonated permanently.

ACT 2: MY INFANT SON ALMOST DIED. IT CHANGED ME.

A regular day at the office. A phone call I'll never forget—rather two phone calls. Not on a cell, mobile, or iPhone, but my office desk's landline.

The first call was perplexing.

- Daycare: "Hi Mom; J is having trouble breathing. Did you send in a nebulizer?"
- Me: "Huh? He doesn't have asthma or a nebulizer. What?"
- Daycare: "Well, he's wheezing. We don't know why. Gasping, actually."
- Me: "Let me call our pediatrician."

I called our pediatrician's office, shocked and dumbfounded. They said: "Sounds like they need to call 911 immediately." Talk about a jolt to the system. I called the daycare back. Thankfully, they'd already made the decision.

Numb, I walked out of my office, looking for my boss to say I needed to leave early. I ran into her (and my former) admin instead. I'm so glad Terry found me. I crumbled and blurted out what I knew.

J is having trouble breathing. They called 911. I need to go...

She called our colleague and friend to drive me to the ER, where they took my baby. Thankfully, my husband was already there.

It was pouring rain. We drove on the highway, inching our way there, only to get a call on my flip phone. They were taking our son by ambulance (instead of helicopter because of the weather) to Children's, literally across the street from the office we had left. So, we turned around.

My boss' boss sent over two pediatric nurses to sit with me. My godsends, they soothed me, telling me what to expect, helping me navigate this surreal moment: "Once they get him triaged and into a room, they'll bring you back. Breathe. He's in good hands now."

Happy spoiler alert: My son is now a healthy, typical 18-year-old teenager headed to college on a merit scholarship.

But so easily, he could not be here.

My husband and I spent all Labor Day weekend in the pediatric ICU with no clue what was going on with our child, being asked "Are you fit to parent?" kinds of questions. They asked about daycare: "Would anyone want to hurt your child? Do you trust them?" They were questions we never thought of and frankly were offended by. But after 20 years in health care, I understand the questioning.

But it didn't help me *at all*. Our ten-month-old next to us with an IV in his head because they couldn't get a vein in his arms or legs.

We didn't know for weeks what was going on with him. Just thinking about it years later makes me want to bawl.

There were more hospital stints—testing for cystic fibrosis, pneumonia, and a bronchoscopy that discovered and confirmed the issue. Turns out he grabbed and swallowed a label that fell off another child's bottle.

My child survived. I nearly got fired, certain I had undiagnosed pneumonia through it all. It changed my outlook on life, solidified my priorities, and sadly, introduced unexpected adversaries—women to other women.

Mind you, I've had my share of male discrimination, but am also fortunate to have a loyal crew of male advocates and mentors.

So, this women-on-women adversity stung. Sharply. It hurt bad. Really bad. Not only was it women on women. But woman to mother. You read that right. Woman to mother.

I never in a million years thought I'd get the "you're not reliable because you're a mother" treatment from another woman. But I absolutely did. Gobsmacked.

She told me, interrogating why I was late to the office after taking our son for lab work (painstaking lab work as they searched for a viable vein in his chubby arms), "If you're going to continue to need to take him to doctors' appointments, we're going to need to consider you going part-time." *What?*

I was out of FMLA protection, and out of sick and vacation time.

*Did she **really** just say that? My son nearly died. Now that I need to take him for appointments to figure out what's going on and make sure he stays* *healthy, I must go part-time? When before I became pregnant, I could do nothing wrong at work?*

Yeah. No thanks.

Even 18 years later, it burns.

But I used that fire to create a new world of leadership.

Call me Pollyanna, but I do believe you can be a mom, a professional, a leader, and, yes, have it **all**!

I have it now. That hate and spite didn't set me back. It fueled me to create a different work environment. One where I don't question the flexibility humans need to take care of their own, whether kids, fur babies, parents, partners, or themselves.

I live my values by example, sharing openly when a family commitment creates a work conflict. If you follow me on LinkedIn, you'll see in full force when I missed a major awards ceremony (where my team earned prestigious awards) so I could see the final varsity soccer game of our son's high school career. Yep, he recovered from his label-swallowing incident just fine to become captain of the varsity soccer team.

Cue my mentor, whom I met after this job, who told me, "We are all adults. I'll treat you like an adult, until you stop acting like one."

I pressed more: "Really? It's okay to leave work early or be late for a doctor's appointment?" She said: "Yes, of course. When else are you going to do it?"

Right. That's leadership. Years later, she held to her word when I encountered two unexpected, traumatic life events.

ACT 3: MY MISCARRIAGE AND MY HUSBAND'S BRAIN SURGERY.

Fast forward a few years: I'm pregnant with our second child, and my husband is diagnosed with trigeminal neuralgia.

We freaked and cried.

I lost the child on Thanksgiving weekend. I experienced a not-great ER experience with my employer. But there, I found hope and influenced change by speaking my voice.

I tried to manage through but found working and processing the loss and the experience to be too much. I remember telling Sandra about it on the verge of tears. "Umm, I had a miscarriage two weeks ago." We both broke down. She gave me a huge hug. Then, she helped me share my story with leadership. I got calls from the hospital, emergency medicine, and obstetrics leaders. Through sharing my experience, I influenced positive changes so other expectant mothers wouldn't encounter the same issues I did.

Another example where vulnerability and stepping out of my comfort zone created growth opportunities.

Then, when my husband had surgery to treat his trigeminal neuralgia (successfully!), she showed her compassionate leadership again. First, donating her own paid time off to help me take time off to be there for him. Inspired by her, the radiology administrator I worked with donated a week of his paid time off, too. Then, intuitively knowing I needed more time after the surgery, Sandra called me, "Why don't you work from home your first week back?" Far before the pandemic normalized working from home, this was a particular gift.

Having the hard experiences described earlier, experiencing Sandra's compassionate, authentic, and accountable leadership was monumental and validating. It showed me there is another way to lead, giving me the strength to be unapologetically me as a leader.

Today, I lead by example, treating people the way I want to be treated. I work hard to be the change I want to see, even if it means being uncomfortable. So, as Rometty said, "You have to get comfortable with being uncomfortable."

After all, growth and comfort do not co-exist.

THE TOOL

HOW TO APPLY MY LIFE LESSONS IN YOUR LEADERSHIP STYLE

1. **Protect your time on your calendar.** Seriously, do it. Block time. Label what it's for, so people think twice about booking over it. For years, I had a recurring daily block from 7-8:30 am saying,

"Take J to School." In health care, early morning meetings are not unusual, but they are difficult for working parents with daycare and school drop-offs.

2. **Take a seat at the table, literally.** Until someone tells you not to. Invite those on the periphery to sit at the table. Early on I would not sit at the table, instead sitting in the seats along the wall. One day, I noticed nearly everyone sitting at the table were men, while women sat along the wall. The next meeting I took a seat at the table. No one said a thing. No one ever has. Today, when I see open seats at the table and people sitting along the wall, I invite them to sit at the table. You can, too.

3. **Be clear why you have conflicts.** One of my male bosses demonstrated this so clearly saying he couldn't make a meeting due to a childcare or family conflict. Seeing him lead by example empowered me to follow suit. I openly share when I cannot make a meeting or have a conflict, going one step further to say specifically I need to pick up my son, take him to soccer practice or a band concert.

4. **Turn off your email when you are on PTO.** Do not work when you are enjoying time off. Set an example for your team by not working. Don't allow people to take meetings while they are on PTO, even if they insist. You set the bar; don't allow your team to lower it.

5. **Allow flexibility, and don't ask questions.** It's hard when you have an underperformer, but you need to be consistent in how you apply your compassion and flexibility, otherwise you undermine yourself.

6. **Speak up for yourself.** Time and again, when I pushed through my discomfort to speak up for myself, it worked out. I successfully asked twice for raises after getting data I was underpaid. After two awkward meetings with board members about marketing, where no one asked me (the marketing person at the table) my opinion, I spoke to my boss about it. I opened saying, "This is difficult and uncomfortable to bring up." He thanked me for raising the issue and doubled down, saying he wanted me to present on marketing at the next board meeting instead of him.

7. **Don't be afraid to let your team see you uncomfortable and vulnerable.** I remember on a few occasions sharing my emotions— George Floyd, the war in Ukraine, my godmother's death. Each time, a team member contacted me, thanking me for sharing my feelings. Recently I reflected on Ahmaud Arbery's murder and our nation's centuries-long pandemic of racism while receiving an award for our coronavirus pandemic work. Audience members came up after thanking me for using my platform to speak out. Be the change you want to see.

8. **Live your values.** Simple as that.

Amy Moudy Comeau, MBA, is an award-winning and acclaimed marketing executive with depth and breadth in health care, non-profit, higher education, and performing arts. As Vice President of Marketing for Emory Healthcare, she leads marketing for a nationally and internationally renowned academic health care system.

Throughout her career, which includes positions at Lyric Opera of Chicago, The Atlanta Opera, Georgia State University's Rialto Center for the Arts, and Emory University's School of Nursing, she's earned accolades being known as a collaborative leader building effective cross-functional teams.

During her years leading Emory Healthcare marketing, she transitioned her team from "marcom" to "martech" integrating data into decision making. An avid sports fan, she's fortunate to build and leverage sports partnerships into the organization's broader strategy, including partnerships with the Atlanta Braves (MLB), Atlanta Falcons (NFL), Atlanta Hawks (NBA), and Atlanta Dream (WNBA).

A Northwestern University graduate with an MBA from Emory's Goizueta Business School, she lives in an Atlanta suburb with her husband and son.

To learn more about Amy's authentic leadership, please buy her book: *Every Storm Runs Out of Rain: Leading a Health Care Marketing Team through a Global Pandemic* at www.everystormbook.com and https://ripples.media/amy-comeau/. You can also book her to speak or consult.

Connect with Amy Moudy Comeau:

Website: https://ripples.media/amy-comeau/

Email: aimer713@comcast.net

LinkedIn: https://www.linkedin.com/in/amycomeau/

CHAPTER 23

CURIOSITY IS YOUR SUPERPOWER

QUESTIONS THAT TRANSFORM TEAMS AND WORK

Camille Strickland

"The important thing is not to stop questioning;
curiosity has its own reason for existing.
One cannot help but be in awe when contemplating the mysteries
of eternity, of life, of the marvelous structure of reality.
It is enough if one tries merely to comprehend a little of the
mystery every day. The important thing is not to stop questioning;
never lose a holy curiosity."

~ Albert Einstein

MY STORY

"We're moving."

The sound of my mother's words was barely louder than the vehicle horns blaring right outside of our living room window. The narrow, winding streets on our little Caribbean island forced drivers to communicate their coming and going with a few honks of the horn, but it was also the same honk used to lovingly greet walking neighbors as they drove past.

My younger sisters and I loved living in our two-story home, where we easily took in the entire scene and even chimed in with our hellos while hanging off the porch chairs. But on this particular afternoon, we sat on the edge of the living room couch so excited by what we had just learned that we couldn't be bothered to run out to the porch and enjoy the bustle of our village street.

Where will we live?

What will our new home look like?

How will we make new friends?

What will you do for work?

What will Dad do for work?

The questions rolled around in my mind and eventually out of my mouth before my mother or father could share much else. As a ten-year-old kid, I had traveled a few times already, but this wasn't a trip. While I couldn't yet imagine what the move meant for my future, I knew it was a significant decision and an important part of my life journey.

Looking back now, I suppose the idea of moving to a new place should've been confusing and somewhat sad for ten-year-old me. But it turned out to be the life event that planted the seed for a powerful mindset, which has become not just a tool for my personal life but also my business relationships and projects.

It wasn't until years later that I understood why my questions didn't seem to unnerve my parents – and maybe even amused them. They were, as it turns out, built for a curious child and had been intentional about the ways they fostered a sense of wonder when my siblings and I were not consciously aware of what they were doing.

"What did you learn in your encyclopedia today?"

There was an Encyclopaedia Britannica set in our home library that I poured over on weekends and holidays. Reading them helped me to paint a picture of a world beyond the one I lived in and opened up many questions that my parents would either answer or encourage me to find the answers to through more reading. Their gift to me was not a set of books but permission to ask questions and use them as a tool to understand people and the environments they navigate or dream new ideas.

At a time when there is much to have anxiety about in the world of business – from dwindling demand and increasing cost to workforce shortages and employee burnout – curiosity has risen to the top of the list as an antidote that can inspire impactful teams and work. Recent studies have highlighted it as a desired skill emerging leaders must have to be effective and viewed positively. But even in our everyday lives, it is the superpower that can help us to bravely explore uncertainty long enough to stumble into the good stuff – the right answer, the innovative approach, the really good friendship you didn't know you needed.

Think of a coworker you typically have a difficult time working with. Now think about approaching a conversation with that person to kick off a project you must collaborate on. Which conversation starter do you think would yield the most productive conversation – one where the two of you agree on a style of collaboration that meets both of your needs: would it be the scenario in which you tell that coworker that your way is the best way to get the job done? Or would it be a scenario in which you first ask your coworker about their thoughts on the project and perhaps what they are most concerned about or looking forward to? I'd venture to say that a coworker who feels heard and even a little understood stands a better chance at being a collaborator you'd enjoy working with than a coworker who feels unheard and misunderstood (or even worse – not seen).

Curiosity is an invitation to shift our focus from the overwhelming and often paralyzing uncertainties and unpleasantries of life and business to a proactive engagement with the unknown. It encourages us to explore, ask questions, and seek out understanding of anything which can transform anxiety into a journey of discovery and learning (and inadvertently, wonder). By adopting and fostering a sense of curiosity, we don't just learn to navigate complex challenges with a sense of purpose and resilience; we also find new and exciting ways to solve them and connect with those around us on a much deeper level. In essence, curiosity empowers us to turn our fears into opportunities for growth and positive change.

"I'm moving to South Korea."

It was 11 years after my parents shared that our family was moving. I was weeks away from my undergraduate graduation and the start of a life independent of them. The irony that I was sitting them down to share that I was moving to another country to work was not lost on any of us.

"You're what?"

My dad was surprisingly the one to speak first. Usually, the more contemplative of my parents, I could hear the nervous excitement in his voice. He was always a big supporter of my love for discovery and travel, even trusting me to spend the summer of my 16th birthday away from home, exploring Leicester and London, England, with my cousins.

Much like the last time we sat down to discuss a major move, they started asking a few more questions.

"Why South Korea?"

"What will you teach there?"

"Where will you live, and is it safe?"

"How will you travel around the city?"

"What company will you be working for?"

Likely the last set of simple questions I'd ever get in my life, but they were very welcomed. My first thought was,

I can't believe they haven't said no as yet!

It was quickly followed with,

I might actually get to do this!

It wasn't so much that I needed their permission as it was a desire to go with their blessing (and a backup plan, as my parents and I would later laugh about).

"I'll have an apartment in Seoul with a roommate."

"I'll be teaching grade school and adult students."

"I can't use any of my electronics without an adapter!"

I excitedly shared what I knew about my job with them, as well as the details I learned about the new country that would become my home for a short while. I was thrilled they hadn't shot down the idea and instead shared my slightly naïve but palpable excitement.

Life in Seoul, South Korea was filled with wonder at every turn, and I loved it. My students were in my class to learn English after their school day, but my fascination with their culture and lives allowed me to pick up some of their language and appreciate their customs, which were very foreign to me as a West Indian girl who had spent the last 11 years entrenched in American culture and the prospects of my future in it. My questions about their world and my embrace of their questions about mine allowed us to work through the language barrier that would otherwise complicate our classroom sessions. In making them comfortable with asking questions, I created an environment where they solved problems and also envisioned new dreams for their futures.

This experience highlighted a powerful truth for me: that curiosity is not just a helpful personal trait but a critical leadership skill. In the context of leadership, curiosity serves as a catalyst for empathy, continuous improvement, and, ultimately, innovation. Through this experience and countless others that followed in my career, I learned that when leaders cultivate a curious mindset, they unlock a wealth of benefits for themselves, their teams, and their organizations.

Curiosity matters in leadership because it drives us to seek out new knowledge, ask insightful questions, and challenge the status quo. This proactive engagement with the unknown is what leads to better problem-solving and decision-making. Numerous studies also support the idea that organizations led by curious leaders tend to be more adaptive and resilient, navigating changes and uncertainties with greater agility.

Leading with curiosity also fosters a culture of learning and development within teams. When a leader models curiosity, they encourage their team members to do the same. This creates an environment where continuous improvement is not just happening but is also valued, and employees feel empowered to explore new ideas and take risks. As a result, the organization becomes a breeding ground for creativity and innovation which helps them to maintain a competitive edge.

Questions—why, what, how, what if—are wonderful gifts that bring ideas and teams together for the greater good. They keep a sense of wonder at the forefront of our minds instead of the crippling anxiety that can make inaction (and, as a result, no progress) all too easy for humans. As you lead, let curiosity guide you, and marvel as it opens doors to new possibilities for your people and your business.

THE TOOL

POWER QUESTIONS FOR CURIOUS LEADERS

Curiosity is a powerful tool that every leader can infuse into key milestones in their work. These three areas—exploration, reflection, and visioning—also serve as a framework for powerful questions they can use to cultivate a culture of curiosity and transform their teams and work.

Instructions:

Use these questions regularly in your work, team meetings, brainstorming sessions, and one-on-one discussions to encourage open communication, continuous learning, and forward-thinking. You can also tailor them to fit the specific needs and dynamics of your team. Use the suggested activities under the questions as a guide for how and where you might effectively use these questions.

Pillar 1: Exploration

Encourages leaders and team members to question assumptions and seek new perspectives. Drives innovation by challenging the status quo and introducing new possibilities.

- What if we approached this problem from a completely different angle?
- What assumptions are we making, and how can we test them?
- How would someone with a completely different background solve this?
- What are the potential unintended consequences of our current approach?
- What questions are we not asking that we should be?

This could look like:

- Conducting small-scale experiments to validate or challenge assumptions.
- Researching/analyzing best practices from other industries, adapting relevant ideas to your context.
- Inviting a guest speaker from a different industry to provide fresh perspectives.

Pillar 2: Reflection

Focuses on learning from past experiences and improving future performance. Ensures continuous improvement and helps teams build on their experiences.

- What did we learn from this project that we can apply to future work?
- What patterns do we see in our successes and failures?

- What were the key successes and challenges, and what did they teach us?
- How can we better support each other to achieve our goals?
- What are the root causes of our most significant challenges?

This could look like:

- Holding a retrospective after a project to discuss lessons learned and document key takeaways.
- Identifying specific process improvements and assigning owners for accountability and traction.
- Performing root cause analyses to address and resolve underlying issues of a persistent execution or team challenge.

Pillar 3: Visioning

- Inspires teams to think big and set ambitious goals. Empowers teams to think creatively and strategically about their future.
- What would success look like if there were no constraints?
- How can we innovate to stay ahead of industry trends?
- What future opportunities can we explore to achieve our long-term goals?

This could look like:

- Facilitating a visioning workshop to create a shared picture of success with your team.
- Creating strategies to leverage organizational strengths in new areas of your/your team's work.
- Seeking and establishing strategic partnerships that accelerate progress toward a specific vision or goal.

What new and wonderful thing might you happen upon today if you lead with a question? I'd love to hear how curiosity is helping to transform your business relationships and projects—send me a note via email or LinkedIn!

Camille (Cam) Strickland is Senior Vice President at BVK, where she provides strategic support to healthcare teams that are challenging the status quo across the industry, their business, and audiences for better care outcomes and experiences. She has supported and led strategy teams at both consulting firms and health provider organizations like Dignity Health, Community Health Systems, Loma Linda University Health, and Orthopedic Institute for Children in alliance with UCLA Health for 17 years. A past board member and active member of the Society for Healthcare Strategy & Market Development, Cam holds a master's degree in healthcare administration from Loma Linda University. She is also the proprietor of a boutique coaching consultancy, which is a passion project that helps health and medical professionals unleash their creativity to solve business challenges and make impactful business decisions.

Cam resides in Miami, Florida, with her husband and two girls who are the loves of her life.

Born on the island of Antigua, she grew up on the island of St. Croix, U.S. Virgin Islands, before immigrating to the U.S. mainland, where the rich cultural heritage of her background helped to shape her interest in healthcare management and her approach to building teams.

This combination of professional expertise, entrepreneurial spirit, and a deep appreciation for her family and culture makes her a dynamic leader and an advocate for transformational change in the healthcare industry.

Connect with Cam:

Camille.Strickland@bvk.com

http://www.linkedin.com/in/comstrick

http://www.creativecostrat.com/

CHAPTER 24

BE THE WATER THAT DRIPS THROUGH STONE

SAVE YOUR BUSINESS
WITH THE POWER OF PERSISTENCE

Daniel Brian Cobb

"It's better to be constant than clever."

~ Matt Bunk

MY STORY

Your fear will destroy your business. Fear can be paralyzing, seeping into every corner of your life, and it can be especially destructive in business. More than any other factor, fear will take your eyes off your goal and put you on a path to self-destruction. If your anxiety doesn't hurt the people around you at work, it will impact your family or your health.

My journey is a testament to the power of conquering fear by choosing to ignore what cannot be controlled.

I've been accused of being an optimist. I confess I'm guilty as charged, but my optimism isn't a misguided emotion I was born with. I wake up every day facing the same fears common to all entrepreneurs. My optimism is a learned technique. It's a choice based on training and experience, and it's powered by persistence. The core of this transformative leadership strategy is built on the power of trust.

"Good news. We lost our home."

I remember when my dad came home excitedly with an opened envelope in his hand. He busted into the kitchen and said, "I've got good news." As we waved a piece of paper, he said, "This letter says God has to do something now."

The letter was our eviction notice.

My dad was the type of father who taught his sons, "Boys don't cry." So, when later that night I saw him with tears in his eyes, I knew something was seriously wrong. As a child, I watched my father build and scale a company from the ground up. Soon after, I watched my father lose everything he once worked so hard to create. Losing a job can be painful, but it wasn't just him who got fired. His dream was fired. Everyone around the company got fired. The once immovable rock I built my confidence upon didn't appear so solid anymore.

My dad demonstrated the ability to quickly find his happy place, he rebuilt his confidence and believed beyond the evidence of failure. Like cream that inevitably floats to the top, he eventually found his way back to success. We indeed recovered, and we were never homeless.

To this day, this memory haunts me—and inspires me. *How do I trust my training when my teacher has failed? How do I maintain the faith of my father?* Recently, sitting with my dad in his comfortable retirement home, he recalled his corporate job prior to being an entrepreneur, saying, "It was nice to have a regular paycheck." I had the opportunity to stay in a "safe" corporate job, but like my father, I didn't choose that path. As an entrepreneur at heart, I'm what we serial entrepreneurs call "unemployable," and I wouldn't change it for the world.

TRUST IS YOUR SUPERPOWER.

There is no power stronger than trust. People who don't understand this truth sadly believe trust makes us naive. It's not my intention to persuade you into believing you can trust everyone or everything, but trust is the factor that separates the good from the great. Consider Warren Buffet, who knows which stocks to trust. If he were a cynic, he'd never invest. Similarly, every brain surgeon or bridge engineer trusts their training. Well-placed trust keeps us all safe.

How do you know what to trust? Make your life a study of patterns:

- Watch the patterns of success at work in business and trust them to work for your company.

- Study successful families and apply their patterns in your marriage and for the sake of your children.

- Trust the science found in the patterns of nature.

- Most importantly, make your life a study of people and greater purpose—study philosophy, history, and religion. And not just from one perspective. Find people who will disagree with you.

As an ad agency founder, I gained more from serving people than I have by managing them. I remember a client at Chick-fil-A that changed the trajectory of my business. Dan Cathy, CEO at that time, said, "Love the people. Don't sell the chicken. If you love the people, the chicken will sell itself." So, we put that statement in the creative brief. The work that came out of this statement was some of the greatest work in our agency's history to date.

When a company dared to love its customers, the customers loved the company back, and the chicken store advocates became famously known as the Chick-fil-A "Raving Fans." In fact, that was the greatest growth period in the history of Chick-fil-A. Today, that franchise stands as number one in every measurable category, especially store-level sales revenue. For me personally, this work proved the law of reciprocity.

Unfortunately, I haven't always been so brave as to trust the law of reciprocity for *my* business.

It's been proven time and again that trusting a value, such as love or the law of reciprocity, can create results. However, trusting people is much more complex. People don't always get things right. The first temptation in business is to simply replace people when they fail. What I found is that when I replaced one imperfect person with another imperfect person, I got even worse results. For my company, the new imperfect person didn't come with the lessons learned from our previous mistakes.

What do you look for? Of course, not everyone is a fit with your culture, but look for values that match yours. When you find people with authentic passion for your company values and goals, trust that as a source of future success. Make those people the priority. They might not be from your tribe, but take them in. Test them with your trust and let them fail early.

Why let them fail? Every team member I ever hired has a weakness. Likewise, I found every human with a superpower has a kryptonite. I'll never learn what that weakness is if I don't first trust them with opportunities to fail. If failure is inevitable, why not get it out of the way quickly? Avoiding failure is simply avoiding life.

"Whether you think you can, or you think you can't, you're right"

~ Henry Ford

Happiness is attractive. Oppression repels. In this way, confidence acts like a self-fulfilling prophecy. As does depression. The greatest challenge I've faced as a leader is keeping my confidence. When things get bad, such as the loss of a big client, confidence can be difficult to muster. I remember trying to express confidence after laying off half my staff. In the aftermath, I stood up to give the state of the agency speech. Between the empty seats on the floor, the remaining staff appeared shell shocked. I remember seeing the same fear in their eyes that I felt deep in my heart. As the face of a company, I've long known that a fearful leader creates a fearful staff in the same way a poisonous seed sprouts poisonous fruit. However, I've also learned a lying leader undermines the culture of trust. I found myself in a no-win scenario.

Facing my team, I knew I couldn't fool them. So, I finally decided, "I must tell them what I feel." Fighting to holding back tears in my eyes, I boldly said, "I never want this to happen again." Admittedly, this was not a bold statement at all. I was clearly exposing my weakness and qualifying my promise with an ill-crafted disclaimer. I choked.

In my feeble speech, I was caught preventing myself from saying "I will never let this happen again." I thought to myself, *Where is my faith? They need me to lead them. They need to know, I've GOT this.* The truth was, and is, that I don't. I guess I finally decided, *I've been doing this long enough to know bad days are beyond my control, so why should I lie to them?*

A few faithfully stayed with me in spite of the risks and in spite of my weaknesses. Years later, those very people run the company as partners today.

After decades of wins and losses, I can proudly say that we've lived through the recession of 2007-2008, through the COVID-19 pandemic and the resulting 2020 recession. Yes, I've mortgaged my home to save the business. Like my dad, I've learned to smile through it all.

IT'S NOT A SPRINT. IT'S A MARATHON.

Now, here I stand, 30 years into a business that should've failed. Countless times, we thought it was the end, yet we just finished our best year. We just launched another 8-figure account last month, so I'm on the upside of that swing. What have I learned?

I learned life is fractal. A mountain looks like the rock it's made up of. The tiny branches within a leaf look like the branches of the tree it lives in. Patterns visible in nature can be visible in business, too. That's why an analogy can be so useful. If we can learn how the universe is engineered, we can learn to master the tiny universe of our business careers, families, and lives we lead.

EVEN WATER DRIPS THROUGH STONE.

New ideas. New innovations. New solutions. No distractions.

Being a creative person, I love making new things. But not every problem can be solved with creativity. My life taught me it's better to be consistent than clever. Over time, even water drips through stone. This is a pattern I've seen in business. In fact, I'm obsessed with the patterns that emerge from observation. I observe patterns so I don't suffer or cause suffering to others.

How do creative people find the balance between innovation and consistency? A well-conceived goal shouldn't be negotiable, but the path to the goal should remain flexible. Rigid pioneers find themselves pushing through mountains rather than climbing them. However, don't be so flexible that you create change for the sake of change. That just wears people out.

My superpower? I trusted the value of hard work.

If trusting in hard work was my superpower, what was my kryptonite? I've often found myself reverting back to behaviors that bring safety to the business rather than pushing forward toward the business goal. If I lose trust in my team, I sometimes turn back to my old role and often do their job for them. Worse yet, I get extremely prescriptive, telling people exactly what to do and how to do it.

I know this is happening when I get that look in the eye from my team members that says, "You are doing my job again." I may blame it on my desire to be creative, but deep inside myself, I'm afraid. My fear of loss of another client drives me to take over. If I do it all myself, I know I can get the job done to the satisfaction of the clients. I can prevent us all from another layoff. Or can I?

If I let go, I allow my team to fail. They learn more by failing than by my incessant teaching of the way. Most likely, their failure won't destroy the business, but giving up on them or getting distracted from the goal surely will.

When I fear failure, I become the workaholic husband/father who spends his nights sleepless on the couch with red eyes glazed over by hours of computer time. I might be present in body but not in spirit. The stress takes me away from my workout time and prayer time. This is how high-performance executives lose their marriages and their families.

When I stop to pay attention to the lessons I've learned, I come to a place of rest. When I meditate on good things, I can see it all clearly. I must be the water that drips through stone. This is how successful businesses thrive. Successful families are the same. Patience and persistence can build trust, so the crazy cycle of the rat race does not take over.

To keep it all simple, success starts with this equation:

Focused Pressure + Time = Breakthrough

Keep your new ideas focused on old goals. Fight the temptation to focus on threats or new shiny objects that can distract you or your cause. Don't give up on your goals or your values to "save" your business.

Be the water that drips through stone. Over thousands of years, water has proven to erode even the most immense monuments of granite or limestone. From the Sphinx of Giza to the rocks of Yosemite, limestone and granite have been sculpted by persistent water flow. When faced with conflict, adversity, or temporary failure, water does not give up or go back to where it came from.

WHAT'S YOUR THOUSAND-YEAR BUSINESS PLAN?

It's often stated that 80% of new businesses fail in the first year. I argue that 100% of new businesses fail in the first year. It's the 20% who proceed past failure that change the world. Failure shouldn't take us by surprise, as it's simply part of the process. I've started countless businesses, and for every one of them, I have had at least one good reason for quitting every year. The only difference between the failed businesses and the successful ones is the fact that we didn't quit. Time is your friend.

In Japan, some family businesses have thousand-year business plans. This concept can be incredibly foreign in the land of fast-food entrepreneurs. The quality of Japanese cars came as a shock to the Detroit automotive machine, where the automotive industry was first invented. In the U.S., we pride ourselves on having better ideas, but generational business thinkers outperformed us. Since those failures in Motown, we updated our mental models, and our cars improved as well.

There is a proverb that reads, "In all work, there is profit." It takes a certain faith or life experience to believe this is true. Sometimes, our efforts seem to yield little to no results. But time can be a great teacher. In a way, failure is an even better teacher.

A good idea can be useful, but unless it's backed by effort and time, that idea will almost always fail. With enough effort and time, even a mediocre idea can succeed. Likewise, consistency rules over genius. In fact, consistency is genius in the making. Like Nelson Mandela said, "I never lose. I either win or learn."

Learning is a superpower. We all build mental models for quick decision-making. Similar to that of a great athlete who acquires muscle memory, experience builds response times much faster than any human processing can understand. This proficiency by way of building mental models happens in business and even personal relationships.

When we dedicate time and attention to a singular effort, our brain adapts to the environment we subject it to survive in. Our minds naturally build "muscle memory" to avoid complex processing of lessons previously learned. This is the essence of wisdom.

THE TOOL

ROUGH WATERS MAKE SHINY ROCKS

As I sit on the beach in Northern Michigan, I'm enjoying the results of hard work. I notice how the powerful currents and rough waters of Lake Michigan have polished the stones into something quite beautiful. Resting in finely ground sand, these colorful and polished stones symbolize the end result of the powerful forces that often push against us all. I have come to believe the struggle of hard work is a good thing. It polishes perspective, humility, and, most of all, gratefulness.

The tool you can use for building trust is gratefulness.

Rather than constantly looking around for something better, be grateful for the people around you and begin to trust them to perform in their superpower. Don't expect them to perform in their kryptonite. That's why they need you.

Gratefulness lives life to the fullest with no regrets. The only thing I would take, back if I could, is the time I wasted worrying about things that never happened. What am I most grateful for? The people I chose to do life with, despite their shortcomings and failures along the way. These are the same amazing humans who stuck with me despite my shortcomings and failures.

That is how we've won so often—together. That is our "drip."

If you have problems, don't turn your focus on them; your drip will get off course, and the problems will only get bigger. First, solve the problems of others, and ultimately yours will be solved. When you find your tribe, make your covenant there. Be grateful, have grace, and trust the process.

Daniel Brian Cobb, is a father of five, grandfather of four, and husband to his high school sweetheart and business partner, Krista Cobb. Author of *Surfing the Black Wave: Brand Leadership in a Digital Age*, Cobb is a seasoned entrepreneur and CEO with over 30 years of experience in the advertising, media, and entertainment industries.

Cobb is a 23-time Emmy Award-winning media executive, innovator, and multiple patent holder of streaming TV and automated advertising. As founder of national media companies, Daniel Brian Advertising, DBA Healthcare, MyStreme, OneDoor Studios, and AdBox.io, Cobb has led and managed more than $500M in ad spend, creating billions of dollars in revenue world-class brands:

University of Michigan Health, Henry Ford Health System, Penn Medicine, Cincinnati Children's Hospital, Valley Children's Hospital, Uhealth, Chick-fil-A, Disney, Warner Bros., Sony, ABC, NBC, CBS, Papa Johns and PizzaAndAMovie.com with Paramount, introducing social media for Disney's Tangled, Warner Bros., The Hobbit, Board Member at Missions.Me

Purpose-driven, under the banner of "Better Brands for a Better Human Condition" framed and hung at the entrance of his Rochester Michigan agency, Cobb is passionate about sharing his insights on leadership and resilience, helping others navigate the complexities of business with wisdom and grace.

Feel free to connect with Dan through his agency at:

http://danielbrian.com/

CHAPTER 25

THE CAGE OF NOT BELONGING

INCLUSION PROPELS SUCCESS

Jean Dougherty

"There is no meaning in this world outside of representation."

~ unattributed

MY STORY

I was never going to slide backward on my career climb, never going to join a sorority, never going to enter a sweat lodge, never attend a native drumming ceremony, never going to a women's retreat, never going to attempt any of the eight limbs of yoga…

Each time I embraced my "nevers," my mind and heart opened. I was wrong about my many misconceptions. My prejudices were wrong. In no way did my experiences match my pre-judgements.

I spent my life knowing I experienced life unlike others. My Gestaltist view of wholeness, believing I lived in *one* world while others saw the world in fragmented parts. Often deemed a puzzle to others, I became accustomed to feeling like an outsider.

Thrust into leadership roles at a young age provided opportunities for "mis-takes" early and often taught me how the world worked. I garnered a thirst for leadership. And where I didn't fit other's expectations, doors opened, showing me a perspective of new worlds.

Resistance, the gatekeeper of my potential, persisted. *Never* became my superpower. A harbinger of what I'd later embrace (often with trepidation) for the enrichment of my heart. Whatever I said *never* to would cling to my superpower cape—the cape of shadows that followed behind me.

False belonging created a cage around me—until I melted my armor and slowly creaked open the gate of my cage. Each trigger I faced, each feeling I felt, inched the door of my cage open, excavating my inner truth from my judgments.

Throughout high school, I hid from my friends that I was in a sorority. Yes, my high school had clandestine sororities, a layover from the nineteen thirties. I, myself, refused to join. Surprisingly, a close family friend invited me. It meant so much to my mom that I felt I had to say yes.

Ugh, this is not me. I just want to be myself (a.k.a. comfortable in my small cage)!

Surprised they invited someone like me (and never asked me to change). I had a blast with these additional friends, raising funds for philanthropies and seeing new possibilities for myself.

Why am I supposed to hate sorority girls? I didn't understand the exclusivity of the group that invited diverse girls to join. *Why can't everyone in the school be invited?* Despite including girls from different backgrounds and races and striving to make them feel comfortable, diverse members usually wouldn't stay long due to the exile they received from their original friendship groups.

Fearing judgment from my original friends, I continued to hang out with them while keeping Tuesday nights a secret. *Am I unique in bridging diverse friendship groups? Why doesn't everyone do that?* I wasn't someone who accepted dichotomous thinking (or even the status quo).

Despite sharing our high school years together, my friends later discovered my secret. "I didn't know you were a snob," they said in surprise. Even though a year had passed, they ghosted me. I was beginning to discover the many faces of exclusion.

In addition to growing my perspective by embracing my *nevers*, I also thrived in places where I felt I belonged.

In second grade, I felt certain I wanted to be a Brownie Scout. If my intuition ever served me, it was the impetus to join Scouting. Wearing my gray plaid Catholic school uniform, I walked to the public school and entered a world of collaborative, cooperative leadership.

I felt at home harmonizing around a campfire. Nature became my best friend. Lighting fires, using knives, hiking, camping, and exploring sparked empowerment within me. I can still shiver remembering the frigid cold of sleeping under a lean-to on mountain snow in my canvas sleeping bag during a weekend of winter survival camping.

If it wasn't for the civil leadership activities of Scouting, I wouldn't have spontaneously spoken before the City Council at the age of nine. Even though the male council members laughed at me, I felt I had done something grand.

I am thankful for the inclusivity and affordability of Scouting. And to the patience, ingenuity, and endurance of the leaders. And, of course, for learning to leave no trace (in nature, business, or energetically with people).

In all the cages of not belonging, I always felt like I belonged and my ideas mattered in Scouting.

This was not always the case in corporate America.

A high performer at a Fortune 500 company, I brought in a forty-million-dollar deal. I was pleased with my influence management—ascertaining a small dose of help from 200 people to create this unique offering. Until I was informed by an interim manager that I likely wouldn't be invited on an upcoming award trip.

Stunned, I stared at him.

What?

Really?

How many of the 125,000 employees brought in a forty-million-dollar deal this year?

Is the Director of Account Management going?

Oh, the empty suit Assistant Director, too?

The division heads at regional headquarters also?

None of them had anything to do with this project.

My heart sank. Roasting in anger, I glared at him.

The manager continued, "People are saying you are too uppity and *expecting* you would go. I'm thinking of sending a new hire as she has the right attitude."

What is happening?

You're telling me that you will be attending on the skirts of my achievement and have decided not to invite me? Instead, you're considering a recently promoted secretary who hasn't brought in any significant revenue and hasn't even been in the position long enough to qualify?

Crestfallen, I stood slowly and left his office.

Fortunately, the Vice President extended an invitation to me. I graciously accepted my award as one of the top two-percent performers in the company. Yet the icy slap took a while to melt.

Overcoming challenging events provided me with new sources of power as I ventured into my realm of "nevers," softening my edges each time.

Seeking a fresh experience for my resilient, long-time lesbian friend who was experiencing her sixth visitation of cancer, I snuck her into a high-tech security company cafeteria on the top floor of a mini-skyscraper.

"I feel like I'm in an international airport in India or Singapore," she quipped.

"I know," I replied, "And you probably think those tall young men with blond hair and blue eyes are from UCLA."

"Yes," she giggled, "they're not?"

"Nope, Ukraine."

No longer able to travel, I knew she'd delight in witnessing a hidden view in this wealthy, homogeneous suburb.

Sparked by diversity and inclusion, the magic happens, and spills into others around us in ever widening circles.

Anxiety permeated the silence. Several applicants' legs shook noiselessly. There wasn't a whisper in the room. Candidates wearing noise-canceling headphones, fixated on their laptops awaiting a familiar ally to escort them to their interview.

In this welcoming conference room, I co-facilitated a hiring project designed for sensitive individuals whose brains process differently. This program opened a portal for individuals who might excel at their jobs yet struggle through a typical screening and in-person interview.

The companies' intention was to recruit fresh perspectives for developing new products and technologies by increasing the diversity of their workforce.

I liked this new non-competitive way of hiring, as there were enough positions to accommodate each applicant as long as they demonstrated the skills required. As an ally, I observed intently while calming nerves and holding space for these neurodiverse candidates.

Smiling assuredly, I provided friendly support with dignity for each of these highly intelligent folks as they stepped considerably out of their comfort zone into a realm of new possibility. My heart lifted during each hallway conversation, each interview I supported, and each post-interview lunch conversation.

For those hired, I continued as their ally and advocated for them throughout the transition to employment, softening the launch into corporate expectations.

As is the case with nearly every adjustment created to accommodate individuals differently abled, corporations and their teams benefit, showing increasing efficiency, effectiveness, creativity, and profitability.

If it's true that attention is power, many neurodiverse folks could outdistance most of us on focus and attention.

I observed that the real winners were the teams who courageously hired someone who benefited their team in a unique way. Many teams collaborated in new ways, replacing the competitive edge that might infect coworker environments by instilling camaraderie. The capacity of employees and managers expanded, as did their hearts.

A director of a multinational corporation commented on his new hire: "I liked his authenticity both in the hiring process and as an employee. He was direct and honest. He didn't try to impress."

The director explained, "It takes many types of people to form a team, and it was refreshing to see how his contributions benefited us in a way we couldn't have predicted. He enjoyed completing necessary daily tasks with focus, consistency, and accuracy. Our team was grateful to have him and his dedication."

As the only white cis-gendered woman attending BIPOC diversity and inclusion events, I felt the stares and wonderment of what I was doing in the room. Yet once I compassionately shared my ally-ship, there was often a pause and a nod.

One of my favorite inclusion experiences was co-chairing a child-designed, neighborhood-built playground. Multigenerational neighbors engaged in fundraising and planning, culminating in a four-day barn-raising style build. All those willing to hammer, paint, shovel bark, provide food or childcare or "supervise" were welcome. Four hundred neighbors rolled up their sleeves to participate in this community-building experience that resulted in a playground.

As I expanded my perspective, I sent an arrow through my privilege and arrogance and received a wave of humility. Humility tones down my ego, leaving me with a superpower of insight, inviting me to ground into accepting what is.

What is for me is a world beyond myself. It includes the joy I feel when surrounded by individuals dissimilar to me, who've experienced an uncommon background, a different skin color, speak a language unfamiliar to me, and have different expectations than I do.

I invite you to consider when *you* felt like you didn't belong, perhaps feeling the chaos of confinement in a cage of not belonging.

My wish is for everyone to be set free from the cage of not belonging and embrace the empowerment to open the doors wide for others as well.

I work in the business of belonging. I get excited at next-level success for everyone's work environment where each member believes they truly belong, and that their ideas belong. Often, when they see others like themselves represented, they feel comfortable and safe sharing freely.

One methodology I use that provides positive outcomes is systemic constellations. The key component is that everyone has a place, everyone is seen, and everyone belongs. Facilitation includes detangling repeated beliefs and patterns, which free individuals and leaders to overcome obstacles and improve team collaboration. Often, the individual who doesn't fit is the one providing an invitation for that organization to grow.

I've been touched to witness:

- Optimism ignited within a group project.
- Writing flowing again for authors who felt blocked.
- Organizational blocks identified.
- Naturopathic doctors uprooting a uniquely challenging prognosis.

One software company president identified the clarity and confidence to delegate significant responsibilities to team members, allowing them to grow through challenges while setting herself free to resign and follow her dreams.

One client stated, "For the first time, I felt I belonged in my family— an elusive sense of welcoming to the world that had plagued me most of my life."

Belonging is everybody's business. Especially those in a leadership role.

I see belonging as a leadership imperative, a transformative leadership essential that pays off for business.

It takes transformative leaders to move from "King of the Mountain" mentality (fraught by historical culture: sports, academia, awards) to creative, collaborative openness (open-mindedness, expansive-heartedness, trusting one's gut).

When I witness diverse leadership teams, my creativity unleashes, and my vitality soars. When I recognize those who represent me, I feel an invitation to belong in the world of leadership (and of wealth, of celebrity, of choices).

Stepping aboard Sir Winston Yacht on Long Beach Port in sunny, windswept California introduced me to a world of financially successful women. This event was sponsored by the Business Relationship Alliance – accomplished women mentoring aspiring female entrepreneurs.

I was moved by the friendly, engaging flow of connections and exchange of this Women of Wealth conference. I was elated to meet financially successful BIPOC and LGBTQQIP2SAA entrepreneurs.

Finally! The representation in transformative leadership I've been seeking.

My experience during this excursion amplified my belief that a diverse group of individuals with differing experiences, views, backgrounds, economic status, color, and gender identity is a ticket to success. During this event, I witnessed individuals step into their power and become vulnerable with one another.

The laughter, fun, and lightness of diverse individuals encouraging others and sharing their success felt invigorating. Each event speaker depicted leadership that inspired. A highlight for me was meeting the affable producer, Catherine Gray, who, at the event, completed her fund-raising goal for her film *Show Her the Money*.

Written and directed by Ky Dickens, the story features rock-star female investors who invest in diverse women entrepreneurs with innovations that will change the world. In a heartwarming way, the film reminds us money is power and women and gender non-conforming individuals need it to achieve true equality.

When the grass-roots film tour finally hit my alma mater, I was ripe with anticipation. Sitting in the seats of my familiar former university lecture hall, I sent a picture of the film screen title page to my friend, entertainment attorney Tisha Morris, who had been a speaker at the Women of Wealth conference.

"Thank you for hosting me at the conference; I just spoke with Catherine Gray, and the film is about to start."

"You're going to love it," she responded.

And I did. I loved it.

And tears.

And poignant silence at the end of the film (before the applause).

Young students in attendance remained after the film to hear local female and gender non-conforming millionaires share their journey to success.

Revealed in the film:

- Less than 3% of venture capital goes to women.
- More than 85% of venture capital companies have *no* female decision-makers.
- Investable assets controlled by women are expected to rise to thirty trillion dollars by 2030 according to McKinsey & Company.

Show Her The Money started as a film and incited a movement. Catherine mentioned that universities have asked her to develop a curriculum for understanding the new face of wealth: women.

Featured in this film is transformative leader and SoGal Ventures co-founder Pocket Sun. Sun reveals that her Venture Capital firm has gained profitably from investing in diverse business owners who were previously turned down by other VC firms. Some of those VC firms are now out of business. SoGal empowers the next generation to succeed and includes a community that connects global entrepreneurs to change the world by investing in diverse founding teams.

What I felt with this film was women and gender non-conforming individuals engaging with a passion for their business. I aspire to learn from ever-emerging heart leaders, leaders of collaboration and cooperation, leaders who nurture—the leaders who embrace inclusion.

Where others might hunger to be "one of the cool kids," I find my inspiration in play. I long to be included by innovators and positive change makers. I pine for adventure, exploration, and novel experiences. I access my creativity most easily through travel. Whether an ocean visit, a road trip through the mountains, or following a mystic through northern India, I gain confidence in my leadership. Sharing beautiful sites, exotic meals, deep silence, invigorating conversations, and laughter inspires my inner landscape and nourishes me to feel whole.

Diversity and inclusion might embody a festival of narratives, yet there is no "somebody oughta." When I desire to improve our world, it begins with me improving myself. I feel helpless waiting for governments or organizations to act a certain way, fix an issue, or do the right thing.

Empowerment arrives when I discover what I can do to trek out of my comfort zone and acknowledge, embrace, and include someone who thinks differently than I do, who has a belief system unlike mine, who doesn't look like me.

Might you join me?

Join me with reverence for life and compassion for others as the predecessors of the upcoming shift of humanity. A future immersed in rugged creativity, discovery, and exploration, fostering the cusp of quantum-level innovation. Believe with me that you can lead something meaningful, something that makes a difference.

The result may be that you become comfortable in more places than you thought possible and explore the world in ways you've never dreamed possible.

THE TOOL

Free someone from the *Cage of Not Belonging*, and you may find you've also freed yourself:

- Make someone feel welcome in your workplace.

- Look for opportunities to provide dignity to someone, especially if it brings you out of your comfort zone.

- Hire someone who is differently abled.

- Introduce yourself to those who are different from you and listen if they're willing to share.

- Hire folks from the LGBTQQIP2SAA and BIPOC communities.

- Be the magic you want to see in the world.

- Become part of the movement:
  https://showherthemoneymovie.com/about/

- Consider revisiting one of your own "nevers."

Dedication: Freeing from the Cage of Not Belonging is dedicated to Molly Dougherty, who welcomed everyone who didn't feel they belonged. She was a transformative leader who encouraged unity through compassion for others. May my beautiful sister live in great joy, with many parties at her new home on her charming, serene lake in her place of rest.

Jean Dougherty is a mentor, life coach, and healer. She encourages clients to bloom into their potential. A longtime proponent of diversity and inclusion, Jean has led marketing teams in Fortune 500 high-tech companies, co-founded a successful internet startup and advocated for differently abled adults.

Among her modalities as a mentor and healer, Jean is a Systemic Constellation Facilitator, healing organizations, families, and individuals by helping them feel they belong. Jean consults on diversity and inclusions and launches products, services and new businesses. Jean loves traveling with companions, groups, and by herself.

Thanks to Two Peacocks Travel for transformative travel empowering and supporting women and students through their amazing trips. Thanks for supporting women-owned businesses in our trip to Morocco.

Connect with Jean:

Website: https://jeandougherty.com

Instagram: https://www.instagram.com/jean_dougherty1

Email: Jean@JeanDougherty.com

THE FINALE

"We shall not cease from exploration
And the end of all our exploring
Will be to arrive where we started
And know the place for the first time…"

~ T.S. Elliott, from "Little Gidding," *Four Quartets*

When I invited 24 brave souls to explore transformative leadership with me, I had no idea what I was really asking of them or of myself. I thought I would describe the defining moments of my career and how they changed me.

Turns out, the writing itself was transformative. Retracing those milestone moments gave me a new depth of understanding and a comprehensive view of my self-empowerment journey and how it developed over time. Mining my explorations, I:

- recognized a pattern of my capabilities, the roots of which were present right from the start;

- traced my view on value as it morphed from an external lens (*they don't value me or respect me*) to an internal view (*I don't value or respect me*) to a self-empowered claim (*I value and respect myself*);

- and witnessed my transformation from yielding power to others to claiming my sovereignty as the leader of my own life.

Finally, I realized that the most meaningful, impactful, and far-reaching work I do is in co-creation with and on behalf of others, where we all rise together.

To that end, I'm grateful to my fellow authors for collaborating on this journey, for being willing to look inward with a sense of curiosity, and for sticking with it through unexpected turns. Ultimately, I'm grateful to them for telling their powerful stories with candor so our words might give voice to others as we have given voice to ourselves, seeing and knowing our stories as if for the first time.

Our collaborative book supports Vox Grata Women's Choir, a non-profit organization that also joins their "grateful voices" on behalf of others. Through their concerts and outreach, Vox Grata's mission is to give voice and visibility to those whose voices often go unheard. Through their songs, Vox Grata (www.voxgrata.org) invites us each to make a difference.

Thank you for joining us on this journey. Whether you're an aspiring or seasoned leader or reluctant to see or title yourself as such, we invite you to continue through conversations with any of the 25 courageous voices who have spoken to you. May you, too, see and know your story for the first time.

For additional tools and resources, reach out to connect at:

www.NewVoiceofLeadership.com

WITH GRATITUDE

To the readers of *Transformative Leadership*, thank you for joining us. This book is now your book. Together with my fellow authors, we invite you to write your new chapter.

To the brave authors of *Transformative Leadership*, thank you for saying yes to this adventure. I'm grateful for the gift of your words, experience, wisdom, courage, and trust.

To all the teams, colleagues, leaders, organizations, clients, and customers I've worked with, thank you for the opportunity to learn from and with you. This book wouldn't exist without you.

To my mentors, coaches, and teachers, thank you for creating, holding, and facilitating a container for me to do the work: Sarah Craft, Kelly Kanski Fisk, Bonnie Gillespie, Bethany Joy, Mary Kipp, Rachel Lang, Tisha Morris, The Stevens, and Melissa Veler.

Thank you to the members of my communities and their leaders for a safe place in which we can be vulnerable, practice our tools, and learn from each other:

Astrology for Creatives, Bonnie Gillespie and Rachel Lang

Dreaming with Bees, Dasha Bond

KBee Fitness, Kelly Kanski Fisk

Live Your Chart, Bonnie Gillespie

Power Path, Jose, Lena, and Anna Stevens

Priestesses of the New Earth, Bethany Joy

True Hunger and Full Life, Melissa Veler

VortexHealing®, Lorraine Goldbloom

West End United Methodist Choir, Andrew Risinger

The Writing Room, Tisha Morris

The Women's Wisdom Circle

To the members of the Healthcare Executive Forum, thank you for your generosity and responsiveness, particularly in support of this project.

To Jeanette MacCallum, founder and director of Vox Grata Women's Choir, thank you for creating and leading such an amazing choir that shares their beautiful voices on behalf of others.

To the members of the Vox Grata Women's Choir, the Board of Directors, and the Advisory Council, thank you for volunteering your time and talents.

For the advice, brainstorming, edits, and patience to listen to me verbally process, thank you to my dear friends Jean Dougherty, Mary Jo Greil, Susan Holt, Mary Kipp, Kiran Lakshman, Kate Loyco, Maureen Nelis, Malana Redpath, and Melissa Veler.

To Dasha Bond, a special thanks for leading the way and believing in me. Your kind-heartedness and fierce resilience take my breath away.

Many lifetimes of gratitude to Mary O'Keef Kipp for walking the paths with me to arrive back to where we started.

To my daughters and sons, Kate and Tim, Jordan and Katie, and Meg, thank you for your love and support.

To my grandsons, Logan and Dean, and granddaughters, Eloise and Sallie, thank you for letting your "GiGi" see the miracles of the world anew through your eyes.

Deep gratitude to Tracy Prentice, my husband, voice teacher, sounding board, first reader, and editor, and the love of my life. You are the yang to my yin and the yin to my yang.

My heartfelt thanks to Laura Di Franco and her amazing team at Brave Healer Productions and Brave Business Books. I'm grateful for your support of this creative, writing, and editing process, for a glimpse into the publication business, for a view of marketing from a different lens, for the chance to recruit, collaborate, and network with other authors, and for the opportunity to share the brave words in this book with the world.

For speaking engagements and podcast interviews, contact me at Jill@NewVoiceofLeadership.com

"There are three essentials to leadership: humility, clarity and courage."

~ Chan Master Fuchan Yuan

"The future ain't what it used to be."

~ Yogi Berra